Dance Music Spaces

Critical Perspectives on Music and Society

Series Editor: David Arditi, University of Texas at Arlington

This book series produces books that present a critical perspective on popular music and the music industry. Two dominant strains of thought exist for the study of popular music. First, many texts in the popular culture tradition celebrate the artists, fans, and cultures that arise from popular music. Second, Music Industry Studies texts give students a "how-to" perspective on making it in the music industry. In both cases, texts rarely address the way that the music industry produces and reproduces power. The purpose of this book series is to provide a platform for authors who explore the social production of music; as such it is broadly interdisciplinary.

The series invites submissions by scholars from the fields of cultural studies, American studies, history, sociology, literature, communication, media studies, music, women's studies, ethnic studies, popular culture, music industry studies, political science, economics, and history.

Specific topics addressed:
• Musicians as Labor
• Identity (Sex, Gender, Race, Ethnicity, Disability, and Sexuality)
• Critical Representations
• Music Industry Studies
• Music in the Global South
• Production of Genres
• New/Old Technologies
• Sound Studies
• Access Inequalities To Music Production and Consumption
• Spaces of Music Production, Creation, and Consumption

Dance Music Spaces: Clubs, Clubbers, and DJs Navigating Authenticity, Branding, and Commercialism by Danielle Antoinette Hidalgo
Mixtape Nostalgia: Culture, Memory, and Representation by Jehnie I. Burns
"This is America": Race, Gender, and Politics in America's Musical Landscape by Katie Rios

Dance Music Spaces

Clubs, Clubbers, and DJs Navigating Authenticity, Branding, and Commercialism

Danielle Antoinette Hidalgo

LEXINGTON BOOKS
Lanham • Boulder • New York • London

Published by Lexington Books
An imprint of The Rowman & Littlefield Publishing Group, Inc.
4501 Forbes Boulevard, Suite 200, Lanham, Maryland 20706
www.rowman.com

86-90 Paul Street, London EC2A 4NE

British Library Cataloguing in Publication Information Available

Library of Congress Cataloging-in-Publication Data

Names: Hidalgo, Danielle Antoinette, author.
Title: Dance music spaces : clubs, clubbers, and DJs navigating authenticity, branding,
    and commercialism / Danielle Antoinette Hidalgo.
Description: Lanham : Lexington Books, 2022. | Series: Critical perspectives on music
    and society | Includes bibliographical references and index.
Identifiers: LCCN 2021051707 (print) | LCCN 2021051708 (ebook) |
    ISBN 9781793607546 (cloth) | ISBN 9781793607560 (paperback) |
    ISBN 9781793607553 (ebook)
Subjects: LCSH: Electronic dance music—Social aspects. | Rave culture. |
    Authenticity (Philosophy) | Branding (Marketing) | Commercialism.
Classification: LCC ML3918.U53 H54 2022 (print) | LCC ML3918.U53 (ebook) |
    DDC 781.648—dc23
LC record available at https://lccn.loc.gov/2021051707
LC ebook record available at https://lccn.loc.gov/2021051708

Dedication
For my Dad,
"You got a face with a view,"
a view that I miss beyond words . . .

Contents

List of Figures

Acknowledgments

This project would not have been possible without the support and guidance of my editor, Courtney Morales. You found me at the perfect moment, patiently listening, reading, and reflecting with me every step of the way. It's been an absolute dream finishing this with you. Thank you also to David Arditi for your support and enthusiasm and for seeing what was valuable here before I fully saw it.

This project also would have been impossible without everything that The Blessed Madonna, Honey Dijon, Peggy Gou, Eris Drew, Octo Octa, and their colleagues bring to dance music. Thank you for guiding, challenging, and inspiring this work and, of course, for bringing me back to the dance floor. Thank you also to all of the clubbers I met along the way. I continue to learn so much from you. Thank you for bringing this project to life.

A number of mentors and colleagues have guided my thinking and supported me while I was still finding my way in academia. Mimi Schippers, you have absolutely moved me intellectually and beyond. Thank you for making me a better thinker, teacher and for encouraging me to "go there" both professionally and personally; this journey has been full of pleasure and so much good, loud laughter with your ongoing guidance and friendship. I would also like to thank mentors, colleagues, and friends from UC Santa Barbara and Montana State University: Beth Schneider, Leila Rupp, Richard Appelbaum, Kegan Allee, Jennifer Rogers-Brown, Debra Guckenheimer, Tonya Lindsey, David Eitle, Tami Eitle, Sara Rasch, and Kristen Lavelle. At Chico State, I want to especially thank Kim Jaxon. Your encouragement has absolutely kept me going. Thank you so much. Thank you also to colleagues and friends in and beyond my Sociology Department: Kathy Vargas, Nandi Sojourner Crosby, Liahna Gordon, Nik Janos, Alex Kokkinakis, Jeff Livingston, Dilia Loe, Brian Oppy, Marianne Paiva, Ryan Patten, Doris Schartmueller,

Suzanne Slusser, Chunyan Echo Song, Eddie Vela, Dana Williams, and Lauren Wilson. For colleagues who provided invaluable feedback along the way, I want to thank Hannah Burdette, Kim Jaxon, James Joseph Dean, Christopher T. Conner, Matthew Thomas, and Tony Waters. Thank you to my research assistants and students over the last few years: Paige Connell, Elizabeth Henry, Tierce Cason, Christina Hammans, Nayeli Iniguez, Lesley Bernabe Martinez, Carina Baca, Lupe Santos, and all of my brilliant spring 2020 Contemporary Social Theory students; working with all of you felt like a party from start to finish. Thank you.

This research was supported by Chico State's Research, Scholarly & Creative Activities (RSCA) funding and the College of Behavioral and Social Sciences. I want to especially thank Anna Allard and Julie Jessen. Thank you for all of your hard work, support, and guidance as I received and explored funding for this project.

To old and new friends, thank you for your expert knowledge and feedback along the way: Michelle Mai, Manuel Gonzalez, Ciara Hélène, JT Taylor, Danny Lee, and Jessica Buchleitner. Thank you also to my wonderful Chico friends: Hannah Burdette, Nathan Heggins Bryant, and Erin Kelly. Hannah, writing with you helped me shape this project. Thank you for always listening and for your razor-sharp feedback. Nathan, I've learned a lot about how to speak up and call "no BS" with you in my life. Thank you. Chico wouldn't be nearly as interesting without you, Hannah, and Avery. Erin, summer 2017 in London was memorable for so many reasons and I blame that almost entirely on you.

The travel for this project would not have been possible without the love and support of my dear family and friends in London, Paris, Glasgow, Chicago, and San Francisco. Maria Cal, thank you for letting me be your couch burrito and for your decades-long friendship. I love being your "little nerd." Laurent, Hakema, and Maylis, thank you for opening up your home and for loving me and Brian. Those trips were so special and I can't wait to get back to all of you. Linda and Ruth, I love you both so much and I'm so happy I finally got up to Glasgow. Thank you for making that possible. Katherine, Pete, Louis, and Francesca, thank you for welcoming us to Chicago. We loved every second of it and miss you. Michelle and Jess, thank you for always letting me crash in your guest room. I miss my pre-SNL naps with you and love you both so much. Thank you also to Amazing and Rudy for taking such good care of my Helen, especially when I was gone for so long.

My first rave would not have happened without Sara Windels. Thank you for introducing me to that world and changing my life forever. Thank you also to Clarke Eaton. I'm so lucky I found you on the dance floor that night. When dancing became extra tough during the pandemic, my pole dancing teacher and dear friend, Natalie Cook, made it all bearable. Thank you for always encouraging me to get out of my head and into my body, and to

Joanna Miller, none of this would be possible without you. Thank you and love you always. To Dr. Sarah Burke, thank you for supporting me through an extremely tough couple years. My post-D&C rambling is all true.

To my best friends and chosen family, I love you all beyond words and couldn't have jumped into this project without your love and support. Mirae and Michelle, thank you for always bringing me back down to earth and loving me fiercely. I'm your Granielle forever. Cinnamon, you're the best wifey a girl could ask for. Thank you for loving me so unconditionally.

Thank you also to the Kress family. Nancy and Steve Kress, thank you for your patient listening and always constructive feedback. If nothing else, I hope you enjoy what I've done here.

To my loving family, thank you for supporting me always. Rich, Amy, Isabetta June, Serafina Perry, Laurie, Rocky, and Buzz, you all have my heart. Your support has kept me going.

Mom, there is so much to thank you for that I don't even know where to start. I love you dearly and wouldn't be the person I am today without your guidance. Thank you for making me a better sociologist and, more importantly, a better person.

Dad, I miss you with my everything and hope you're proud of what I've done here. Your lust for life is all over this book.

To my sweet loves, Helen, Frieda, and Meole, thank you for being the best writing buddies a Momma could ask for and always lifting my spirits.

And to my love, my sweetheart, my Brian. Is it really this cool to be in your life? Loving you is so much fun and I know I wouldn't have made it to the end of this book without you. Your patience, wicked smart feedback, and love is so big. So ready for more of all of it and you.

Introduction

"This Must Be the Place": Making Sense of Dance Music Today

She was only 16, determined yet shivering with nerves.[1] While she was pretty seasoned at this point, butterflies flew up and down her body anyway. As she made her way to the massive warehouse, a large crowd gathered and pushed her up against the fence separating the parking lot from the coveted entrance to the party. She was always unsure about what the outcome of the night would be. Would the party get shut down? Who would she see? What would happen? How would she feel as the night progressed? Perhaps her butterflies reflected years of teenage angst and her relentless longing for everything she loved about these parties, spaces that she never experienced anywhere else, spaces that opened up so much for her. Perhaps the butterflies were also a deeper reflection of what was literally saving her life. The dance floors she found in these warehouses, the people with whom she shared collective moments of pleasure, and the way she was able to move through her body offered a long, ongoing, life-affirming exhalation.

She finally made her way past the entrance and into the first "room" of the warehouse, her head held high, back straight, shoulders back—a posture that was unnatural in most other areas of her life. Here, she moved with confidence. This space felt like home, these people felt as freaky as her, and this music moved her in ways she had never been moved before. While she was still in the parking lot, long before she finally made her way into the party, the music literally shook her car, a familiar feeling now that always rushed through her system like a lightning rod, electrifying her completely: "It still gives me a rush thinking about those moments" (Bratches 2020).[2]

And that electricity also sparked her desire for other dancers, other bodies, for her own expression of desire and pleasure in and around the dance floor. In these spaces, much like the first rave she ever experienced, she felt fully realized in a way that she had never accessed before. That first night, like

1

so many nights that followed, meant sweaty dancing and sometimes sweaty kissing, often with people she met only for a moment, never to be seen again. As she writes this, she's remembering moments like this: walking through a crowded dance floor, exchanging a desirous gaze with another dancer and total stranger, and then falling into a deep, long French-kiss before she pulled back and smiled wide as she continued to move through the rest of the crowd:

> Suddenly, I belonged somewhere with people who loved the same thing I did. What thrilled me most, and still moves me now, was being a part of an underground party where you could let loose, smile at a stranger across a dance floor who was feeling it like you were . . . before the beat dropped and the whole room went nuts. (Bratches 2020)

And then there was the dancing. Above and beyond nearly everything else, she found herself on the dance floor, a space that felt sacred, safe, and finally, one that she could claim as her own. And while hierarchy certainly made its way into the scene in a number of ways, often in competitive dancing on the actual dance floors, she often avoided this altogether by finding her own space in the multiroom warehouses. Within minutes of entering the party, she would leave her group of friends and venture off on her own, getting a sense of the space and looking for the "perfect" spot to dance with her own shadow.

I begin with this vignette in order to reveal how deeply embodied, emotional, and sensuous[3] moving through dance music spaces can be: "[c]lubbing does not 'happen,' but is experienced" (Malbon 1999, 184). How are these spaces embodied and what do these embodiments reveal about their ongoing social and cultural components? Similarly, what are the social and cultural contradictions that emerge from contemporary dance music[4] spaces? These are the questions that animate this project.

THE PROJECT AND ITS SIGNIFICANCE

This book[5] is about the ongoing production of social and cultural physical and digital spaces, spaces that share features of *both* rave authenticity[6] *and* electronic dance music (EDM)[7]/club culture commercialism.[8] Fully aware of Thornton's (1996, 115) early critique of research that analytically conceptualized authenticity and commercialism as "universalizing, ahistorical, abstract and/or overly reductive" (Butler 2012, xxvi),[9] my research builds upon her critique by paying attention to how scene insiders (such as DJs), clubs and clubbers *perform, produce, maintain* and, in some cases, *resist* authenticity.

What is marked as authentic is as interesting as how it is used. Similarly, I treat commercialism as an ongoing process, locating the complicated interplay between, for example, "performing real-ness" and selling one's brand;[10] capturing what is *performed, produced, maintained,* and *resisted* as one engages in *branding* and other commercial practices opens up space for conceptualizing commercialization as *social and cultural practices* rather than a static thing.[11]

Directly addressing sociologist Tammy Anderson's (2009a, 2009b, 2009c)[12] call for future research on the "social and cultural space between [perceived] authenticity and mainstream commercialism" (Anderson 2009a, 168), I use those social and cultural spaces as my starting point, showing that *both* authenticity *and* mainstream commercialism are dynamically present, vying for more or less power or working together, depending upon the context.[13] This *both/and*[14] approach is also consistent with how I analyze DJs' and clubs' *branding.*[15] Utilizing Banet-Weiser's (2012, 4) definition of "brand," I conceptualize *branding* as the ongoing social and cultural processes that connect marketing, product, and consumers, processes that DJs and clubs are constantly navigating. Instead of writing branding off as gross commercialization only, I use Banet-Weiser's (2012) work on brand cultures to open up space for ambivalence, "where *both* economic imperatives *and* 'authenticity' are expressed and experienced simultaneously" (5, my emphasis).

Given this ambivalence and its contradictions, this book also fills a major gap in dance music literature, providing readers with descriptions and analyses of *actual dancing* and *moving bodies* as clubbers *perform, produce, maintain,* and *resist* the ongoing contradictions they must navigate in today's dance music spaces. As clubbers navigate clubs and their dance floors, they are confronted with spaces that share *both* "authentic" *and* commercial features, a reality that often requires employing a complicated set of social and cultural practices.

Finally, branding makes sense here as it seamlessly connects to the emotionality so inherent to dance music storytelling. As I show throughout the book, DJs and clubbers often construct their experiences playing and/or dancing to music as other-worldly, blissful, and emotional (e.g., DJs talk about loving their fans and clubbers talk about "losing it" on the dance floor). As Banet-Weiser (2012) argues, something becomes "brandable" when "it inspires affect and emotion from individuals, [a process that is] needed to create a relationship between the branding company and consumers" (220).[16] Given the proliferation of branding in dance music, coupled with the pervasiveness of *both* authenticity *and* commercialism in dance music spaces, this book analyzes the ambivalent social and cultural practices that DJs, clubs, and clubbers must negotiate to navigate this terrain.[17]

The Literature and Methods Used: "I Just Believe House Is the Mother of Them All"

In the documentary, *I Was There When House Took Over the World*,[18] dance music historian Tim Lawrence explains one of the main ways that house music started to go global:

> During the summer of 1988, I was studying at Manchester University and a friend said, "Let's go to the Hacienda . . . it's this kind of amazing club." We walked into the venue and it was like this level of energy that I had never witnessed before. The music was an outer-worldly, deconstructed, postmodern samples coming in and out. Many of us had never heard anything like this at the time. The music happens to coincide with the arrival of ecstasy in the United Kingdom and that particular drug combined with a sound becomes a kind of explosion of house music in the summer of 1988, the summer of love.

While dance music literature offers a long and often conflicting list of theories for how dance music is realized and where house music[19] fits into the larger dance music oeuvre, this book analyzes the opinions, experiences, and (social) media discourses of three "house music" DJs and their colleagues,[20] using these contributions as a starting point.[21] The following chapters take us on a journey from city to city,[22] primarily following The Blessed Madonna[23] (@theblessedmadonna), Honey Dijon (@honeydijon), and Peggy Gou (@peggygou_), all DJs who have worked together and use similar reference points to discuss their love of the scene, its history, the music, their fans, and their own contributions and collaborations.[24] While house music is constantly changing ("there is no end to it" (Rietveld [1998] 2018, 213)), all three DJs have talked about the importance of house music to their identities as DJs and used house music cultural markers and a rave ethos[25] to talk about their own contributions to dance music. Rather than capturing some so-called "truth" about house music, this book captures a snapshot of the legacy of house music, realized via these DJs' stories and physical spaces that connect them.

In recent years, TBM, Honey Dijon, and Peggy Gou have exploded onto the scene with awards, new singles, and opportunities that have exposed them to much wider audiences, thus requiring them to engage in nearly nonstop *branding practices*, practices that require carefully dancing with *both* authenticity *and* commercialism. The Blessed Madonna earned *Mixmag* DJ of the Year in 2016 and took her "We Still Believe" tour across the globe.[26] Honey Dijon has performed with TBM, as Black Honey, events that always draw large audiences, and was named Best DJ of North America by @djmagofficial (May 29, 2019).[27] Peggy Gou's rise has been referred to as Gou-mania: she has over 2M *Instagram* followers, was credited as the first South Korean DJ to play Berghain (a legendary club in Berlin, Germany (Mitchell 2018)) and was named a *Mixmag* DJ of the Year in 2018.[28] Given a typically nonstop tour schedule, Gou—like TBM and Honey Dijon—physically slowed down quite a lot since March 2020. Before the pandemic, all three DJs tirelessly traveled the globe; thus, their perspectives and ongoing critiques of dance music provide any researcher with a wealth of on-the-ground data worth analyzing and making sense of.

Additionally, I conducted autoethnographic[29] research in multiple clubs throughout the United Kingdom, other European countries, and the United States, capturing a particular type of embodied knowledge that would have been missed if I had only conducted interviews (Takahashi and Olaveson 2003). Building upon my dissertation research (Hidalgo 2009) in nightclubs throughout Bangkok, Thailand, I utilized a methodological approach I call *spatiotemporal embodied relations* for studying clubbing behavior,[30] an approach that simultaneously considers space, time, and clubbers' embodiments in order to better understand the social and cultural relations taking place in any one club.[31] Following this logic, Phil Jackson's (2004) *Inside Clubbing: Sensual Experiments in the Art of Being Human* highlights why an autoethnographic approach to clubbing research makes sense:

> The knowledge found in clubs is an embodied knowledge that you can feel deep in your guts and it must be lived if it is to be truly comprehended. It is both social and sensual. . . . *Clubbing is a profoundly visceral and corporeal phenomenon*, it is a leisure activity that allows us to shake off the body of the everyday world and subsequently recreate our experience of the world. This sensual shift grants us access to the succulent and carnal modes of social encounter, which arise in the hours of darkness. (1, my emphasis)

Everything about clubbing is experienced as an extraordinary connection to embodied knowledge,[32] one that is undeniable in almost every way.[33] Given this fact about clubbing and experiencing a dance floor, while there are certainly exceptions,[34] the vast majority of studies of dance music culture—particularly recent ethnographic studies—tend to do a poor job of actually describing and analyzing embodied knowledge in and through dance music scenes and spaces.[35] As Malbon (1999) stated over twenty years ago, "[e]thnographies of clubbing are especially scarce" (180). This dearth of ethnographies of clubbing has largely continued; for example, there are only a handful of ethnographic clubbing/dance music, book-length studies—sociological research, in particular—that have been published over the last twenty years (Thornton 1996; Malbon 1999; Buckland 2002; Anderson 2009a; Conner 2015). While there is certainly interdisciplinary dance music research that takes an ethnographic approach (St John 2012), the analyses are largely drawn from interviews even when the researcher completed (auto) ethnographic fieldwork (Rietveld [1998] 2018; Pini 2001; Jackson 2004; Sylvan 2005; Hutton 2006; Wilson 2006; Farrugia 2012), a pattern that often failed to answer spatiotemporal embodiment questions I had about what was actually happening in dance music spaces.[36] Malbon's (1999) ethnographic study of clubbing[37] is, to the best of my knowledge, the only book that comes close to the (auto)ethnographic work I was looking for yet, once again, his analyses draw heavily from his interviews.[38] While journalists' books on dance music (Reynolds [1998] 2012; Collin 2009, 2018; Matos 2015) offered a bit more on-the-ground accounts, their work often lacked a clear sense of how their data was collected and analyzed. My research fills these gaps and calls for future research on embodied knowledge in the context of contemporary dance music.[39]

Utilizing autoethnography,[40] my research shows on-the-ground, ethnographic examples of sociologist Chris Conner's (2015; Conner and Katz 2020)[41] arguments about EDM;[42] in other words, what does "spectacular subculture to culture industry"[43] actually look and feel like in and through dance music spaces—both physical club spaces and digital promotional spaces such as *Instagram*? As Conner and Katz (2020) argue: "EDM culture serves as a prime example of how subcultures become commodified through its history of transformation in response to legislation" (450). Analyzing transformations that occurred from 2004 to the present, Conner (2015) shows that "EDM has become corporatized" (166) via "a full blown culture industry" (ibid.). Building upon Horkheimer and Adorno ([1944] 1972), Conner describes the culture industry[44] as "the increasing tendency for culture to be commodified and organized using standardizing practices, which are masked by superficial differentiating characteristics they refer to as pseudo-individualization" (166). My work shows how this transformation is actually realized and resisted in physical and digital spaces today.[45]

I also extend and update Anderson's (2009a) groundbreaking ethnography of dance music with contemporary data, specifically data that include social media activity and the use of new technologies in and around dance floors.[46] Furthermore, while Conner's research primarily utilizes interviews to answer his research questions, my research primarily utilizes thick descriptions of autoethnographic fieldwork and extensive content analysis of social media activity. I use both of these methods in order to capture both the feeling and carnal import of dance music in real time and the emergent import and significance of digital technologies and communication in dance music today.

The Data Collection

My desire for an in-depth understanding of physical and digital spaces in between authenticity and commercialism required multisited, physical, and digital ethnographic methods. After completing preliminary research in summer 2017, I embarked on four years of in-depth research, particularly intensive fieldwork over the New Year's Eve (NYE) dance music season,[47] following TBM, Honey Dijon, Peggy Gou, and their colleagues and attending venues in the following cities: London, Manchester, Glasgow, Edinburgh, Amsterdam, Berlin, San Francisco, Chicago, and New York. Following the lead of TBM, Dijon, and Gou, I also treated the NYE season as a busy and important time of the year, one that includes back-to-back events over a three- to five-day period.[48] There are a few reasons why I closely studied clubs rather than large spring and summer festivals: (1) club culture (rather than festival season) is more central to the NYE season; (2) festivals are typically far more expensive than club events and therefore less accessible to a wider, more diverse audience; and (3) while house music is certainly present at large dance music festivals, it's typically not the central feature of festivals or the headlining act. While the spaces I studied did not neatly fit into either *main-streams* or *undergrounds* (in fact, many of the spaces shared a combination of features in both *mainstreams* and *undergrounds*), how Fiona Hutton (2006) describes these particular types of nightclubs is worth mentioning. Outlining her interviewees' descriptions of these spaces, *mainstreams* are "commer-cialized spaces for clubbing with musical styles that are often in the music charts, popularized and widely dispersed throughout youth cultures and wider society" (Hutton 2006, 9). Additionally, Hutton's (2006) *mainstreams* typi-cally have the following features: large clubs with clubbers ranging from 16 to 22 years old; highly sexually charged; use of amphetamines and alcohol; dress codes such as "no trainers, jeans, or baseball caps" (9); "less tolerant attitude towards those who are different" (10); and increased commercial-ization and "corporatization" of club spaces. In short, "[m]ainstreams were associated with high prices, chart based music, and poor sexist attitudes towards women" (10). *Undergrounds*, on the other hand, typically included the following features: more experimental music played, thus "offering . . . 'something different' from mainstreams" (Hutton 2006, 9); less sexism and macho attitudes with regard to women; lack of alcohol use; an overall *attitude* or inclusive ethos that felt "right" to women clubbers; an "anything goes" (9) approach to fashion realized in less or no dress codes; a PLUR-like ethos or "free atmosphere" (9) that supported queer intimacy and less sanctioning with regard to behavior; and smaller, less commercial venues with creative décor, an older crowd (25 and older), and a far less sexually charged atmo-sphere. Given the fact that the spaces I studied shared more or less features of Hutton's (2006) *mainstreams* and *undergrounds*, those shared features gave me a window into precisely the kind of research that Anderson (2009a) called for 13 years ago; spaces that *shared* the features of so-called "mainstreams" and "undergrounds" point to physical (and digital) dance music spaces that are increasingly *both* authentic *and* commercial, a compelling finding in and of itself.

Beyond completing on-the-ground fieldwork, I also followed TBM, Dijon, Gou, and other important actors in the scene (other DJs, promoters, managers, and venues/clubs) on social media. This means that I checked social media feeds (*Instagram, Twitter, Facebook, TikTok,* etc.) at least 30–50 times per day, archiving pictures and videos as data collection for future analysis.[49] In addition to this data collection, I also reviewed and collected data from dance music magazines (both digital and physical copies),[50] recently released records, books and memoirs, short and long documentaries, and any other pieces of data that addressed my ongoing research questions.

While the methods used for this research are fairly standard sociological methodology, the ongoing analysis of new technologies (both in physical and digital spaces) has forced me to engage in innovative and flexible ways of collecting data. For example, using *Instagram* and *Facebook* has sometimes meant that I have direct contact with key actors such as the DJs I followed and clubbers I met. For example, I interacted via *Instagram*'s direct messaging function with a number of DJs in this book, interactions that were often initiated by the DJs themselves and revealed additional information about how they accomplish their work as a DJ and artist. Finally, while the title of this chapter might not be immediately obvious now, its significance will be clear and obvious by the end of the book.

CHAPTER SUMMARIES

Chapter 1 provides context for the rest of the book, emphasizing how peace, love, unity, and respect (PLUR) continues to reverberate in dance music today at the same time as all aspects of contemporary dance music are impacted by ongoing commercialization. The chapter explores the significance of respite, release, and transcendence in dance music, themes that are often discussed by DJs and clubbers alike.[51] If, as TBM often says, "love is the message," what does that message actually produce? This chapter begins to answer that question, paying attention to a few central themes often experienced on dance floors: slipping into another space, crossing boundaries, and leaving better than we arrived. Highlighting how *both* rave authenticity *and* EDM/club culture commercialism (Anderson 2009a) are always present, these themes are *both* bound by friendly, warm interactions between clubbers *and* fractured by new technologies that pull clubbers away from each other. The chapter ends with an initial analysis of toxic patterns (such as DJs' grueling tour schedules) that the entertainment machine (Marcuse 1964) often makes invisible, a tactic that keeps the machine running.

Chapter 2 takes a closer look at the three DJs I followed for this book—The Blessed Madonna, Honey Dijon, and Peggy Gou—describing how they have shifted house music and the wider dance music industry and outlining how each DJ is "doing DJing" differently from how it is done in the mainstream, more commercial end of the industry. TBM and Honey Dijon are politically and socially outspoken, while Peggy Gou's political and social contributions are implicit and typically coupled with her efforts to monetize her brand. Focusing on the DJs' actual practices, this chapter lays the groundwork for a closer analysis of the brand-building that all three DJs must engage in. Once again highlighting the ongoing presence of rave authenticity and EDM/club culture commercialism, these DJs have to strategically navigate this new terrain and do so in a way that positions them as more or less authentic, a precarious dance that requires careful curation.

Chapter 3 highlights how the social and cultural space between authenticity and mainstream commercialism is physically realized, negotiated, and resisted on dance floors. While dance music floors have certainly shifted since the 1990s, especially with the introduction of new technologies, they remain sacred, a place where "church-like moments" can happen. Mapping the cultural components (norms, behaviors, and activities) of today's dance floors, PLUR practices are just as present as anti-PLUR practices. PLUR-ness/rave authenticity is realized via a "love fog" that encourages friendliness, connecting with strangers, and reconfiguring masculinities and femininities; anti-harassment policies that impact how clubbers interact; and smartphone restrictions that encourage dancing and connecting with other clubbers. These patterns reflect the institutionalization of a PLUR/rave ethos, supported by the venues, events, and clubbers themselves. Anti-PLUR practices are also present and realized via subtle or "underground" harassment and usually intersect with alcohol consumption as well as a lack of connection on the dance floor, a pattern that often intersects with the widespread use of smartphones and the treatment of DJs as celebrities. These findings show that *both* rave authenticity/PLUR practices *and* EDM/club culture commercialism/anti-PLUR practices have been normalized and accepted, reflecting the ongoing institutionalization of both extremes on contemporary dance floors. Clubbers can lovingly embrace strangers one minute and the next minute clear out the front of the dance floor after a celebrity DJ ends their set—both extremes are present and often at the same time.

Returning to TBM, Dijon, and Gou, chapter 4 analyzes how these scene insiders make a living in dance music without undermining their ongoing commitment to its culture and collective identity (or, in Gou's case, at least her performance of that commitment). Utilizing a practice I call *authenticity maneuvering* or employing strategies to gain and maintain legitimacy, all three DJs carefully navigate a dance music industry that is increasingly interested in the bottom line over any gradations of PLUR, a reality that makes it difficult to preserve authenticity. Thus, *authenticity maneuvering* is required and strategic—especially for house music DJs—in an increasingly commercial industry. Mapping the DJs' behavior along a continuum from rave authenticity to EDM/club culture commercialism, their *authenticity maneuvering* is either constant and explicit (TBM), fairly constant and either explicit or muted (Honey Dijon), or implicit and muted (Peggy Gou), largely reflecting how they build their brands. TBM and Dijon are far more willing to have tough conversations about social and political issues they care about, especially as these pertain to their industry. Gou, like TBM and Dijon, has to engage in *authenticity maneuvering* to stay in the game, yet she does so by focusing on taste only (in music, her DJing, her fan base, and her performances). Focusing on taste rather than the social and/or political ramifications of her business decisions allows her to avoid difficult conversations entirely, yet it often leaves her open to criticism ("selling out"). For TBM and Dijon, their skillful *authenticity maneuvering* as they engage in branding makes their business practices less obvious, leaving them open to far less criticism for "selling out" than Gou.

The Conclusion brings us back to my fieldwork at NYE events, focusing on three events/clubs during the 2019/2020 NYE season, two that featured more commercial/anti-PLUR practices and one that offered a model for "creating a positive environment"/PLUR practices that all clubbers were encouraged to enjoy. Analytic themes covered in the preceding chapters are solidified as I consider what needs to change for dance music to find its way back to a rave ethos that doesn't position money-making over and above everything else. The chapter ends with reflections on the future possibilities of dance music, possibilities that will—hopefully—continue to disrupt pervasive "money over love" practices, behavior, and decision-making on the part of DJs, producers, clubs, clubbers, and dancers alike.

NOTES

1. This vignette describes the author's rave experiences in the 1990s, particularly in California's Bay Area.

2. https://www.residentadvisor.net/features/3584

3. Stoller's (1997) *Sensuous Scholarship* is utilized throughout this book; "the sensuous body—its smells, tastes, textures, and sensations" (xv) constitute important social and cultural components of dance music spaces, a reality that often requires an ethnographer to "reawaken" their body (xvi) and remain sensitive to these sensations throughout their fieldwork. See also Pink (2009).

4. While Conner (2015) and Anderson (2009a) use EDM as an umbrella term for dance music, I use dance music as an umbrella term and position EDM as one

of many genres in dance music. Following the lead of the DJs I followed, calling their work EDM would be incorrect; they do not call themselves EDM DJs and position their work as very different from what they perceive as the more commercial EDM music, DJs, and events. A number of terms have been used to reference dance music such as electronic/dance music (McLeod 2001), electronica (Butler 2012), and electronic dance music (Reynolds [1998]/2012; Rietveld 2013; Collin 2018), to name a few; thus, I use *dance music* (like Thornton 1996; Gilbert and Pearson 1999; Fikentscher 2013) over these other terms in order to avoid any confusion and use the term that the DJs I followed often use.

5. Like Malbon's (1999) book on clubbing, "[t]his book [also] represents only the beginnings of an understanding of the countless meanings, interpretations, practices, rewards and experiences" (188) of dance music spaces today.

6. In Conner's (2015) interviews with DJs, promoters, and other industry professionals, they defined authenticity as "commitment to the music, prioritizing artistic excellence, building community, expressing concern for the future (especially environmental concerns), and rejecting the idea of placing profits above the values of the subculture" (64) in addition to "supporting their friends" and thus supporting the scene and an underground economy, innovation, making significant money and time commitments, and owning "rare, pre-release records called 'white labels'"(67). These definitions are consistent with a rave/PLUR ethos (described in this Introduction and chapter 1) and also reflected in the social and cultural practices DJs engage in.

7. As one of this book's reviewers noted, EDM is not made up of a single scene and, relatedly, dance music is made up of a full range of scenes (see especially Anderson 2009a, 2009b). This book, therefore, captures spaces that are primarily connected to the DJs I followed and therefore also connected to "house music" and other related genres that the DJs and their colleagues identify with and play during their sets.

8. Combining Gilbert and Pearson (1999) and Banet-Weiser (2012), I consider "the extent to which 'dominant' and 'non-dominant' cultures and formations interact with each other, not simply 'winning' or 'losing' their mutual struggles, but negotiating complex and usually *ambivalent* outcomes" (Gilbert and Pearson 1999, 160, my emphasis).

9. Relatedly, Thornton (1996) also problematizes "mainstream" as ambiguous and contradictory; yet, like Takahashi and Olaveson's (2003) use of the term, depending upon the context, it also makes sense to use it to "refer to the dominant and visible cultural forms and products of North American and European society" (90).

10. Building upon Banet-Weiser (2012), this project includes "thinking through what it means that authenticity *itself* is a brand, and that 'authentic' spaces are branded" (11). How do these processes play out in the context of dance music culture?

11. I analyze and remain sensitive to the social and cultural practices attached to authenticity and commercialism, thus treating these concepts as ongoing, contextual, and/or embodied—authenticity and commercialism are socially constructed and shift across time and space (Thornton 1996). Thus, I am less interested in finding some so-called "truth" about either authenticity or commercialism and far more interested

in making sense of the discourses (Foucault 1978) that circulate around these terms and their emergent social and cultural practices: What do these discourses produce?

12. In order to avoid homogenizing urban nightlife, Anderson (2009c) suggests putting "bars, parties, restaurants, and nightclubs on a continuum based on the cultural components (e.g., ethos, organization, identity markers, norms, and behavior/ activities . . .) each possess" (919). This was a productive approach, especially because all of the events I attended included some combination of *both* "underground/ independent" (music appreciation, dancing, socializing with friends, some but much less sexual courtship, and less harassment) *and* "commercial/corporate branding" (popular music, "an atmosphere of elitism and clearly defined cliques, an overemphasis on social (scene) status and style, loose hierarchical status ordering, and highly sexualized interactional styles featuring 'hook-up' objectives," (920) sexual and racial harassment) features. While Anderson (2009c) ends her article by differentiating between "the city's High streets and brandscapes . . . [and] the other end of the nightlife continuum" (920) or between commercial venues and independent, smaller and more intimate spaces, her analysis still fails to do what she suggests—addressing the in-between spaces. Thus, that's precisely what I do here, paying particular attention to how a combination of the features listed on either end of the continuum combine and impact what clubbers, DJs, and clubs negotiate and accomplish.

13. This *both/and* approach also connects to how I conceptualize power: "[P]ower does not always work in a predictable, logical way, as something either corporations or individuals can possess and wield" (Banet-Weiser 2012, 12). Taking up Banet-Weiser's approach to brand cultures, I approach dance music culture as "ambivalent, often holding possibility for individual resistance and corporate hegemony simultaneously" (ibid.). Initially, this ongoing ambivalence where contradictory dynamics were present in dance music spaces seemed confusing and chaotic. Over time, I realized that the contradictions were the story; the ambivalence *is the story* about how *both* rave authenticity *and* EDM/club culture commercialism are dynamically present in dance music today.

14. This approach is also consistent with Gavanas and Rietsamer's (2013) interviews with women DJs; when talking about the sexualization of women artists, their answers included *both* feminist *and* anti-feminist themes (67).

15. As Farrugia (2012) shows, DJs' branding became especially significant as dance music got increasingly more commercialized: "[B]ookings then grew increasingly dependent on a combination of skills *and* image. In this context, having a recognizable brand helps DJs stand out from their competition, which in an increasingly hyper-competitive DJ market has become more and more important over the years" (43). Montano (2013) shows how DJs have essentially become brands, "selling not only their club performances but also music, equipment and mix compilations" (181) and are used by promoters to sell their events and/or clubs.

16. Utilizing Berlant's (2008) thinking, Banet-Weiser (2012) asks: "Individuals may indeed be 'empowered' through their participation within brand cultures, but if this empowerment is directed toward normativity because they desire the 'utopic' feeling of belonging, what is its value?" (221). In other words, if branding practices do not challenge or disrupt capitalism, then what we're talking about is a reproduction

of normalizing practices that simply hold up the status quo and ultimately bind us to discourses and outcomes that rarely or only temporarily sustain us.

17. This approach also aims to fulfill—even partially—Gilbert and Pearson's (1999) request for "more precise accounts of the power relationships existing within and between cultural formations, dominant and non-dominant, accounts which recognize that there is no one single locus of power in society, but rather a multiplicity of points at which power is condensed and dispersed" (160).

18. For the quote above, see Screamin' Rachael Cain in *I Was There When House Took Over the World*, https://www.youtube.com/watch?v=9Rah1F1zq1k

19. For an excellent, concise review of house music, see Gilbert and Pearson (1999, 73–74).

20. The DJs I followed and the related spaces and events where I conducted fieldwork impacted the data I collected; that is, the music they play and how they brand themselves draws a particular crowd, one that would be different if I had followed a jungle/drum'n'bass DJ like Goldie, for example.

21. Following the lead of these DJs, I use an inductive method and grounded theory approach (Glaser and Strauss 1999) that samples and builds theory as data is collected and analyzed. Adopting this theoretical sampling method, my research aims to "fit [sampled theory to] some of the rhythms and moods" (Rietveld [1998] 2018, 5) of the DJs I followed and related social and cultural spaces between authenticity and commercialism (Anderson 2009a). While a number of studies have specifically focused on DJs (see a full range of DJ research in Attias, Gavanas, and Rietveld's (2013) edited volume; Brewster and Broughton 1999; Farrugia 2012; Fikentscher 2013; Gadir 2016), to the best of my knowledge, no studies have specifically focused on DJs' *branding practices*—particularly with regard to their social media activity.

22. This approach is also meant to capture the research journey (Pini 2001) I have taken, where I did not "fail to be surprised, to change direction, to occasionally get swept away, get stuck or get propelled in an unanticipated direction" (17). As my loved ones, editor, friends, and colleagues can attest, this was a wild ride and one that I will continue to travel after this book is finished.

23. Throughout the book, I will typically use The Blessed Madonna's abbreviated name, TBM. On occasion, I also use her given name, Marea Stamper.

24. Building upon Farrugia (2012), I am interested in how the "tastes and practices" of these women DJs and their colleagues "are challenging assumptions and reshaping beliefs about [the larger dance music industry and] where women's interests in EDM lie" (10) while, at the same time, navigating a commercial industry that often puts gendered pressures on them. Also, using Farrugia's (2012) language, these DJs would be considered "full time DJs/producers" (12).

25. See chapter 1 for more on this ethos, particularly PLUR values. As Conner and Katz (2020), Anderson (2009a) and others have shown, PLUR and/or a rave ethos is central to the origins of the EDM subculture in the United States and, as I show, it continues to proliferate throughout the world (not just the United States). Even if the acronym PLUR is no longer used, its ethos is present and used in a number of conflicting ways, patterns I analyze throughout the book.

26. During the pandemic, she released a Dua Lipa album titled "Club Future Nostalgia (DJ Mix)," a move that exposed her to Dua Lipa's fan base and undoubtedly raised her profile.

27. Over the course of the pandemic, she released multiple singles including a decidedly queer single and music video titled "Not About You," and worked with a number of artists such as Madonna, Lady Gaga, Jayda G, and Kiddy Smile (see https://www.youtube.com/watch?v=3fzuzLkzL2w).

28. Since 2019, Gou also released two music videos, moves that were always coupled with a video release party: see https://www.youtube.com/watch?v=kD0en-6bbJPI and https://www.youtube.com/watch?v=XKJgVg7Eux0

29. Autoethnography is a research approach that "puts the self at the center of sociological observation and analysis . . . the autoethnographer uses . . . her engagement in the interaction, or reflections about the interaction, as the data" (Warren and Karner 2005, 15). I also used this method for my research in nightclubs in Bangkok, Thailand, because it helped me capture the materiality and physicality of nightclub behavior such as dancing and it "forced me to consistently reflect on my research questions, a process that is vital throughout data collection" (Hidalgo 2009, 73). Additionally, this research required putting myself in the middle of the action; thus, my extensive personal experience in California's rave culture in the 1990s and my multiyear nightclub research in Bangkok provided me with the embodied social and cultural capital I needed to blend right in.

30. As Malbon's (1999) research shows, "[c]lubbing is constituted through a complex inter-weaving of continually unfolding practices, spacings and timings" (182).

31. See Hidalgo (2009) for an extensive discussion of this methodological approach.

32. Extending Turner (1967, [1969] 2017), Rill (2006) describes how "Unity and Acceptance of Diversity" or a PLUR/rave ethos is *felt* and "is not merely an ideological fantasy that exists in the minds of participants" (651–652). Instead, it is a sensual, embodied ideal: "[W]hen we humans feel something that touches us deeply, it adds a tremendous meaning to the experience" (652). Also highlighting the importance of embodied experiences, Takahashi and Olaveson (2003) outline the "rave experience," one "[r]avers identify [as] *the vibe* . . . a kind of energy or pulse which cannot be expressed or understood in words but as something which can only be physically experienced" (81).

33. Despite the importance of embodiment in dance music spaces and Takahashi and Olaveson's (2003) call for research where ethnographers use "empathetic participation" or their "entire person" as a "research tool," a full-bodied study has not yet happened; as St John (2006) adds, "I have yet to see a full-bodied penetration of a dance scene informing scholarship outside perhaps that which Phil Jackson, attending to 'the social and sensual knowledge of the night' (2004, 2), performs on clubbing" (15).

34. Olaveson's (2004, 269–272) excellent description of how people typically embodied and embody raves offers an exception to this rule. As Takahashi and Olaveson (2003) argue, "an experiential methodology is essential for any investigation into the deep structures and inherent meanings of rave culture and the rave

experience" (74), a methodological and theoretical approach that we share. Ironically, although their article sets up the methodological import of experiential embodiments and embodied knowledge, they do not actually provide the reader with any extensive examples of how ravers actually moved through raves and primarily used data from surveys and informal interviews for their theoretical analyses.

35. As Ferreira (2008) writes: "There is a corporeal dimension of IDM[/Intelligent Dance Music] that is usually neglected by most theorists" (19). Butler (2012) also makes this argument, emphasizing the fact that "*specific movements* of *specific people* at *specific times and places*" (xxii) is largely missing from the literature; he describes Buckland's (2002) *Impossible Dance: Club Culture and Queer World-Making* as the only direct observation ethnography that considers all three factors—movements, people, times, and places—listed above. My autoethnographic approach addresses the methodological and theoretical import of these factors without losing site of what clubbers are actually doing.

36. In considering what he would have changed or added to his book, *Energy Flash*, Reynolds ([1998] 2012) says he would have included the more "experiential side of clubbing and raving" (533), precisely what I wanted to see more of in the literature and what I begin to do here. As he describes it, these experiences include "[t]he crowd reactions and the relations between intimate strangers on the floor—those pursed, knowing smiles of people on E[/ecstasy]. A big part of what dance culture is about as an experience is hard to capture and convey" (533). While difficult "to capture and convey," experiential social and cultural processes are not impossible to capture and my methodological approach—spatiotemporal embodied relations—made that challenge much easier.

37. Butler (2012) elucidates Malbon's (1999) geographical approach well, noting how its "subtly expressed . . . in his descriptions of dancing as a set of '*concurrent spacings*' . . . one that while communal also enables participants to 'trace unique paths through the clubbing experience'" (xxx). Given how skillfully Malbon (1999) addresses ongoing, contextual, spatiotemporal embodiments in and through clubbers' social and cultural practices, I was disappointed that (1) he primarily analyzed interview data, (2) offered only a few accounts of *actual dancing bodies* in club spaces, and (3) that other dance music scholars had failed to build upon his work and include actual dancing/moving bodies in their own research.

38. For example, halfway through Gilbert and Pearson's (1999) *Discographies*, they write: "We have already seen how dance offers a way of experiencing music which cannot help but foreground the materiality and physicality of that experience" (105). Thus, the lack of dance music research that actually includes "the materiality and physicality of that experience" has been especially frustrating. Olaveson's (2004, 12) PhD dissertation is a welcome, though dated exception.

39. On especially cynical days, I assign blame to an academic system that historically and consistently privileges the so-called "mind over the body" (Hidalgo 2009), even in dance music studies, an area that should have included a full range of accounts of *actual moving bodies* decades ago.

40. As a queer, cisgender, Latinx, middle-class woman who is primarily read as "white," my identities undoubtedly impacted how I interacted with clubbers and

dancers in and through my fieldwork; those interactions are analyzed and interrogated throughout the book and especially in the chapters that draw heavily upon my auto-ethnographic fieldwork (see chapter 3 and the Conclusion). While my age (39–43) during the research certainly positioned me as a Gen X clubber (those born between 1965 and 1980; see Anderson 2009a, 2009b) and was mentioned by other younger clubbers on occasion, given the events I attended and DJs I followed (their fan base, in particular), it was not an issue that negatively disrupted my autoethnographic work.

41. See Conner's (2015) dissertation, titled "Electronic Dance Music: From Deviant Subculture to Culture Industry" and his coauthored article, titled "Electronic Dance Music: From Spectacular Subculture to Culture Industry" (Conner and Katz 2020).

42. Once again, in this book I use dance music, rather than EDM, as an umbrella term.

43. Given Anderson's (2009b) desire "to move beyond culture industry narratives toward a broader explanation of cultural change" (307), she asks questions such as: "Does commercial intrusion cause music scenes to evolve or decline? What else besides commercialization explains scene transformation?" (308). Both Anderson (2009a, 2009b) and Conner's (2015) work addresses these questions about dance music's ongoing transformations; thus, using their work as a guide, my research aims to better understand how these ongoing transformations are realized, maintained, and resisted in physical and digital spaces. Anderson's (2009a, 2009b) research focuses on rave culture's alteration and/or decline before 2009; I am less interested in replicating her work and more interested in analyzing *how* DJs, clubs, and clubbers are actually navigating these transformations. Also, Conner's (2015) work extends Anderson's (2009a) in that she theorized dance music's decline prior to 2009, a transformation that did not persist: "[A]fter 2009, a shift occurred in the United States which catapulted the EDM subculture into a billion dollar industry" (Conner 2015, 2). Dance music is even bigger throughout the world—in Europe and the UK especially—and once again following the lead of this book's DJs, the fact that they're based in London (TBM) and Berlin (Dijon and Gou) and primarily perform outside of the United States reflects this pattern. Also, while Conner's (2015) work on dance music's culture industry is used throughout the book, the Conclusion offers detailed analyses of how it operates via DJs' and clubs' branding practices (particularly the practices of Steve Aoki, Peggy Gou, and others and club branding practices that sharply contrasted a "non-mainstream" club in Amsterdam).

44. Throughout the book, I also use the term "entertainment machine," developed in Marcuse's (1964) writings. As Conner (2015) explains, Horkheimer and Adorno's ([1944] 1972) concept of the culture industry, a culture that is "becoming increasingly imposed in a top down, or administered, manner" (24) offers a useful starting point for thinking about dance music today. A culture industry includes both standardization (e.g., "the quick, cheap, and profitable reproduction of cultural commodities" (ibid.) and pseudo-individualization (when cultural products such as dance music are "marketed as unique, when in fact, they are all derived from a common formula" (ibid.)), processes that are fully realized in the form of today's dance music entertainment machine. As Conner points out, however, Adorno's later writings "concluded that the

culture industry can never fully erase the critical potential that it promises but does not deliver" (ibid.). Thus, my treatment of authenticity and commercialism as dialectical ("dialectical thinking reminds us that power dynamics are always in motion" (Berg 2021, 4)) or that branding is used to both feed into dance music's entertainment machine and disrupt it, opens up space for these ongoing contradictions.

45. While Conner's (2015, 110–111) work outlines *the context* for how EDM/dance music turned into a culture industry, my study shows how EDM/dance music as culture industry actually looks and feels in physical and digital spaces. Now that we're firmly in it, what is it like to swim in it? What do we learn and, given these lessons, what can we change or, at the very least, imagine changing?

46. Unlike Anderson (2009a), I did not study "rave culture" in Philadelphia and do not replicate her overall project. Instead, I take up her call for future research on the social and cultural space between authenticity and mainstream commercialism and compare my findings against hers in order to make sense of how dance music spaces have shifted since she published her book.

47. In a discussion of useful practices and methods used in dance music research, Garcia (2013) insists that he must write within two to three days of an event in order to "recall the small gestures, facial expressions, overheard comments, recognized tracks and other details that make ethnography come alive" (9). My data collection process is similar; I track these details in the Notes section of my *iPhone* over the course of the NYE season and make sure I get to my laptop and begin writing thick description fieldnotes within 24 hours of the 3–5-day trip. When I attend a single event in cities like London, San Francisco, and New York, I track details in Notes and record fieldnotes within 24–48 hours of the event.

48. Since these research trips were at least three weeks long, I also attended clubs and events in London before and after the NYE season.

49. Utilizing digital sociology, my digital data collection "focuses on the enabling and constraining dimensions of the use of objects and how objects shape or discipline users just as users reconfigure objects" (Lupton 2015, 38–39). See Lupton (2015) for a thorough review of methodological approaches in digital sociology; Waisbord (2014) for a thorough edited volume on media sociology; and Snickars and Vonderau (2012) for an edited volume on iPhones and the future of media.

50. My use of media sources such as *Mixmag* and *DJ Mag* is sensitive to the way these sources "construct, consolidate and perpetuate discourses surrounding DJs as artists" (Jaimangal-Jones 2018, 223), particularly, how the discourses "serve to elevate and sustain the cultural status of DJs" and "validate and perpetuate a wider range of ideological notions within dance music culture" (ibid.).

51. See St John (2006) for a thorough review of this literature.

Chapter 1

Experiencing Bliss

Spaces of Respite, Release, and Transcendence in Dance Music

As young as 16 years old, I attended my first rave in San Francisco, California, an experience that left a deep, lasting impression on me. It was a small venue, a space no bigger than 1,500 square feet, with an energy that felt bigger than anything I had ever experienced. The walls, ceilings, and dance floor literally shook with the music's vibrations, smoke filled the air, and dancers' sweaty bodies rubbed against mine as I relentlessly moved to the beat: "You could feel the ball of heat just rise through the floor" (May in Matos 2015, 35). Finding space on the dance floor, I remember vibrating with energy, sweat dripping off my nose, my face flushed. I completely lost track of time and space, let my body find one beat after another as I raised my head and closed my eyes, the wave of beats rushing in and out of my torso, head, and up and down my limbs.[1]

Feelings of euphoria, again and again and again, swept through my body like a fever. Never before had I felt so completely in my body—on my own terms—in control of my movements and interactions with others.[2] Never before had I really, truly felt this free.[3] There was an electricity that turned me on that night and that inner light has stayed on for decades. This first impression was so lasting that I can still remember what I was wearing, how I was moving, with whom I danced, how I felt, and what I saw, a quarter of a century later. Endless flashbacks of that night are still so vivid and fresh. Now, at 43 years old, I think about that night every time I attend a new dance music party. Will it feel like it did back then? Will similar moments of transformation and bliss enter into and around my body? Will I, quite simply, be moved? These are ongoing questions, desires, and experiences that people in the dance music scene often draw upon to describe its relevance to them and their community; they either lament its loss or reflect upon its iterations today. In this chapter, I show how experiences of respite, release, and transcendence have and continue to inform dance music culture. I will begin to investigate the sociological implications of these experiences with the goal of better understanding what is accomplished in and around dance music spaces. If "love is the message," what does this declaration actually feel like? What does it accomplish? These are questions I return to throughout this book.

PLUR AND CONTEMPORARY DANCE MUSIC

Rave culture's PLUR philosophy, an ethos that centralizes peace, love, unity, and respect, was often deployed during rave's peak in the 1990s. It has been described as "beliefs and attitudes that give raves their unique culture and group or collective identity" (Anderson 2009b, 310), "[t]ypified by notions of inclusion, acceptance, communality, and a celebration of difference" (Maloney 2018, 231), and an ideology that "persists in club culture and electronic dance music (EDM) at large today" (ibid.).[4] In Matos's (2015) *The Underground Is Massive: How Electronic Dance Music Conquered America*, he connects PLUR to both the widespread (especially in the 1990s) use of the drug ecstasy and the overall vibe of the early rave scene:

> On ecstasy, one's perception sharpens, but so does one's level of empathy; on it, nearly everything seems wonderful, almost indiscriminately so . . . the hug-your-neighbor vibe began a sea change in popular music and popular culture. House music was no longer a novelty; it was the future. (Matos 2015, 25)

DJ Seth Troxler offers his own thoughts on PLUR, writing:

> In the US, there's this term PLUR. It's got a crappy reputation now, but *it stems from the values of original club culture: respect, being positive, communal unity. Once you have those values, they spread in how you conduct yourself and view the world.* I was in a club recently, and there was this guy there with one of the original Paradise Garage tee shirts on. We got talking, and he said the major difference with dance music now and back then, is *real* diversity. You had social, class, race, sexual diversity—and that's cool. That's what dance music culture is about. Everyone under one roof, exploring their own and each others [sic] identities. A celebration of something more, something outside of received norms. Not having a giant glow stick and getting on it. The Red Bull Music Academy street party for Paradise Garage and Larry Levan Way last weekend was beautiful for that exact reason. *You have a huge block party in a huge city, full of white, black and Asian people, young and old. Nobody looked wasted, and hardly anyone was on their damn phones.* They were just dancing and

singing together to beautiful music, for hours and hours. *That* is club culture.[5] (Troxler 2014, my emphasis)[6]

Anderson (2009a) draws some conclusions about PLUR:

> The cynical accounts of PLUR in the past and its denial in the present likely earmark a fundamental change in rave consciousness and identity. Why do scene insiders define the ethos this way? Why did PLUR not resonate more broadly or work its way into popular culture? As I mentioned in Chapter 1, this ethos was one thing that attracted me to EDM early on. I was troubled, then, to hear that PLUR was silly and on its way out. PLUR was, after all, raves' socially conscious ethos and the heart of their collective identity. (25)

Has PLUR and/or a rave ethos[7] that celebrates inclusion, acceptance, communality, and difference actually been on its way out? Anderson found that "[p]eople also described PLUR's relative absence in the contemporary scene . . . [y]ounger EDM fans even lacked the consciousness about it all" (Anderson 2009a, 24). My research tells a slightly different story.

While the commercialization and corporatization of dance music have certainly put a strain on the practice and awareness of PLUR, careful attention to the messaging that continues to come out of dance music scenes reflects an ongoing PLUR presence.[8] Admittedly, PLUR might be especially present in my study because of the actual DJs I'm following (The Blessed Madonna and her colleagues typically play house music and use PLUR/rave ethos identity markers; see chapters 2 and 4) and because it is showing up in different ways, with a new lexicon and new representations. Following The Blessed Madonna and her colleagues means that a particular subscene—arguably more aware of its own history—is front and center. While The Blessed Madonna and Honey Dijon are firmly planted in an admittedly fluctuating "house music" scene, the larger dance music industry is made up of a massive range of music and dance tastes (see Matos 2015; Collin 2018); The Blessed Madonna and Honey Dijon occupy a slice of dance music that harkens back to the PLUR/rave ethos, particularly given the fact that they play house music and are historically connected to the early rave days. Reflecting on her deep connection to rave culture's history, in a 2017 *Instagram* post TBM writes:

> Tonight I turn 40 years old. I also celebrate 25 years in dance music in the city which gave birth to house: Chicago, my home since college. A quarter century ago this week I was nosing around my first warehouse party, knowing deep inside that my life was changing forever. (@theblessedmadonna, October 21, 2017)

For those who reflect on their entry into dance music spaces, how "life-changing" it was is a common sentiment. The Blessed Madonna, again, remarks on this sentiment:

> "Nobody falls into dance music; everybody's there for a reason," she says, her voice cracking with emotion. "However you found your way there, if you're coming to house music you're coming to be relieved. I don't know each person's story, but I do know what house does. People tend to over-romanticise dance music, but those moments of transformation, those moments are real." (Brailey 2016)

For many, house and dance music spaces offered a new world of possibilities. As I will show in the analyses throughout this book, even if PLUR wasn't explicitly referenced, its philosophy was present.

PLUR also emerges in critiques of the current dance music industry. Commercialization and capitalism are often cited as "killing dance music," particularly rave culture's early emphasis on inclusivity.[9] As an obvious example, ticket sales (particularly for the large festivals that are now so popular every spring and summer) automatically exclude large numbers of people without the financial resources and time needed to attend the event. In a recent *Facebook* post, Derrick May (a key though fraught DJ in dance music)[10] bemoans capitalism in the dance music scene. Posting an article titled, "KFC Bought Colonel Sanders a DJ Slot at Ultra Music Festival in Miami," (David G. 2019) he writes:

> There seems to be NO limit on the lack of commonsense or ethics, business is business but this is really to[o] much! At the expense of creative people, corporate + over zealous [*sic*] mindless promoters are destroying dance music! Greed will kill dance music!

DJs' social media posts, especially those who experienced early rave culture, often reflect on their shared history, how "DIY" everything was back then, and what today's industry is like for the fans, music, and the actual labor of DJs. "Greed will kill dance music!" sums up a fair share of the critiques. Some fans in the comments section of Derrick May's *Facebook* post further highlight their frustration with the current scene:

Greed *has killed* dance music!
There, I corrected that for you!

Coming from the 90's myself . . . loving the music . . .
we have lost the beauty of the underground . . .

these kids have no idea where we started. It was pure, and amazing . . . festivals don't hold the same value as a[n] old school warehouses party, map point event.

Sounds no different to the rest of EDM shite. Who cares whether it's Steve Aoki or Colonel Sanders throwing shit into the crowd, it['s] still shit.[11]

PLUR, represented in other ways and via a different lexicon, seems alive and well in the messaging that The Blessed Madonna and her colleagues put out and in her fans' enthusiasm for her shows and related music (discussed at length in chapter 2). Thus, PLUR/rave ethos messaging—notions of love, respite, release, and transcendence, for example—continues to reverberate throughout dance music spaces at the same time offering direct and indirect challenges to corporatization and capitalism, both on an institutional level (in and through the industry) and a personal level (rethinking how we navigate our world today). As DJs, clubs, and clubbers continue to sample "the mythos of PLUR" (St John 2012, 244), what do these samples produce?

THE "LOVE" MESSAGING

Rethinking Our Temporal Dimensions: "Leaving time behind for a little while"

To start, DJs often use the language of respite, release, and transcendence[12] to describe their own understanding of what dance music culture accomplishes or should accomplish. In another *Instagram* post, The Blessed Madonna writes (in reference to *smartbar* in Chicago): "[T]his space became a home and a proving ground for the most brilliant minds in dance music, countless sweaty hugs, tears on the dance floor, wild incantations, loss, joy, transformation . . . my intention is that together we can slip into another space. We can tear down the walls and leave it all on the floor. Leave time behind for a little while. And when it's all over and the world comes back, we can say good morning and leave better than we came."[13] Malbon's (1999) "playful vitality" captures what TBM describes here, an ineffable sensation—often experienced on the dance floor—that entails both controlling and losing control of one's body in the process of merging with the crowd and euphoric sensations that intersect with spacelessness, timelessness, and the temporary (116).[14]

Notably, The Blessed Madonna's quote highlights the temporal theme[15] that often peppers accounts of dance music spaces today and in recollections of its early days—*timelessness* or losing oneself in the moment and therefore losing track of time. Malbon (1999) articulates how time often operates in clubbing and especially on the dance floor: "Time passing is superseded by music playing" (102). That is, timelessness is aided by rhythmic, loud music that makes it nearly impossible to communicate verbally (especially on the dance floor) and the context of nightclubs (music, use of space, dancing, typically late at night and/or during the weekend, etc.) also brings clubbers *to the present* and temporarily away from their lives *"outside* clubbing" (Malbon 1999, 102).[16]

Those writing about timelessness connect bliss and transcendence to slow practices, often using the practice of timelessness or flow to describe what slowing down actually means. Bliss, they argue, is intimately connected to and realized when we slow down. In Carl Honoré's (2004) book, *In Praise of Slowness: How a Worldwide Movement is Challenging the Cult of Speed,* he offers some advice we might consider for slowing down, for living in the moment, and cultivating balance rather than tracking every moment of our lives for maximum productivity:

> [W]hat the Slow movement offers, is a middle path. . . . The secret is balance: instead of doing everything faster, do everything at the right speed. Sometimes fast. Sometimes slow. Sometimes somewhere in between. Being Slow means never rushing, never striving to save time just for the sake of it. It means remaining calm and unflustered even when circumstances force us to speed up. (Honoré 2004, 275)

Berg and Seeber (2016) offer similar advice, reviewing literature that emphasizes the importance of *flow* and *timelessness*. They explain:

> This experience of "flow" is so elusive that it can only be captured retroactively, once it's all over . . . "Timelessness is the experience of transcending time and one's self by *becoming immersed in a captivating present-moment* activity or event. Scholars and poets have suggested over the years that the timeless intensity of the present moment is a gateway to creativity and joy (548)." (27, my emphasis)

According to Berg and Seeber, flow and timelessness promote creativity and joy, allow us to think without pressure and expectation, and is desperately needed in our age of constant distraction and high-speed communication. In the space of flow, we calm down and prepare our embodied selves for re-entering our distracted world with more clarity, the ability to navigate problems with more ease, and the tools we need to start directly challenging corporate control of our lives. They add: "[w]e need, then, *to protect a time and a place for timeless time,* and to remind ourselves continually that this is not self-indulgent but rather crucial to intellectual work. *If we don't find timeless time, there is evidence that not only our work but also our brains will suffer"* (28, my emphasis). Honoré (2004) agrees. Our embodied selves need time for timelessness; without timelessness, we fail to cultivate the tools that we need to resist the culture of speed.[17]

The Blessed Madonna's description echoes these themes of timelessness, flow, creativity, and joy. She sees the scene, particularly dance floors, as offering a space unlike those that we usually find ourselves in. "Together we can slip into another space" that is not overlaid with work, anxiety, and consumption; on her dance floor, we can hop off the hamster wheel for a couple hours.[18] We can turn our back on capitalism, even for a moment. "We can tear down the walls and leave it all on the floor," crossing boundaries that we don't often cross in everyday life, connecting with strangers and expressing love and connection rather than indifference and disconnection. And, finally, "when it's all over and the world comes back, we can say good morning and leave better than we came." These are some themes that emerged in fieldnotes from her and others' events, were featured in social media posts, and offered a general template for goals that dance music actors emphasized. Even if not entirely realized, these themes have been central to the physical and digital spaces I studied.

Slipping into Another Space, Even Momentarily

In a club called *Geluk*[19] in Amsterdam, featuring The Blessed Madonna as the headliner, the following sign was posted in one of the bathroom stalls:

In our perfect world
you would stay
until the sun comes
up and come back
every weekend.

If something makes
you feel unwelcome
or unsafe, please let a
member of staff know.

While this sign points to the ongoing sexual harassment theme that many of the clubs and events are directly and indirectly addressing (covered in chapter 3 and the Conclusion), what stood out to me was the first sentence: "In our perfect world you would stay until the sun comes up and come back every weekend." There are a few messages delivered here, particularly the act of losing yourself in the moment: "Together we can slip into another space," one unfettered by deadlines, money-making, social and cultural expectations, career-building, family obligations, and a growing list of stressors that have such wide-ranging implications that entire books are being written about the deteriorating mental health of entire nations (Hari 2017). In Johann Hari's (2017) *Lost Connections: Uncovering the Real Causes of Depression—and the Unexpected Solutions*, he argues that our contemporary societal expectations are hampering our ability to really, truly live full lives. In other words, we are half awake, distracted by our smartphones, unwilling and unable to truly connect—face-to-face—with the people in our lives. And given the fact that so much of our time is spent disconnecting or connecting on a superficial level (Turkle 2011), when close and loving connection—even with strangers—is made available to us, those in dance music spaces describe these (even temporary) connections as transformative, freeing, and even life-changing.[20]

The themes TBM lists in her quote above are similarly described by her colleagues. For example, Honey Dijon describes freedom, timelessness, and, perhaps most notably, pleasure as she discusses her work as a DJ:

[Interviewer:] For me, dancing works out a kind of physical intelligence that I don't access in other places. Like, a mind-body connection. How does DJing make you feel?

[Honey Dijon:] Free. It's almost like when you're having really good sex with somebody, and there's no inhibition, or there's no thought. You're not thinking, you're feeling. I have no concept of time. When I'm DJing sometimes, I don't know if 10 minutes have gone by or 10 hours. *I feel really free, and I feel really lustful. I get so sexually turned on when I get in the zone.* (Wray 2017, my emphasis)

Honey Dijon's description of "the zone"[21] intersects with Malbon's (1999) playful vitality or a flow state wherein "you're not thinking, you're feeling"; thus, one experiences a combination of timelessness, spacelessness, and, in the process, pleasure and joy. DJs and the crowd often experience these embodied connections together, connections that can be transformative. Returning to my description at the beginning of this chapter, that moment at my first rave was life-changing because even though technology had not fully entered into our lives as it is now (via smartphones and social media, for example), there were social practices in U.S. society that made it increasingly difficult to connect with other people, particularly experiences of alienation inherent to capitalism. The ambience and dance floors at my first rave and so many raves and related events after offered such a comparative difference that, of course, I saw and continue to see that experience as different, transformative, and even blissful. There were/are so few opportunities for me to experience and share those connections with others that the rave scene served as that one single space both in the moment and, perhaps most importantly, in my own personal history.

I'm not the only person to describe this other dimension and its lasting impact on me.[22] Those who experienced the early rave days also describe its pull and what they saw and experienced in those early days:

> "The humidity and the heat—it was like a jungle in there," says Ollivierra. "Nobody was there to get laid. Nobody was there to get drunk. Nobody was there to make a presentation of style with respect to hair, their makeup, their clothing" . . . .[Carl] Craig attended the night [Derrick] May premiered Inner City's "Big Fun." "I've never seen a room, before that, explode—really, almost spontaneous combustion," says Craig. "These people lost their freaking minds." . . . . Craig was also impressed by the fluid, expressive dancing[:]... "they weren't doing flips, but, God, you thought they were going to. They were dancing together—not like, 'Can I have this dance?' You just kind of joined in. It was really exciting."
>
> [Ollivierra references this feeling again in a description of another party:] "When Derrick [May] plugged the set with all the familiar cues, people were crying. You could see it in the strobe lights."

In an early rave in 1990, another raver describes how it felt to be there:

> "I remember feeling like part of something that wasn't obvious to the world," says Vanessa. "I remember looking at the crowd and feeling like somehow this event brought together a subculture, because it was like home to a lot of people. It became the language that we were all understanding and speaking. There was something profoundly understood that was way beyond the music. It wasn't even like 'It's us against them.' It was like, 'It's *us.*'" (Matos 2015, 35–36; 42; 60)

In the documentary titled "I Was There When House Took Over the World," DJ Traxman describes his introduction to *The Music Box* in Chicago, vividly bringing us back to how it felt:[23]

> When I first went to *The Music Box*, I was about 16 and when I went I heard music playin' like, WHOO, WHOO, WHOO, WHOO . . . walkin' up. The closer I got, the harder it felt. Like, whoo, whoo, whOO, WHOO! I never heard anything like that in my goddamn life.

Honey Dijon often reflects on these moments of transformation or slipping into another space, particularly when, as she describes it, a "masterful" DJ makes that magic happen. One of her *Instagram* posts reads:

> A truly great DJ, just for [a] moment, *can make a whole room fall in love. Because DJing is not about choosing a few tunes.* It is about generating shared

moods; it's about understanding the feelings of a group of people and direct-
ing them to a better place. In [the] hands of a master, records create rituals of
spiritual communion that can be the most powerful events in people's lives. (@
honeydijon, June 2, 2019, my emphasis)

TBM makes a similar argument in a 2019 interview with *TimeOut London*:

Given how worldly you are now, if you were randomly plonked in a DJ booth
and had no idea where you were, could you work it out just by reading the
crowd?
    "I think so. You become hyper-aware of body language in a crowd. Reading
a room and being aware of people's feelings and what their deal is, is a real
quality. I could probably work out if they'd had too much to drink, or were having a bad week, or were fighting with their girlfriends or boyfriends." (Ravens
2019)

Again, themes that pepper these accounts include temporary moments of
individual and collective transformation and the often life-changing, "most
powerful events in people's lives," experiences that are certainly heightened
by a DJ's ability to read the crowd. These temporary moments have been
referred to as "Temporary Autonomous Zones" (Bey 1991), widely referenced in the literature (Wilson 2006; Rill 2010; Collin 2018). Wilson offers
a useful definition:

Theorists like Hakim Bey (1991) take the neo-tribe concept even further,
describing periodic, spontaneous, and often hedonistic communal formations—
raves, for example—as "temporary autonomous zones," as parties or gatherings
that *explicitly challenge mainstream value systems* associated with consumption
and social order by virtue of their status as unsanctioned get-togethers in illegal
venues. (158, my emphasis)

Obviously, the contemporary use of the term "rave" and the context in which
most so-called "raves" now take place are far from this definition and have
everything to do with why DJs like Seth Troxler have so little patience for
the intense commercialization of dance music today.[24] Yet, DJs like TBM and
Dijon often draw upon these ideas—losing it on the dance floor with a DJ
that can take you there—in order to emphasize their work and, perhaps most
importantly, frame their work in relation to a PLUR/rave ethos. Much like the
media discourses that Jaimangal-Jones (2018) analyzes, DJs often use a rave
ethos and their unique contributions to that ethos as a way to emphasize their
authenticity, originality, and "special" performances—moves that make sense
ideologically (as these are common discourses in dance music) and position

them as emotionally invested and connected to their fans, dance floors, the music, and so on (see chapter 4 for more on these authenticity moves).

At the same time that these discourses are circulating and people continue to describe their dance floor experiences as extraordinary, many argue that one's ability to slip into another space on the dance floor has become increasingly more difficult with the introduction of new technologies (a theme I address in chapters 2, 3, and the Conclusion). DJs like Honey Dijon often talk about what she sees on her dance floors now (a lot of people looking at their smartphones, for example) that has fundamentally changed how people experience dance music spaces. Slipping into another space is still accessible and certainly experienced by dancers/clubbers, but the context in which dancing and community happens on dance floors has shifted, especially with the ongoing use of new technologies, a pattern I analyze closely in chapter 3.

Crossing Boundaries: "Where You're Absolutely Free"

In The Blessed Madonna's quote, she claims that "[w]e can tear down the walls and leave it all on the floor," representing what I so often see and experience on (house music) dance floors.[25] At a New Year's Eve in Glasgow, Scotland, connecting with strangers was so common that it felt normalized throughout the night and especially during the countdown to 2019. Exchanging glances, hugging, kissing, and simply talking to strangers are extremely common social practices that are often even more likely when the music (the lyrics, especially) and the particular context of the situation (a New Year's countdown) support those connections. The following field notes offer examples of the connections to strangers that so often happen in and around the dance floor. At the NYE event in Glasgow, strangers on the dance floor literally hugged me as we celebrated the New Year:

> Soon after I watched multiple queer women couples kissing around me, two women on the platform above me made a point of hugging me and wishing me a Happy New Year, a total stranger on the crowded dance floor. I was taken aback but instantly felt warm and held, smiling so wide and returning the New Year's wishes as we embraced.

Wide smiles are exchanged on the dance floors, representing very quick connections that strangers often make with one another. At a post-NYE event in Manchester in 2018, exchanges like this were common:

> This happened at least 5 times tonight (usually with women on the dance floor): I exchanged a wide smile with a woman to my right and another woman to my left, especially as the music got extra intense and "danceable." I would be

dancing, look over into the eyes of another dancer, smile wide, my eyes bright, and she would look back at me and also smile wide before we would both look up at the light show and DJ booth again.

This also happened while I was in Rotterdam (at a NYE event the night before), exchanging wide smiles with dancers on the dance floor, mutually showing one another that we appreciated the music we were hearing, were vigorously and passionately dancing to that music, and were happy to share this moment with each other: total strangers dancing next to one another at a club.

Mutual appreciation for the music is another way that strangers come together and connect. At a London club in Shoreditch, I experienced yet another mutual appreciation for the DJ's music with another stranger on the dance floor:

> As the clock approached 1:45 a.m., Joe Goddard played two fabulous songs in his set, Madonna's "Hung Up" and another song about how women are taking over the world. After he played those songs, a woman on the dance floor looked over at me, gave me a massive hug and said, "OMG, that last song brought tears to my eyes!" I smiled wide and agreed.

The emotionality of these connections—even and perhaps especially with strangers—represents crossing boundaries and "leaving it all on the dance floor," even temporarily. It is also an on-the-ground representation of the emotionality that TBM consistently references in her interviews: "[l]ess heart-hands, more hand on heart" (Brailey 2016).

Therefore, what does "Love is the Message" actually produce? At house and related dance music shows, it is often reflected in loving connections—typically temporary—that clubbers make with each other. During the NYE event in Glasgow, for example, another set of strangers befriended me (now *Instagram* and *Facebook* friends); they were two men with whom I proceeded to dance and spend time throughout the entire evening. Notably, one of the men (gay-identified POC/person of color) approached me first, exclaiming that "I was "SOOOOOOOOOOO fabulous!!!" soon after he watched me dance and then started dancing with me. In a NYE party in Rotterdam, a queer woman of color—Carina—approached and befriended me almost as soon as I arrived, a connection which directly led to a full night of meeting new friends, learning how to navigate the fairly complicated token system for purchasing water and access to the bathrooms, and connecting with other dancers on the multiple dance floors with her by my side. Additionally, the exchange with women dancers in the middle of the 2019 countdown above was initiated by them, not me. Finally and perhaps most notably, during my first introduction to TBM at a club in Shoreditch, London (see chapter 2), I became fast friends with another dancer—Alejandro; we became so close, so quickly that we proceeded to spend the entire weekend together, hopping from one dance party and club to the next over a three-day period and have continued to send sweet, loving messages to one another over *Instagram* and *Facebook* for the last four years. On our way to yet another club, he posted a picture of us with a caption that read, "We dint not go. #oldfriends #new-tings," playfully marking us as new friends acting like we had known each other forever.[26] Thus, emotional interactions with strangers are a common theme. In all of the cases above (except Alejandro, who was visiting London from Toronto), the strangers who approached me were "locals," interested in either temporarily connecting with me for a few seconds or the entire evening and often interested in why I was there to begin with.

"Love is the Message," therefore, is not realized as an empty mantra. Instead, there is often a "love fog" that clubbers enter when they step into (house) dance music events, one that holds up and supports PLUR and is more or less pronounced in any one space. In Christine Siokou's (2002) study of Melbourne ravers, for example, she found that "the party atmosphere and collective 'vibe' quickly became apparent" (13). Referencing Ben Malbon's (1999) *Clubbing: Dancing, Ecstasy and Vitality*, she highlights his definition of this vibe or group feeling

> through movement, proximity to and, at times, the touching of others, and (crucially) a positive identification with both the music and other clubbers in the crowd, those within the clubbing and especially the dancing crowd can slip between consciousness of self and consciousness of being part of something much larger (p. 74). (quoted in Siokou 2002, 13)

Chapter 3 extends this discussion, outlining more examples of how this "love fog," vibe, or group feeling permeates dance floors and how other clubbers and fans often challenge anyone who fails to follow its rules and regulations.

Leaving Better than We Came: Timelessness as Necessary

Returning to TBM's quote, "love" is also realized in how it impacts clubbers/dancers at any house music and/or dance music event: "When it's all over and the world comes back, we can say good morning and leave better than we came." This theme connects to the love fog I discussed above. There are rules and regulations for interacting on dance floors that often have a lasting impact on how those in (house)/dance music scenes talk about conducting their lives in and beyond the dance floor. In chapter 3, I analyze a number of examples of how these rules and regulations played out on the dance floors, contributed to warm and loving interactions on the dance floor, and, in some cases, resulted in clubbers/dancers aggressively highlighting the rules (to other clubbers) in order to keep a PLUR-like ethos present.

WHERE THE DANCE MUSIC INDUSTRY FAILS

Even though timelessness, flow, creativity, joy, and love are often highlighted by DJs and clubbers as they describe certain dance music spaces and their experiences in those spaces, dance music—EDM[27] or otherwise—can also contribute to a grueling, unhealthy schedule and lifestyle for actual DJs. Avicii's tragic story is a case in point.[28] While his nightly fees were as much as $250,000 or higher (McIver 2018), his tour schedule was extremely stressful, topping about 250 shows per year. In a documentary about his life as a superstar DJ and producer (titled *Avicii: True Stories*), when Avicii started taking his mental and physical health seriously, no amount of money or fame mattered to him. In a number of painful scenes, we see him relentlessly trying to advocate for himself while those in the industry (booking agents and his manager, for example) remained far more worried about the financial cost of his canceled shows:

> *Even after a long break, Avicii could no longer handle the stress of performing:*
> I'd been away for—for—it's eight months, six months. Now, I've—I've literally done everything I can. And straight away, I still . . . I still get stressed out. I still don't like this.

> *Yet, the industry failed to support Avicii's decision to retire:*
> I've been very open with what I've been through, what I've felt, and . . . what I've done. You know, everyone knows, uh, that I've been anxious and, you know, everything, and that I've been trying. So I-I . . . I didn't expect people to try to push me to—to do more shows, when it really. . .

> When they'd seen how shitty I felt . . . doing it. So—So I did get a lot of resistance when I wanted to stop doing the shows.
> *As one friend describes it:* "The problem is that your agency is so concerned with their own money that they can't take in what you're saying and then explain it to the promoters." (Tsikurishvili 2017)

Again and again, Avicii faced an industry that cared far less about his mental and physical health than the bottom line.[29] In 2014, the tour schedule and lifestyle (drinking, in particular) that became so normalized for Avicii eventually caught up with him, putting him in the hospital with "alcohol induced pancreatitis" (Musgrave 2020, 95). "I realised that my body and mind couldn't handle it any more," he told *The Guardian* (McIver 2018). Ironically, dance music's entertainment machine (Marcuse 1964) often paints a picture of pure bliss and transcendence (for audience members and in order to generate ticket sales), while DJs' actual labor is often marginalized, ignored, or simply made invisible. Given how mainstream, successful DJs are now firmly planted in the commercialized music industry, it makes sense that they're often treated as commodities, experiencing labor exploitation as much as other musicians with coveted record contracts (Arditi 2020).

While Avicii's tour schedule seemed extreme, a quick glance at the tour schedules for The Blessed Madonna, Honey Dijon, and Peggy Gou tells a similar story. In May 2019, for example, Peggy Gou released her tour schedule with a list that included shows in a wide range of locations (Amsterdam, Malta, Brooklyn, Arizona, and Tokyo) within the first 12 days of the month. While she's on tour, Gou's *Instagram* story posts are often dizzying, reflecting a schedule that rarely seems to slow down. Soon after Avicii's death, The Blessed Madonna (2018) published an article titled "The Black Madonna's[30] guide to protecting your mental health when touring." In it, she writes:

> Recently, I've done something I almost never do: cancelled two shows due to illness and exhaustion. Normally such a decision would be fraught with additional anxiety and guilt; I'd be driven to self-care only after my husband, parents, tour manager, and friends begged me repeatedly to go to the doctor and stay the fuck in bed. But for once, I just did the right thing without being prompted. I put my own mental and physical health first, and if you're an artist on a seemingly never-ending world tour, I hope you will take a moment and think about your own wellness plan too. (The Black Madonna 2018)

She goes on to list her own self-care work, emphasizing practices that put her mental health front and center, such as getting a regular therapist, practicing mindfulness, cutting out or down on drinking, no drug use, making time for her most trusted friends, and physical wellness.

Another DJ, Laidback Luke, also reflects on toxic patterns that are experienced in the dance music industry:

> *Don't you want to warn them sometimes? Are you in a position to give them fatherly advice, or does that not happen anymore?*
> It still happens sometimes. I was backstage with The Chainsmokers the other day, who are just starting to tour heavily. I'm the first person to tell them: "You think this is hard? Wait until you have to tour outside of America, in Australia and Europe." Then I give them some tips. Somehow I still feel responsible for them.

Do you think more people should take that responsibility?
Yes. A lot of people, maybe also in the underground, are only concerned with their own ego; getting drunk, using drugs, fucking girls. But you forget that you got into it for the music, for the people that also like your music and that you feel connected to.

Do you worry about them?
Yes, I do worry. I care about my fellow human beings. I went up to those Nervo girls not too long ago at Ultra Korea. I asked them like: "Are you okay? I see you drinking a lot and touring a lot, how are you holding up?"

What kind of response do you usually get?
In general, people react very well. I hope they sense that I'm being sincere. But anyway, DJs still end up in hospital if they're not looked after. And there will always be as many DJs getting into the music business as there are dropping out. And they will also think: "Fuck it, sex, drugs and rock 'n' roll!" That's supposed to be super cool. It's nothing new or special, but that is not what it's all supposed to be about. (Friedman 2014)[31]

THE "BRO" SIDE OF DANCE MUSIC V. ITS DIY HISTORY AND HOUSE MUSIC

A Resident Advisor ("the influential online publication and clubbing community hub" (Vincentelli 2017)) video reflects on dance music's DIY history:[32]

But perhaps more than anything, punk also influenced dance music on a philosophical level. *Like a punk concert, the ideal dance floor is a temporary autonomous zone, one with different rules and different behavior from the world outside which is part of its thrill. But the most important connection is the DIY ethic.* As Carl Hyde of Underworld once put it, "Rave was more punk than punk. Ten thousand people in a warehouse, making records in your bedroom, pirate radio . . . You could have a career entirely outside the conventional music business." This is still true today. As production software and free resources like *YouTube* tutorials lower the barrier to entry even further empowering anyone who wants to jump in and see what happens. This idea of self-empowerment of attitude and ideas over trained skill was born not only in disco clubs or warehouse parties but in the brief explosion that was the original era of punk. (my emphasis)[33]

As I discuss throughout this book, distinctions are consistently made between the "more 'bro' side" (Vincentelli 2017) of dance music or EDM and other, far more inclusive and reflective strains of dance music. For example, house music—via its history and fan base—is usually positioned as counter to the spectacle of EDM at the same time that EDM artists certainly use house and talk about house music as central to their work. In other words, while house is not necessarily "owned" by any one strain of dance music, house music and its history consistently link up with PLUR-related practices, practices that often include a direct and unapologetic rejection of EDM-centric music and its scene.

My on-the-ground research combined with ongoing debates about the future of dance music points to some ongoing shifts in dance music, in general. Some of these shifts are hopeful and PLUR-related, while other shifts are less hopeful, far less reflective and critical, and what many have started to refer to as "rager"—"code for frat boy" (Matos 2015)—rather than rave culture. DJs have seen this massive shift—from DIY raves to massive, EDM-centric festivals—over the years and often reflect on where they see the scene going:

> *Do you think that feeling of positivity from the 90s is in the air again?* [John Digweed:] Well, when you think about places like Twilo, there was definitely not a bottle service culture. It was 90 percent about the dancefloor. There was no place to sit and if you weren't dancing you were at the bar. It really was either one of those two options. I think that's what was nice about it—people went there because they wanted to cut loose for nine, ten, eleven, twelve hours—however long they wanted to stay. *I think that's what's happening now again. The underground culture is having a resurgence and people are experiencing the palettes of a lot of new DJs. The confidence is there, which is healthy for the scene.* (Garber 2014, my emphasis)[34]

Chapter 4 and the Conclusion build upon this section, outlining how the house music scene and DJs I'm following critically think about and try to institutionally and individually address the problems and possibilities in the larger dance music industry. In many ways, Avicii's death reflects how thoroughly taxing (in terms of DJs' labor and business travel) and corporatized dance music is today. Thus, the book's Conclusion discusses how these problems are being addressed, exploring new and perhaps less grueling ways to do dance music.

CONCLUSIONS

Beginning with a vignette of my first rave, this chapter explored how PLUR/rave philosophies (peace, love, unity, respect, respite, release, and transcendence) have continued to impact dance music spaces. In particular, it emphasized how DJs like TBM and Honey Dijon are reflecting on and still using these philosophies without actually making any direct references to the acronym PLUR. The Blessed Madonna is often referred to as a different kind of DJ, one that speaks up, looks different, and contributes to genre-bending music in her sets (Vincentelli 2017). How she deploys PLUR/rave philosophies parallels her difference and direct challenges to the larger dance music industry. While TBM, Honey Dijon, and Peggy Gou have unique ways of approaching their careers, all three of them are committed to changing dance music (making it more inclusive, for example) and thinking critically about what they can do differently and what they see as missing from the larger dance music milieu. Thus, chapter 2 takes a closer look at what TBM and her colleagues are navigating, accomplishing, and resisting in dance music.

Additionally, this chapter explored how PLUR emerges in frequent discussions of the ongoing corporatization of dance music scenes, taking a closer look at what both DJs and fans have to say about these trends. Chapter 3 and the Conclusion offer a closer analysis of how these challenges are realized and negotiated in and around dance floors.

Further building upon PLUR, this chapter also explored the "Love" messaging frequently referenced in TBM and others' house music events. In particular, it showed how timelessness, slipping into another space, crossing boundaries, and leaving better than we came are all themes that circulate in and around "house music" and physically and emotionally on dance floors. Even in the face of new technologies that make it increasingly more difficult to have transformative experiences on the dance floor, these themes are still realized and reflected upon.

Finally, the chapter ends with some reflections on "Where the Dance Music Industry Fails," again, pointing to dance music's ongoing corporatization, how it has and continues to impact both dance music spaces and DJs' labor and well-being. Once again, we see TBM doing something different here as she shares her own practices for staying physically and emotionally healthy in her career and while on tour. This book's Conclusion brings these discussions together, offering some reflections on where dance music is going and what needs to be done to continue to challenge its commercialization.

Laying out the context for how rave authenticity and EDM/club culture commercialism is realized from the standpoint of three successful women DJs, the next chapter takes a closer look at how TBM, Honey Dijon, and Peggy Gou are shifting the dance music landscape, paying particular attention to how they're *performing*, *producing*, *maintaining*, and *resisting* authenticity and commercialism in the larger dance music milieu.

NOTES

1. As Malbon (1999) cogently describes, "this [loud] music is as much felt by the whole body as simply heard" (123). Similarly, Honey Dijon often talks about loud music and its embodiments in real life: "To feel the bass or to see how other people's bodies react to different frequencies in music, you just can't get that in front of a fucking computer looking at YouTube" (Shukur 2021; https://www.crfashionbook.com/culture/a35509582/honey-dijon-kim-jones-cr18/).

2. In this vignette and throughout this chapter, I discuss a process that Malbon (1999) calls "playful vitality" or "the exhilarating and often ineffable sensation of strength or vitality. . . . These sensations appear to result from this simultaneous losing and gaining of control over the body, through the feeling of merging with the crowd (or *exstasis*), and through the experiencing of 'glowing moments' . . . or sensations of euphoria, spacelessness, timelessness and the momentary" (116).

3. In my early 20s, I remember reading McRobbie's (1993)'s "Shut Up and Dance: Youth Culture and Changing Modes of Femininity," a chapter that helped me articulate why I loved raves and dancing so much: "What kind of image of femininity, for example, is being pursued as female ravers strip down and sweat out? Dance is where girls were always found in subcultures. It was their only entitlement. Now in rave it becomes the motivating force for the entire subculture. This gives girls a new-found confidence and a prominence" (419).

4. While its often assumed that the PLUR ethos emerged in the U.S. rave scene and was coined by DJ Frankie Bones and/or his friends and colleagues (see http://hyperreal.org/raves/spirit/plur/Origin_of_PLUR.html), Maloney (2018) offers another possibility, one that recognizes the historical connections between disco, house music, the Civil Rights Movement, Stonewall, and gay liberation; in his article, he "asserts that disco's use of gospel elements created a quasi-religious *proto-PLUR* . . . ideology on the dance floors of the 1970s, and that this was an expression of those made Other by aspects of either race or sexuality" (231, my emphasis). As Rill (2006) explains, PLUR "is echoed across websites and in participants interview responses, and is the 'fantasy' that participants wish the external world could embrace" (656).

5. A defining feature of dance music today is the ongoing and often contradictory debates about authenticity (e.g., are you into the scene for love or money?). I take up the issue of authenticity and other features of these debates throughout the book and specifically in chapters 2, 4, and the Conclusion.

6. https://www.vice.com/en_uk/article/bmb953/seth-troxlers-guide-to-dance-music-festivals-clubbing-and-notbeing-a-terrible-human

7. Even though the acronym PLUR is rarely used, its set of values—inclusion, acceptance, communality, and difference—are often used by key actors in dance music, specifically the DJs featured in this book. Also, given the fact that rave ethos (Heath 2019) is another term used for this philosophy, I often use PLUR/rave ethos to capture that connection.

8. As Anderson (2009a) adds, "[s]ome antagonism between people from different subscenes has become well established, and this compromises the larger goal of diversity

acceptance as well as the endorsement of peace, love, unity, and respect" (173). As I show throughout this book, as dance music grows (economically, socially, and culturally), DJs and clubbers are constantly navigating *both* authenticity *and* mainstream commercialism, often finding themselves somewhere in-between both extremes, a complicated position that makes it increasingly difficult to access peace, love, unity, and respect.

9. Critiques like this are consistent with rave culture's history; as Anderson (2009b) reminds us: "the rave scene's ethos of peace, love, unity and respect . . . and celebration of anticorporate values and underground music was viewed as an antidote to mainstream conformity" (316).

10. "[A]lleged victims of the Detroit techno pioneer describe a string of incidents over the last two decades in the US, Europe and New Zealand" in an investigative report by journalist Annabel Ross (2020); see https://ra.co/features/3780.

11. My emphasis in the first quote.

12. Fritz (1999) cited transcendence as the central reason why people attended raves; thus, given TBM's personal history and connection to 1990s raves, her quote above draws out themes that were central to that time (such as transcendence) and are inherent to her "We Still Believe" tour and approach to dance music.

13. March 31, 2018. Goulding and Shankar (2011) also emphasize these processes, showing that "clubbing has a quasi spiritual element to it based on the components of; mythology, formulism, sacredness, communitas, and transformation" (1435); for example, "[w]ith clubbing there is an emphasis on the sacralization of time or 'living for the weekend'—a sense of separation and clear distinction between the working week and the clubbing weekend that offers a sense of release and an alternative way of being" (1444). St John's (2006) review of existing EDMC/electronic dance music culture literature describes these processes as an EDMC-specific "'spirituality of life' [wherein a] context for truth, authenticity and self-realisation [is] sought outside traditional religious frameworks" (15).

14. Notably, playful vitality also seems to intersect with BDSM "bottoming," described by sexuality journalist Tracy Clark-Flory (2021) as the following: "Researchers have preliminarily proposed that 'bottoming' . . . is associated with 'transient hypofrontality,' which is the short-term impairment of the brain's executive function. This state can be associated with 'reductions in pain, decision making activity, logic, and difficulty with memory, along with increased feelings of floating, peacefulness, and living in the here and now'" (108). While all of these feelings and embodiments might not be present at once, clubbers who describe losing themselves on the dance floor often also describe a combination of floating, peace, timelessness, spacelessness, and being very present/in the moment.

15. This continues to be a theme in dance music research (see Jaimangal-Jones, Pritchard, and Morgan 2010).

16. Malbon (1999) connects timelessness to our embodied, everyday lives, emphasizing what clubbing often does: "Time and its intense regulation of bodily actions *outside* clubbing—through the demands of working, of traveling, of general sociability and interacting—is replaced by music and its regulation of bodily action *within* the spaces of clubbing—through dancing, through spatial selection, through bodily expression of emotional and identificatory responses to the crowd" (102).

17. Malbon (1999) also addresses flow and uses dancing as a way to explain how flow is realized for clubbers: "Turning to the dancing that is so central to clubbing, it is clear that clubbers feel 'better' or more competent at dancing after some time practising, and that as they feel 'better' at dancing so their enjoyment of that activity increases. . . . With practice, play requires less 'work'. As sensations of competency at playing increase, a sense of 'flow' becomes possible" (138). While flow is definitely not a given and depends upon whether or not a clubber is able to access flow or is distracted by boredom, anxiety, harassment, or any number of other disruptions, in chapter 3, I reflect on how flow might be more difficult to access, particularly for women who often experience harassment on dance floors, especially in venues that do not actually curb sexual harassment.

18. Reynolds ([1998] 2012) describes the anti-capitalist, anti-rationalist features of raving: "Raving is totally unproductive activity, it's about wasting your time, your energy, your youth—all the things that bourgeois society believe should be productively invested in activities that produce some kind of return: career, family, politics, education, social or charity work. . . . That's the glory of rave. It's about orgiastic festivity, splendour for its own sake" (537).

19. This is a pseudonym.

20. While "feeling the love," "losing it," and transformation on the dance floor is widely supported by dance music research, "[o]thers never feel anything they would describe as liberating or mystical" (Rill 2006, 655). Transformative experiences are certainly not a given and are largely dependent upon context.

21. Similarly, Fikentscher (2013) discusses Csikszentmihalyi's "seamless flow experience" as resonating "uncannily with the DJ practice of programming dance music" (142).

22. These themes are also widely discussed in dance music literature (see, in particular, St John 2001; Rill 2006, 2010).

23. https://www.youtube.com/watch?v=9Rah1F1zq1k

24. Even with the commercialization of dance music, temporary moments of pure bliss—what Malbon (1999) calls "extreme flow experiences" (141)—are absolutely accessible today and largely depend on the context (see chapter 3 and the Conclusion). I describe these temporary moments of pure bliss in the vignette at the beginning of chapter 2 and again in my analysis of dance music's dance floors in chapter 3.

25. While I do not intend to offer "over-romanticised and idealistic visions of the supposed annihilation of social differences upon the dance floor" (Malbon 1999: 135), this section reports on patterns that emerged in my fieldnotes. In the Conclusion, I complicate this finding a bit more, thus emphasizing how social differences often became especially significant in particular dance music spaces and with particular crowds. Malbon's (1999) research also flips the script here a bit, arguing that "to some extent *it does not matter* whether the clubbing crowd is actually diverse in terms of identities or not . . . what matters is that many clubbers *understand* the clubbing crowd, of which they are a part, to be diversely constituted, and they crucially find this understanding a rewarding and enriching experience" (186).

26. *Instagram* post, June 18, 2017; not including html or *Instagram* handle because Alejandro is a research informant.

27. Matos (2019) offers a fairly typical definition of highly commercialized electronic dance music (EDM): "[As] *Mixmag* wrote in the summer of 2015, [EDM] 'means the drop-heavy, stadium-filling, fist-pumping, chart-topping, massively commercial main stage sound that conquered America. It means Dayglo vests, EDC [Electric Daisy Carnival], Ultra [Music Festival, in Miami], Vegas pool parties, and flying cakes. It's possibly somewhere between electro and progressive house, directed by Michael Bay, and like many music genres, trying to pin it down exactly is like trying to grab a fistful of water. Or should that be a fist-pump of water?'"(https://www .npr.org/2019/11/13/778532395/the-mainstreaming-of-edm-and-the-precipitous-drop -that-followed)

28. Avicii was considered an EDM DJ; as this book will show, "house music" and PLUR/rave philosophies are often positioned in direct opposition to the practices, actual music, DJ, and crowd behavior that takes place via commercialized EDM. For example, the DJs I followed do not describe themselves as EDM DJs precisely because the EDM label does not reflect the music they play, the brand they want to cultivate and—especially for TBM and Honey Dijon—the venues and events they play.

29. In a review of the documentary, Musgrave (2020) offers an astute reading of Avicii's tragic story: "What the documentary appears to show, to my reading at least, was the tragic story of a shy and anxious young man, who loved making music and the deep, meaningful joy it brought to him, propelled into a world reliant on the ever more avaricious exploitation of his labour in order to support the development of an economy which had formed around him, where simple human care and compassion had been decimated by the compulsion to keep going and market his music, and against which he tried to fight back" (97).

30. TBM changed her name in July 2020, a move that was precipitated by negative media attention about her previous name (The Black Madonna). This is how she describes her decision to change her original "name . . . a reflection of my family's lifelong and profound Catholic devotion to a specific kind of European icon of the Virgin Mary which is dark in hue. People who shared that devotion loved the name, but in retrospect I should have listened harder to other perspectives. But now I hear loud and clear. My artist name has been a point of controversy, confusion, pain and frustration that distracts from things that are a thousand times more important than any single word in that name. We're living in extraordinary times and this is a very small part of a much bigger conversation, but we all have a responsibility to try and effect positive change in any way we can. I want to be able to feel confident in the person I am and what I stand for" (https://www.instagram.com/p/CC3BKAQnc2S/). She made this move only a couple months after George Floyd was murdered by Derek Chauvin and the #BlackLivesMatter protests exploded throughout the world, thus directly speaking to and acting on that moment.

31. https://www.vice.com/en_us/article/mg4zn3/laidback-luke-i-got-sucked-into -the-mainstream

32. In Chris Conner's (2015) dissertation, he includes an analysis of "bro culture" in dance music today—specifically in EDM. In the Conclusion, my analyses

interrogate how "bro culture" emerges in particular dance music spaces and how it's supported and resisted. Future research in this area is also needed.

33. Resident Advisor video located here: https://www.residentadvisor.net/features/3192

34. https://www.vice.com/en_us/article/qkmgy5/how-to-dj-with-integrity-according-to-john-digweed

Chapter 2

The Blessed Madonna, Honey Dijon, and Peggy Gou

Different Kinds of DJs

How do The Blessed Madonna, Honey Dijon, and Peggy Gou disrupt the dance music status quo? What are they doing to shake things up? Answering these questions requires carefully teasing out and making sense of their ongoing work, how they talk about their work, and how they have to constantly negotiate *both* rave authenticity *and* EDM/club culture commercialism to accomplish their DJing today. TBM's quote below reflects one of many examples of how she navigates and speaks up about these ongoing negotiations:

> Dance music needs riot girls. Dance music needs Patti Smith. It needs DJ Sprinkles. Dance music needs some discomfort with its euphoria. Dance music needs salt in its wounds. Dance music needs women over the age of 40. Dance needs breastfeeding DJs trying to get their kids to sleep before they have to play. Dance needs cranky queers and teenagers who are really tired of this shit. Dance music needs writers and critics and academics and historians. Dance music needs poor people and people who don't have the right shoes to get into the club. Dance music needs shirts without collars. Dance music needs people who struggled all week. Dance music needs people that had to come before midnight because they couldn't afford full admission. *Dance music does not need more of the status quo.* (Couvreur 2015, my emphasis)[1]

As I began this research project, I literally stumbled upon her approach to DJing, captured in the quote above, and experienced on one of her dance floors.

In summer 2017, I received research funding to study nightclub life in London, a project that built upon dissertation research I had completed in nightclubs in Bangkok, Thailand (Hidalgo 2009; Hidalgo and Royce 2016).

43

Much like the preliminary research trips I had completed in Bangkok before I started intensive ethnographic fieldwork, my summer 2017 trip to London was entirely preliminary and exploratory. While I had plans for how I might want to study London's nightclub life, with particular questions about how it differed or overlapped with Bangkok's nightclubs, I had no idea what I would stumble upon and subsequently obsess over for the next four years of my life.

This journey and the topic of this book began that first Friday night in London. I had officially started my on-the-ground preliminary research, dragging my best friend, Maylis,[2] to a nightclub that seemed like the most appropriate first place. At this point, I was looking for spaces that catered to queer clubbers, so house or techno music seemed like an obvious first start. I was also trying to get a general sense of the nightlife scene, so some time in Shoreditch, an increasingly popular, though gentrified, area of London, seemed like another obvious first start. For the first couple of hours, Maylis and I spent most of our time on the upper floor of the club, people-watching and trying to get a sense of the music, ambience, and type of clubbers.

I remember feeling less than impressed with all of it, wondering where something phenomenal was happening, where people were actually moved by the music or one another. This first floor level of the club felt more like a fraternity party than a rave (see reference to "rager"/bro culture in chapter 1) and I certainly didn't see any clubbers losing themselves or experiencing flow on the dance floor. As a clubber/researcher in Bangkok for so many years, I half expected to find a similar trend: nightclubs that felt more like places to be seen and "get messed up" rather than actual spaces of community that even marginally reflected a PLUR/rave ethos.

It was approaching midnight as Maylis and I started talking about leaving. "Maybe this place was a bust?" I frowned. We started making our way to the front door when, suddenly, I heard that sound, so familiar given my very early days in the 1990s rave scene: whoo, whoO, whOO, WHOO![3] As the ground moved and bounced beneath our feet, my heart started to race as I turned to Maylis and said, "Wait! What's that down there? Let's go check it out." To the right side of the entrance to the first level dance floor, we saw stairs and literally followed the music. I remember tentatively, though excitedly, making my way down those stairs, my heart thumping madly in my chest. The stairs wrapped around and down, depositing us into an underground area that opened up to a much larger dance floor, completely packed with dancers. "Welp! I think we found something!" I exclaimed, hardly containing my excitement. We immediately made our way closer to the DJ booth where a large white neon sign above it read: "WE STILL BELIEVE." At this point, I simply had no idea who The Blessed Madonna was and had been so removed from dance music scenes and house music for so long, that my point of reference for everything I was seeing and experiencing that night connected to 1990s raves. While I frequented nightclubs that played dance music in Thailand (from 2005 to 2008), the city of Bangkok was not a dance music destination (and certainly not a destination for house music), so there wasn't really a dance music scene to follow when I was there.

Maylis and I made our way into the middle of the crowd, as close to the DJ booth as we could. I vividly remember that everyone on that dance floor and upon raised stages to the left and right of the DJ booth was dancing. The space vibrated with moving bodies. Although Maylis ran out of steam about an hour after we discovered this underground area, I remained. Mirroring the transformative dancing experience I described in chapter 1 (at my first rave in the 1990s), I literally lost any sense of time; I was completely lost in the moment as I danced to The Blessed Madonna's set for the very first time. Sweat poured off of me, dripping off my nose, my black jeans soaked. This night with The Blessed Madonna and the dancers she brought together set me on a trajectory. While I still did not yet know where this research was necessarily going to take me, I knew, without any doubt in my mind, that I was going to return to this club again and again and again, as long as I could hear and experience her music again. Not surprisingly, the energy she consistently brought to this particular club and how dancers/clubbers responded to her felt different.

THE BLESSED MADONNA: A DIFFERENT KIND OF DJ

The Blessed Madonna continues to introduce a different way of DJing to dance music, one that appears to be less focused on its commercialization and more focused on how those in the industry can impact social change and contribute to warmer social relations. She illustrates this difference in her 2016 DJ of the Year interview with *Mixmag*:

> As we hitch a ride on the final weekend of a grueling European tour, *Mixmag* is immediately struck by her warmth and sense of humour. But then it's these very qualities that, she claims, have facilitated her success. "We were just coming out of the age of steely, emotionless techno guy," she smiles, over a restorative pot of Earl Grey the day after her birthday celebrations. "Then I come in and I'm like, 'Hey, what's up you guys! Love yooooou!" Less heart-hands, more hand on heart, *Marea is the inverse of emotionless techno guy*: excitable, articulate . . . maternal? "You know, there's a little mom thing in it too. Totally. Totally!" But if she's dance music's mom, she's a rad, weird and decidedly cool mom. (Brailey 2016, my emphasis)[4]

Additionally, she is often cited as bringing back or, at the very least, re-introducing moments of PLUR:

But if dance music, and society in general, is far from a utopia, to be at the front of a Bl[essed] Madonna gig is to be transported somewhere far better. Buried among the sweaty, jubilant mass—there's lots of girls, but guys too—it's impossible not to feel The Bl[essed] Madonna loving each and every one of us right back. Is it too broad a stroke to conflate her own sense of not belonging with her all-encompassing love for those who join her in unburdening themselves? She agrees completely. "For so much of my life I have felt like I was not supposed to be somewhere. Being able to relieve people of that feeling of being on the outside looking in—if I can take that from them and welcome them . . ." It seems corny, but in an age of divisive politics, new conservatism and unremitting darkness, we need people like The Bl[essed] Madonna. To help us, on the dance floor, transform hurt into resolve, pain into release, tears into sweat . . . but also show us that the realities that we live in can be so much better, too. (Brailey 2016)

In addition to an inclusive vibe she aims to create on her dance floors, The Blessed Madonna has consistently used her platform to make social and political statements: "[w]hile still committed to dance music's utopian vision of inclusivity and care, she has not shied away from *calling the electronic music community to do better*, to be more welcoming, and to respect its historical origins in marginalized communities" (Trax Magazine 2016, my emphasis).[5] In June 2019, for example, her Field Day London show featured the following messages in large block letters above and behind her DJ booth. These pictures were posted (via *Instagram* stories) by fans on her dance floor and then subsequently posted by her:

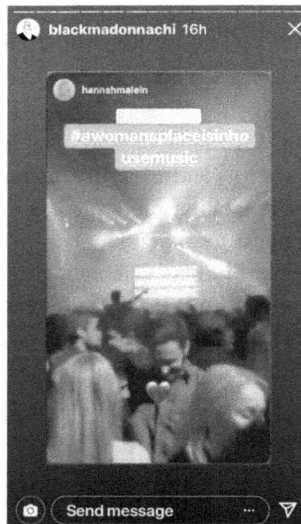

Figure 2.1   Clubbers' *Instagram* **Stories from The Blessed Madonna's Dance Floor:** #awomansplaceisinhousemusic.

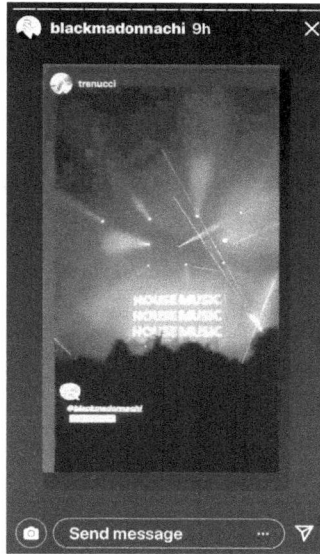

Figure 2.2 Clubbers' *Instagram* Stories from TBM's Dance Floor: House Music Projection.

Figure 2.3 Clubbers' *Instagram* Stories from TBM's Dance Floor: House Music is Disco's Revenge.

Figure 2.4   Clubbers' *Instagram* **Stories from TBM's Dance Floor: #believewomen.**

Additionally, the following messages were also blasted on the screen above her DJ booth: LOVE, FUCK WAR, BLESSED, and GENDER BENDER. In your face, social and political messaging is how The Blessed Madonna navigates DJing, often wearing black T-shirts with statements such as "DONALD TRUMP IS A WASTEMAN," "BLACK LIVES MATTER," or "JESUS WAS A REFUGEE."

A *New York Times* article titled "The Black Madonna, an Activist D.J., Wants to Turn Dance Music Upside Down" describes her success and "openness of spirit—and musical tastes" as a welcome counterpoint to "the more 'bro' side of the commercial dance-music scene known as EDM" (Vincentelli 2017). This article—like most media representations of her—positions her as a different kind of DJ.[6] Describing the time she spent DJing in Chicago in the mid-2000s, she says:

> The things that were popular were not the things I was into. . . . There was this real emphasis on extremely white, extremely male minimal [music]. I love minimal techno but there was a kind of wash to all this stuff that was so similar—very emotionless, without peaks and valleys. That was never me. (Vincentelli 2017)

Additionally, TBM and Honey Dijon often make references to the past, pointing out how their contributions to dance music either challenge mainstream narratives or simply highlight what the music they play means both historically and in the present.[7] References to house music, in particular, offer an example of these reflections. In the images above, "HOUSE MUSIC IS DISCO'S REVENGE" points to a clear repudiation of mainstream attacks on disco. For example, "one of the most ill-conceived, successful promotions in sports history" (Redford 2016) a baseball double-header at Comiskey Field called "Disco Demolition Night" serves as one of the most infamous mainstream attacks on disco. In an article titled, "'Disco Demolition Night' Was a Disgrace, and Celebrating it Is Worse," Josh Terry (2019) recounts the epic failure of "Disco Demolition Night," outlining why any commemoration misses the mark:

> On Thursday, Dahl [a Chicago shock jock who also organized the original event] is set to throw the first pitch and the Sox will give out 10,000 free "Disco Demolition" t-shirts. It's strange for a professional sports team to lovingly remember one of its biggest non-baseball mistakes in its history. . . . Disco was a genre mostly created by and made for Black, Latino, and gay people, and other marginalized groups. While Dahl has vehemently denied it as merely a harmless stunt, its execution was racist and homophobic. *Rolling Stone* critic Dave Marsh who attended the promotion wrote at the time, "Your most paranoid fantasy about where the ethnic cleansing of the rock radio could ultimately lead . . . . White males, eighteen to thirty-four are the most likely to see Disco as the product of homosexuals, blacks and Latins [*sic*], and therefore they're the most likely to respond to appeals to wipe out such threats to their security."

Thus, "HOUSE MUSIC IS DISCO'S REVENGE" is in reference to how house music brought back a scene and music that directly challenged the status quo, much like what disco had done in the 1970s.[8] TBM consistently makes references to these challenges, highlighting how the "emotionless techno guy" and emotionless, minimalist music, for example, wasn't her thing. Both how she interacts with her fans and the actual music that she plays in her sets all point to on-the-ground expressions of PLUR, regardless of whether or not that term is still being used. The philosophy, as embodied, declared, performed, and used for historical reflections, all point to her performance of difference, the way she isn't quite like mainstream DJs and their commercialized dance music scenes.

Additionally, like a number of other DJs today, TBM's sets are genre-bending and reflect the vast range of sounds across multiple genres in dance music. As Anderson's (2009b) research shows, genre-based scene fragmentation accounts for one of the central ways that rave culture transformed (its alteration and decline) and challenges "the very core of what generated the PLUR ethos of the rave scene: musical diversity and mutual appreciation" (329); given this trend, when DJs talk about playing with genres and get frustrated with the genre-based cliques that can form in dance music, they're resisting this trend and, inadvertently, using a PLUR ethos to do so. House music is no different; DJ Octo Octa articulates this well in the following tweet:

House music doesn't get enough credit for being a genre that has so much weird and experimental elements to it. The number of bizarre, off-the-wall house records I have in my collection is amazing. If you think it's all the same then you should start listening more carefully. (@octo_octa, May 27, 2020)

Genre-bending is a term that a number of DJs have been using, thus trying to avoid the pigeonholing that can happen when the larger music industry attaches a particular dance music genre to them, a tactic that fails to align with a PLUR/rave ethos (Anderson 2009b). Peggy Gou, for example, also talks about genre-bending:

You know I used to care loads about genres—you know, "I wanna be a house DJ! I wanna be a techno DJ!" But I don't care about the genres anymore. I go by the year and some people call my music "indie." Some people call it "disco." Some people call it "house music." Whatever, you know? And then, I think . . . I'm planning to do my album this year and I am planning to produce a lot of different kinds of genres I like. It can be downtempo, it can be pop, it can be house music, Italo disco, you know, so, if I like it I like it. So, I don't really go follow by the genre anymore. (*Oxford Union* 2020)[9]

TBM's difference also connects to what she values and wants to see reflected back to her in dance music spaces: "I'm personally invested in seeing a shift in power, even if that sometimes means shifting away from me," Ms. Stamper said. "Maybe if I hadn't spent as much time on the other side of the glass, I wouldn't be as empathetic to the needs for all kinds of people."[10] Her empathy is also realized in how she interacts with her fans, often giving out hugs after her set[11] or directly contacting and reporting people who scam her fans with fake tickets. She posted the following exchange on her social media:

$AndreaGalterio

Acting up lately....Please send $25
three times

Thanks

Do you Understand?

> Cool. So my name is Marea. And
> you might know me as The Black
> Madonna. This Facebook profile
> had been ripping off people selling
> fake tickets to my show all
> weekend. I put everyone you
> scammed on the list. So, get this:
> I'm reporting this info to CashApp
> and the police for fraud right now.
> You should be embarrassed for
> stealing from people who now more
> than ever need to be around good
> folks. Find a new show to rip off.
>
> Do you understand?

theblessedmadonna • Following
Los Angeles, California

theblessedmadonna ✪ Pro-tip:
Don't fucking scam my fans. If you
sell fake tickets to my show I will
personally find you, come for you
and call the police. You may think I'm
the one but I'm not the fucking one.
See you all at Lot613 today. If you
got taken by the person who was
doing this, please let me know so I
can personally make it right.

111w

lydiamthompson BOSS
111w Reply

Liked by brianscottkress and
8,275 others

OCTOBER 21 2018

Add a comment...

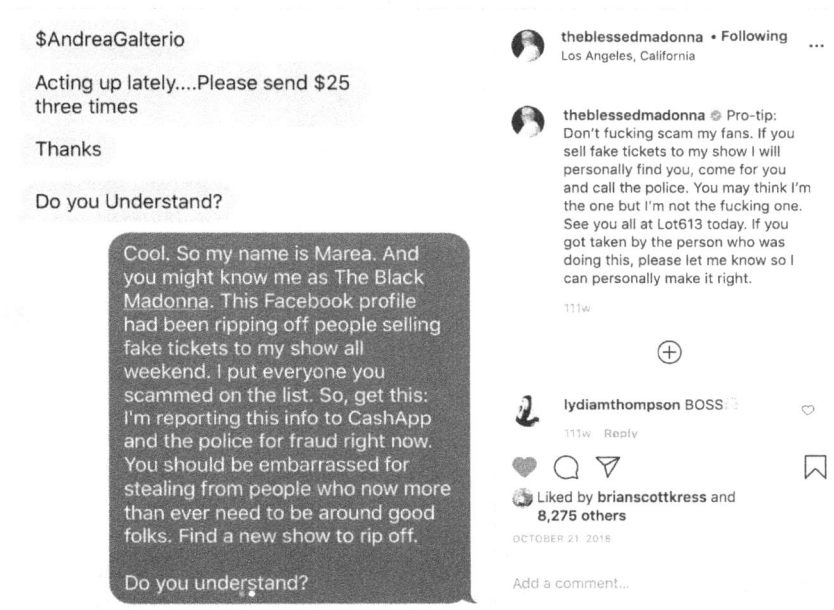

Figure 2.5   The Blessed Madonna's *Instagram* Post, October 21, 2018.

In an interview, TBM discusses her connection to her fans:

I definitely would say that I have some of the most intense fans. *They are the people that love me a lot and I love them a lot too*, and maybe some of that comes from being a person willing to listen and reflect some of the cares and concerns of people who have felt nudged out. If I have made them feel good then I am really happy and honoured. I am maybe not the best person to do it, but I am happy to do that to whatever degree I can. And as much as I have meant to any of them, they have meant much more to me. I'm still trying to figure out how to do this new thing at the ripe old age of 38, and I have been lifted up by the people who have been there, along for the trip. I would say as much as anyone has a special relationship in dance music, I do with the people that come to my shows. *It is personal and emotional and they are very special to me.* (Trax Magazine 2016, my emphasis)

Once again, love, emotionality, and personal connection are central to TBM's DJing and related branding. As she describes it, being "emotionless . . . was never me." About a year after the pandemic made its way across the globe, she released a single titled, "Marea (We've Lost Dancing)"; notably, as soon as she released this song her fans started posting and tagging her in old dance floor videos, reflecting her ongoing emotional connection to them, an uncanny skill she's acquired as a different kind of DJ and one that allows her to successfully engage in branding, a dialectical combination of *both* self-promotion and marketing *and* pulling at her fans' heart strings—certainly an ideological imperative in house music.

As another example of utilizing a PLUR/rave ethos, TBM also remains committed to promoting and supporting up-and-coming DJs, particularly DJs who do not fit the mainstream mold. Kiddy Smile, for example, a queer, French DJ talks about her relentless support, writing:

> The Way This Woman Got My Back and It's mutual! She threatened in the past to cancel some of her gigs so she could make me stop working for a minute and make me rest! She was one of the first to support "Let A Bitch Know" . . . and I mean SUPPORT like making my track her track of the year in dj mag and putting my tracks on mixes when we haven't had [*sic*] met yet! She is a sweet and kind soul like you encounter [*sic*] not so many in this industry! Happy to have you in my life @blackmadonnachi. (@kiddysmile, February 28, 2019)

Similarly, Honey Dijon is positioned as a different kind of DJ, one that celebrates her identity as a trans woman of color, critically reflects on the history of dance music, and looks for ways to directly challenge social and cultural patterns she sees as negative both in dance music and society, in general.

HONEY DIJON: #HONEYFUCKINGDIJON
TAKES ON DANCE MUSIC

In a January 29, 2019, *Facebook* post, Honey Dijon emphasizes a number of PLUR/rave ethos themes, particularly the shift she has seen in how people actually interact on dance floors. She writes:

> The minute you become more than the music, you're through!—Frankie Knuckles
> I am proud to announce my very first party alongside the Percolate crew called Blackout. The concept behind this party is to *bring the focus back to the dancefloor, music and sound, DJs unseen. Inspired by the roots of clubbing when people connected and danced with one another to create memories that last a lifetime.*
> Leave your hang ups at the door and let your inhibitions free to get lost into the sound. (@honeydijon January 29, 2019; my emphasis)

In another *Instagram* post, Honey Dijon, again, laments the loss of club life dance floors. Posted with a photograph of a dancer on her knees, her head tossed back, eyes closed and lips pursed as she rubs her inner thighs, Honey Dijon's caption reads:

> Oh you know that time when people used to dance at the club and get so lost in the music that they fell out on the floor cause it was too much! Too much was the goal. Yes, this actually happened. #onceuponatime #clublife #nyc. (@ honeydijon, April 24, 2019)

There are a number of reasons why the dance floor actually shifted since the early rave and clubbing days. First, events such as Organic '96 (Matos 2015) in San Bernadino, California, and other large events corporatized and shifted the rave scene.[12] These events were "more concert than dance. It was more set up to stare at a stage rather than be part of this ritual" (Gerard Meraz quoted in Matos 2015, 224). Second, much like what we see now, DJs were becoming celebrities. Again, in 1996, DJs Sasha and John Digweed experienced early examples of this where there were "three thousand people cheering us Friday nights" (Matos 2015, 225). Their popularity, however, was coupled with a shift that physically and spatially changed what was actually happening on the dance floor. Another Matos (2015) interviewee explains:

> Still, the effect of that celebrity status could be unnerving to longtime dancers. "It was, rather unfortunately, the first place that I saw people just standing and facing the DJ booth—maybe moving around a little bit, but not dancing with each other, certainly," says Bruce Tatum. "They were just looking at the guy playing the records." (Matos 2015, 225)

Today, this is even more pronounced. For example, if cell phones are allowed in the venue, when the music reaches a peak or a popular song or lyrics enter into the DJ's set, instead of dancing together, clubbers often pull out their smartphones and take photos or videos of the moment. That is, people on the dance floor literally turn away from one another, looking only up at the DJ booth or the lights, focusing only on what they are capturing on their smartphones and, perhaps most dramatically, not really dancing alone or certainly not dancing together.[13] While this might seem minor at first glance, it matters and kills any vibe and related connections typically created by collective dancing. For example, in Takahashi and Olaveson's (2003) discussion of the often intimate connection between the DJ and dancers, "[t]his intimate relationship highlights the ritualistic aspects of events as ravers are fully participating in the performance, rather than being passive spectators watching from the margins" (86). When clubbers on dance floors essentially stop dancing or "fully participating in the performance" by looking down or up at their phones, they often become "passive spectators watching from the margins" or even worse—not really dancing in the middle of the *dance floor*. Instead of "records [becoming] the tools for rituals of spiritual communion" (Brewster and Broughton 1999, 5) achieved by "breaking the audience/artist boundary" (ibid.), the use of smartphones fortifies this audience-artist boundary. The act of archiving the event on smartphones positions the artist/DJ and their performance as a commodity to be consumed elsewhere (shared out via social media, placed in photo libraries, or any other reason clubbers have for taking a picture or recording a video on the dance floor) and puts up new glass-screen walls between artist and audience.

Notably, as I address again in chapter 3 and the Conclusion, clubbers pulling out and using their smartphones on the dance floor is especially pervasive in crowds and venues that are far more "rager" (Matos 2015) than "rave"; that is, when the crowd/clubbers + venue + DJs directly challenge this "rager" behavior, much less of that behavior is present. On the other hand, when "rager" behavior is far less challenged or even encouraged, it permeates the dance floor, the surrounding areas of the dance floor, and the general ambience or feeling of the club. Nonetheless, the use of smartphones on dance floors today across all spaces is pervasive, especially if phones are permitted. This means that clubs have been forced to restrict smartphone use, reflected in the following *fabric* (a well-known London dance music nightclub) *Instagram* post:

> fabric is London's home for underground music, always aiming to create a feeling of self-expression on the dance-floor. As we approach reopening, we are introducing a strict no photo, and no video policy at the club. Stay in the moment and put away your phone, enjoy the night. (@fabriclondonofficial, June 28, 2021)[14]

In Honey Dijon's remix of Jayda G's "Stanley's Get Down (No Parking on the DF[/Dance Floor])" the lyrics literally call clubbers out for being on their phones. The first two lines emphasize the fact that clubbers often have their phones out on the dance floor, scrolling rather than actually dancing:

Hey, you, I see you!
With your phone

Next, the lyrics shame clubbers for not only pulling out their phone on the dance floor but also doing it to mindlessly scroll through *Instagram*:

Looking at *Instagram*
This is a dance floor, baby!

Finally, it ends by saying what should be happening on a dance floor— "groovin'" and actually connecting with the music rather than connecting with your phone:

This is where you're supposed to get dowwwwwwwwwn.
This floor is for groovin'

Sherry Turkle's (2011) *Alone Together: Why We Expect More from Technology and Less from Each Other* shows how technology is keeping us *both* better connected *and* more isolated than ever. That is, we are digitally connected at the same time that our use of technology physically pulls us away from one another.

DJs such as Honey Dijon are sensitive to how our social practices have changed with new technologies and vocal about how she wants to challenge any changes she sees as problematic and as dance music grapples with the COVID-19 pandemic:

> *Nightclubbing has gone from cultural spaces to entertainment. DJs have now more or less become the new rock stars. It's a conflicting thing for me. I experienced clubbing pre-internet. These were places for people not only to be a part of a musical movement. They were also places for people to meet, mate, create, elevate, participate. These were places, if you were not a part of mainstream society to find work, find yourself, express yourself, to find other likeminded people who didn't fit into the straight world.* Nightclubbing isn't just about entertainment. When I came of age in New York and Chicago, these were places where fashion designers, artists, drug dealers and prostitutes were really breaking down social class systems. So, for me, nightclubbing is beyond 2010 and the beginning of Boiler Room, you know? It moved into entertainment and, on the one hand you cannot stop evolution but, on the same hand I kind of feel like something is being lost. *You can't replicate human contact, no matter how many platforms or Zooms you have. It's just not the same experience.* (Flynn 2020, my emphasis)

A study of dance music livestreams during the pandemic (Vandenberg, Berghman, and Schaap 2021) backs up Honey Dijon's point about human contact. While livestreams digitally brought "ravers" together, the fact that they weren't physically on the dance floor together made them long for those moments, thus "hamper[ing] the establishment of a renewed sense of social solidarity" (S141). Without the physical presence of other clubbers on a sweaty dance floor, livestreams failed to measure up to those experiences, often leaving clubbers feeling melancholic and frustrated.

Similarly, Honey Dijon often expresses some sadness and frustration when she reflects on club culture before dance music exploded. Much like

Seth Troxler's quote in chapter 1, Honey Dijon often talks about what happened before dance music went mainstream and got highly commercialized. While this critique of dance music's commercialization is complicated by the fact that Dijon is absolutely embedded in its current entertainment machine (Marcuse 1964), her work in and through it continues to push up against the status quo; that is, she often calls out dance music for its ongoing inability to be more inclusive and recognize its own history. Notably, these critiques are not just empty words; the ongoing contributions she's making to dance music are unapologetically Black, queer, trans, sex-positive, and deeply connected to house music's history. She often talks about how deeply her identities informed her experiences and continue to dictate how she does dance music now: "My transness definitely informs what I do because it's allowed me to walk in so many worlds. If I was just a regular heteronormative girl, I would not have been able to go to those types of clubs, those queer places where we went to hear that amazing music. And I feel like I carry the DNA of that culture with me. It's awesome, you know" (Collin 2018, 354).

In addition to her unapologetic reflections (i.e., like TBM's reflections, they actually help her branding and often utilize rave markers such as "inclusivity, acceptance, communality, and a celebration of difference" (Maloney 2018, 231)), Honey Dijon often uses her social media platforms for branding too—explicitly, implicitly, or some combination of the two. For example, she might promote herself as a DJ (explicit) at the same time that she offers her own take on what it means to be a DJ (implicit). In the following conversation with Stewart Copeland of The Police, she talks about the role of a DJ (notably, this video was posted in her *Instagram* stories):

> Honey Dijon: . . . bringing together people through sound and vibration and . . . trying to channel shamanic, ritualistic sexual energy in people . . . I try to do that through music . . . *I am a facilitator of debauchery*, I'm a facilitator of people's good time. For me, *the music is the star of the show*[15] so I wanted to do a party where people dance with each other and celebrated and had a laugh and tried to get laid and make out in the corner and be in the dark where they can release all of their inhibitions. That, to me, is what a proper nightclub is like.
>
> Copeland: What is it about music that makes them release their inhibitions and start thrusting their pudenda in each other?
>
> Honey Dijon: Awwwwww, you know, I think real life is complicated. I think we all need dreams and fantasy and release from the everyday and I think music brings people together.[16]

Goulding and Shankar's (2011) clubbing research mirrors Honey Dijon's description above, describing DJs as "the new shamans" where there "role is to whip up the crowd, heal their anxieties, and exorcise their demons, and as such, attract near cult like following" (1445). These are consistent, ongoing themes in dance music: "A really good DJ can send the crowd into a frenzy, work you up and then bring you down again gently, they are in control, they're the ones with the power and they know it" (Goulding and Shankar 2011, 1445; research respondent's quote). Honey Dijon is not only acutely aware of this power but she also takes it extremely seriously; as she sees it, as soon as she steps into the DJ booth she is "responsible for creating the atmosphere, setting the mood, and dictating the tone of the night" (Goulding and Shankar 2011, 1445; see also Sylvan 2005).

In terms of Honey Dijon's more implicit branding practices, she often uses social media to promote #selflove, her particular contributions to dance music, and what she sees as missing in dance music spaces. In another *Instagram* post, she clearly outlines what's missing:

WE NEED MORE BLACK FEMALE IDENTIFIED AND QUEER PEOPLE OF COLOR DJS ON LINEUPS AT CLUBS AND FESTIVALS. WITHOUT US THERE WOULD BE NO HOUSE OR TECHNO.[17]

Honey Dijon also uses her platforms to give her followers history lessons. For example, one of her *Instagram* posts quotes Kiddy Smile: "House music today has been stolen. Whitewashed. Completely. People don't even know it's originally black. I didn't even know." Her caption reads:

@chez.damier asked me once what was my reason for being a dj . . . I realized that I carry within me a legacy that is slowly eroding. It has taken me twenty years to achieve the visibility that I now receive and during that twenty years I was studying. Studying a craft that was created by queer and trans people of color. A craft that has now become my turn to pass on because there are so few of us with that information on how to present music in a context born out of pain and [marginalization]. *The music and the culture were safe havens for colored folk who were not welcomed in white gay and queer spaces. The music was about love, community, release, and sex and not getting fucked out of your mind [for] days on end. You didn't need to get fucked up because the music got you high.* You used your whole body to release fear and stress and express your connection to music. You danced with each other instead of shoulder to shoulder or with the flick of a wrist because the music demanded that of you. To think that music that has gone on to change the world that was created by inner city black youth and queens with the most forward thinking ideas would be colonized into entertainment for the white middle class with agendas to push social media entertainers instead of artists (a term used too fucking loosely if you ask me), which it has become, it's important for me to honor the real pioneers that have gone before. That is my reason for doing what I do. Thank you @kiddysmile for saying in @i_d what so many of us DJs and producers of color feel and think. #blackgirlmagic. (@honeydijon, November 9, 2018)

   Her history lesson is clear: house music was created by "queer and trans people of color" and later "colonized into entertainment for the white middle class." Additionally, she uses rave ethos language: "the music was about love, community, release, and sex and not getting fucked out of your mind [for] days on end." Honey Dijon also often speaks to exactly what I'm seeing at dance music venues, on their dance floors, and all over social media—a largely white, cis- and heterosexual audience:

[Interviewer:] We were speaking earlier about how audiences have changed . . .
They're straight and white. We can go there.

[Interviewer:] Let's go there, then. What do you think changed that—
The music changed! People of color and queer people have a certain sound that's really emotional and spiritual. *I'm not saying that what other people do isn't, but there's a certain sound and a certain technique and a certain emotion that comes from disco and early house. The music has become more monotonous.* We have technology now where DJs don't actually have to know the craft of DJing—that changed. I'm not saying things should stay the same, obviously you need to evolve, but, sonically, music changed, and *you don't see a lot of people of color at the club anymore. You don't see a lot of people of color dictating parties, or festivals, or record labels, or editing magazines. It's funny how people that create the change very rarely get to experience the change. This music and this culture has been colonized by heteronormative, cis-gender, white people, and I think we're just seeing a reflection of that heteronormativity.*
(Wray 2017, my emphasis)

As Honey Dijon constantly reminds us, superfluous activity such as how frequently a DJ posts on their social media "takes away from the music, which is what it should fucking be about in the first place!"[18] (Abraham 2019).[19] Additionally, my research reflects exactly what Honey Dijon describes above: "This music and this culture has been colonized by heteronormative, cis-gender, white people, and I think we're just seeing a reflection of that heteronormativity" (Wray 2017; see chapter 3 and the Conclusion).
   Much like what I described in chapter 1 and what TBM, Honey Dijon, and Peggy Gou refer to when they talk about what they do and the scenes they want to create, using your "whole body to release fear and stress and express your connection to music" is central to dance music. Honey Dijon further describes how she sees her work:

[Interviewer:] The most important thing about getting older, for me, has been get-ting more comfortable with how unimportant I am in the grand scheme of things.

You could say the same thing about what I do. I'm not curing cancer, but at the same time . . .

[Interviewer:] You make people happy.

There you go. So, it's not important, but it's extremely important because it brings people joy. And bringing people joy is just as important as curing cancer. (Wray 2017)

That joy is what rushed back into my body on TBM's dance floor that late summer night, well over twenty years after my early rave days—this rave ideology is *felt*, even if it can sometimes make the more exploitative features of the industry less visible. There is a *both/and* quality to these dynamics—much like the presence of *both* authenticity *and* commercial-ism throughout dance music culture. Similarly, this is where TBM, Honey Dijon, and Peggy Gou's dance music philosophies intersect; although they each have their own unique contributions to the larger industry, they are similarly committed to taking the music and its messages (love, commu-nity, and release) seriously.[20] Peggy Gou, though far less vocal and political than TBM and Honey Dijon, is also a very different kind of DJ, one that is, like her colleagues, introducing new possibilities to the larger dance music milieu.

PEGGY GOU: THE AGE OF GOU-MANIA

My first introduction to Peggy Gou occurred a week after I stumbled upon TBM in Shoreditch, London. TBM invited Peggy Gou to open for her Friday night residency at the Shoreditch nightclub. At this point, Gou was certainly up-and-coming but not nearly as globally popular as she is now. Before I saw her, Gou was the first "female" Korean DJ to play at Berlin's infamous Berghain nightclub, an opportunity that she saw as a critical step-ping stone.

Much of her popularity is reflected in her shows, of course, but also via her social media accounts. On June 19, 2019, Gou had 836,000 *Instagram* fol-lowers against TBM's 103,000 and Honey Dijon's 128,000.[21] In other words, Gou-mania has certainly impacted the dance music industry. In a *Mixmag* article titled, "Peggy Gou: Welcome to the Age of Gou-Mania," Aurora Mitchell (2018) offers some examples of Gou-mania:

[A]long with hundreds of people chanting her name so loud she can't hear the music she's playing, and/or waving their shoes at her in time, the arts and creativity are certainly a big part of what's best described as Gou-mania. Take this scene at a recent UK gig: "This guy kept on opening an umbrella in the club. Security kept ordering him to put it away. I know in England that's bad luck. They got freaked out!". But then she spotted that the umbrella said 'I love Peggy' and took things into her own hands, going down to fetch it and perch it on the booth. "If you can't do it, I will do it for you!" she grins.

Even a cursory review of Peggy Gou's *Instagram* feed indicates her fans' enthusiasm for her: T-shirts and even an arm tattoo with a Gou version of the Nike swoosh that reads "JUST GOU IT"; another T-shirt that reads "IN GOU WE TRUST"; and fans chanting "Peggy FUCKING Gou!" during her sets. Gou-mania transported Peggy Gou into a celebrity, superstar DJ. Additionally, an *Instagram* account, @peggystshirts, is entirely dedicated to "posting any fan pics of Gou pun tees."[22] In her interview with *Elle* magazine, she describes Gou-mania a bit more: "Even my agent said to me: 'Peggy, I've been partying for 20 years and I've never seen anything like this,' she smiles, almost not quite believing it herself. 'I feel very lucky to have my crowd'" (Donovan 2019).[23]

While Peggy Gou is far less vocal than TBM or Honey Dijon about politics and social issues, she is shifting the dance music industry through her music. For example, her award-winning singles have included Korean-language lyrics, "incorporating traditional Korean music" (Mitchell 2018), a music practice she continues to use in recent releases. The playfulness and experimentation she brings to her music set her apart as different, in addition, of course, to the fact that she is the only Korean cisgender woman DJ with her level of success. The larger dance music industry continues to take notice, describing her work as notable for a number of reasons:

In a funny way, the South Korean DJ's approach is very universal—Gou doesn't submit herself to the rules and regulations of any certain subgenre of electronic music, she simply vibes. . . . Her music is the first techno-house hybrid that seems truly approachable to the layperson in our times, disregarding the proven commercial success of something like EDM or dubstep in lieu of her own unique musical sensibilities. It's Gou's individualism that makes the DJ's mixes so integrated into her listener's lives—we can all see ourselves in her music, our heartbeats replicated by the BPM in her most popular songs, our footsteps slowly meshing with the pulsing bass as we walk along the street. You could say that about many electronic artists, yes, but Gou has mastered it. She deserves every praise that has flooded both niche and general channels in the years since her debut in London. Each mix of hers seems to reach inside the listener and pull out a rhythm that they were never aware of, controlling them like a marionette through an expert blend of sound, emotion and pure fun. Her fans' homemade t-shirts say "Just Gou It," and it's easy to hop on the bandwagon of Gou-ing it too. (Scott 2020)[24]

As the above quote elucidates, media discourses perpetuate the Gou-mania that her fans engage in, doing some of her branding work for her. Building on her success, Gou also started her own label, *Gudu*, a project she sees as a way to further contribute to and change dance music from within:

> I'm hoping that 2020 . . . I've been thinking about . . . what to give back . . . how can I support more artists? Not just female and that's also one of the reasons why I started my own label as well . . . I did that because I wanted to support the artists because I have an experience of like I said in the beginning it was hard for me to break through because all this obstacle I've been you know rumors and my opinion was not valued and I know that feeling so I wanted to support the artists as they want . . . [and now there are] a lot of new female DJs coming up . . . there are a lot of killer woman DJs . . . I'm trying to look for newcomers from my own country as well. (*Oxford Union*, May 18, 2020)

Like TBM and Honey Dijon, Gou has been especially sensitive to marginalized identities in dance music, particular women DJs and has been vocal about her own ongoing struggles as a woman DJ. For example, when a former friend and DJ posted negative stories about her on his *Facebook* page (stories that included sexist comments about how much perfume she wears), other DJs and fans—including TBM—immediately came to her defense, emphasizing the gendered double standard that women DJs are forced to navigate (see Middleton 2020; Farrugia 2012; Gavanas and Reitsamer 2013).[25] Nevertheless, this example of "giving back"—a rave ideology practice no doubt—is also connected to building her own label; Gou rarely "gives back" without also monetizing it.

Reflecting her meteoric rise over the last few years, she headlined her own London show, called *The Pleasure Gardens*, on August 18, 2019, in Finsbury Park. Like TBM, Gou is now headlining her own shows and inviting up-and-coming DJs to her lineup. Again, if Gou is "giving back" to the scene (promoting up-and-coming DJs, for example), she often couples it with the monetization of her brand, a practice that TBM and Honey Dijon engage in but carefully curate. Overall, they are much more strategic than Gou, often using rave ideology identity markers as they do their branding.

Gou's ascent, therefore, has not occurred without controversy. Given the fact that she plays house music (not the highly commercialized EDM), those in house music circles have been turned off and critical of her Nike sponsorship and other decisions she has made that are obvious examples of the commercialization of her image. She has also received criticism for being an *Instagram* celebrity, constantly posting photos of herself wearing designer clothes and accessories. The fact that she unflinchingly engages in consumer culture and the commercialization of her image (without doing the strategic work that TBM and Dijon have cultivated) does not sit comfortably beside house music culture; her actions are often read as counter to the history and goals of house music and/or a PLUR/rave ethos. Sexism, however, often plays an insipid role in the criticism she receives. In chapter 4 and the Conclusion, I take a closer look at Gou's branding tactics, interrogating and better understanding some recent business decisions that were positioned as especially problematic and tone-deaf.

CONCLUSIONS

Beginning with a vignette of my initial introduction to The Blessed Madonna, this chapter outlines how TBM, Honey Dijon, and Peggy Gou are transforming current house music scenes and dance music, in general. For TBM and Honey Dijon, they are constantly making political or social statements, creating music, and engaging in social practices that challenge the status quo and their industry. Notably, while their activity often aims to disrupt the dance music status quo, it also either explicitly or implicitly contributes to their branding; their activity is curated, much like our own curated *Facebook* and *Instagram* accounts. As Banet-Weiser (2012) explains, the "traversing of boundaries involved in branding" is not about whether or not the "branding process transforms or taints" TBM, Dijon or Gou, "but is an articulation of a politics of ambivalence, which enables [that which is being branded] to be potentially subversive even as it is branded as a consumer product" (220). Via their branding, TBM, Dijon, and Gou can and do potentially subvert and disrupt "business as usual" in dance music at the same time that they are branding themselves as a product to be consumed by their audiences.

In chapter 4, I revisit the branding practices that all three of these DJs engage in, practices that often complicate their connection to house music (always for love, never for money or at least an iteration of a PLUR/rave ethos) and, in some cases, perpetuate and support the commercialization of dance music. As Banet-Weiser (2012) reminds us: "The specter of 'selling out,' or . . . 'cashing in,' and its subsequent undermining of authenticity haunts all brand endeavors, as the notion that authenticity cannot easily exist within the space of corporate profit continues to have public and cultural currency" (220). These DJs certainly walk that tightrope and use *authenticity maneuvering* (defined in chapter 4) to circumvent criticism or somehow mask any profit (especially corporate profit) connected to their branding.

Also, I address the ongoing fact that dance music spaces, dominated largely by heteronormative, cisgender, white people, impact the work that TBM, Honey Dijon, and Peggy Gou have to do with regard to their branding. My ongoing analysis of these three DJs shows that they are constantly navigating *both* authenticity *and* commercialism (Anderson 2009), often landing in a space in-between both extremes.[26]

Additionally, "[w]hen a scene's insiders categorize others involved in the scene (i.e., create ideal types) [or discuss what they see as missing from the scene], they are making statements about authenticity and defining norms for style and behavior" (Anderson 2009a, 171). All three DJs engage in these forms of boundary-making, revealing where they put their energy, how they also create rules and regulations for dance music, and where they land on the continuum that runs from authenticity to mainstream commercialism. In chapter 4, a close analysis of their boundary-making reveals how they brand themselves, how they categorize others and/or "authentic" practices, and how all of these dynamics reflect how scene insiders are navigating, reproducing, and/or shifting dance music's entertainment machine.

For Peggy Gou, while there is far less political and social commentary on her part, she is, nonetheless, introducing new kinds of music to the industry. Also, the fact that she is an award-winning, highly successful South Korean woman DJ is certainly an accomplishment, especially in an industry so heavily run by cisgender white men (Farrugia 2012; Attias, Gavanas, and Rietveld 2013). All three of these DJs are navigating a dance music world that is run by cisgender, white men, and is increasingly heteronormative in terms of the audience, the typical venues and events, and via social media. That is, navigating this world as a woman is decidedly difficult; thus, gender inequality as it intersects with race, sexuality, class, and body size exacerbates an already hostile world. Each one of these DJs has been forced to contend with various levels of discrimination and has been saddled with challenging the wider dance music milieu, largely on their own. I continue to make sense of this issue (e.g., how individual DJs have to challenge an industry that rarely makes room for them) throughout the book.

In the next chapter, I will bring us directly to the dance floor, thus navigating some of these challenges on the other side of the DJ booth. I will take us on a journey through the New Year's Eve parties I attended over a three-year period, returning to the themes outlined in the preceding chapters and further investigating how "house music" and dance music spaces, in general, have shifted since the 1990s.

NOTES

1. https://www.djbroadcast.net/article/121812/the-black-madonna-manifesto
2. All names are pseudonyms.
3. DVS1 captures this full embodiment of sound, a feeling that literally moved me: "With clubs, I've said this a hundred times before, I was influenced by the most

amazing soundsystems in the Midwest—like full physical objects—where the sound was the star. To experience music on that level is like taking drugs for the first time, you chase the dragon, and I always chase that experience now" (Heath 2019). That sound instantly transported me back to my 1990s rave days, when the sound—not the DJ—pulled me onto the dance floor. As Gilbert and Pearson (1999) recognize: "These vibrations are registered on some level *throughout the body*. No one knows this better than today's clubber" (44).

4. https://mixmag.net/feature/the-black-madonna-is-the-dj-of-the-year

5. https://www.traxmag.com/the-black-madonna-jai-decouvert-underground-resistance-avec-le-premier-mec-qui-ma-frappee/

6. In chapter 4, I further interrogate how the authenticity moves and emotional references she utilizes often seamlessly intersect with a PLUR/rave ethos and thus further contribute to her successful branding; as she points out in the quote above: "these very qualities . . . have facilitated her success."

7. Referencing the past and their connections to it is an excellent example of *authenticity maneuvering* or utilizing so-called "authentic" practices to build one's brand or simply prove one's worth and insider knowledge (see chapter 4). Also, utilizing a PLUR/rave ethos is certainly part of this dynamic; the closer a DJ gets to actually practicing this ethos, the more authentic they become. Of course, if a DJ fails to adequately adopt a PLUR/rave ethos, critics will literally call them "fake," something that often happens to Peggy Gou.

8. See Maloney (2018, 235–237) for an excellent review of the "[n]umerous contradictions [that] exist within the discourse of" Disco Demolition Night. Also, one of Malbon's (1999, 85) research informants describes why he likes house music, emphasizing how appealing the combination of uplifting lyrics, disco, and funk is to his overall experience with the music and dancing.

9. https://www.youtube.com/watch?v=gESqFUcia6o

10. https://www.nytimes.com/2017/11/30/arts/music/the-black-madonna-dj.html

11. For example, after she performed in San Francisco (October 2018), I was one out of at least 10 clubbers she hugged immediately after her set, something I have rarely seen any DJ do and especially not men DJs. This is a quintessential example of how TBM uses emotionality and connection to her fans to accomplish her DJing, especially via her face-to-face and online interactions.

12. While dance music scholars have been writing about this shift for decades, see Conner's (2015) dissertation for an historical and sociological analysis of this shift.

13. Although this is a pattern, it isn't always the case when clubbers have smartphones in their hands. During a "postpandemic" event with Jayda G, for example, clubbers were crushed at the front of the dance floor dancing wildly with her, some with smartphones; the few clubbers who used their smartphones to catch a quick selfie continued to dance and cheer as wildly as the other dancers (see @jaydagmusic, July 24, 2019, https://www.instagram.com/p/CRtyQU8AWfg/). Given what I saw in Jayda G's post, more research needs to be done on how dance floors might be shifting postpandemic.

14. https://www.instagram.com/p/CQq8qaxFRsh/

15. I return to this point again in chapter 4 and the Conclusion, especially as I consider how EDM DJs such as Steve Aoki have been criticized for *not* making "music

the star of the show," a cutting criticism when "music appreciation" is so central to the authenticity work that DJs are supposed to do (Jaimangal-Jones 2018).

16. @honeydijon, March 4, 2021, my emphasis.

17. @honeydijon, June 5, 2018.

18. Once again, DVS1's quote about soundsystems also makes this argument: "I was influenced by the most amazing soundsystems in the Midwest—like full physical objects—*where the sound was the star*" (Heath 2019, my emphasis).

19. https://www.dazeddigital.com/music/article/45643/1/honey-dijon-dj-club-culture-comme-des-garcons

20. Similarly, given their review of dance music research, Redfield and Savard (2017) make the following argument: "[T]he potential for enhanced wellbeing on participants should no longer be considered a negligible piece of information, having been empirically documented by several independently conducted studies in the past two decades" (60; see, also Malbon 1999; Hutson 1999, 2000; and Sylvan 2005). As I show throughout this book, although commercialism largely dominates the scene, participants continue to express and experience enhanced "personal and psychosocial wellbeing" (Redfield and Savard 2017, 52) particularly on dance floors, via fans' reflections and shares on social media, and—perhaps most notably—as fans/clubbers and DJs have expressed how much they miss being on dance floors together during the pandemic.

21. Gou's *Instagram* follows increased at a phenomenal rate. For example, her numbers jumped from 836K to 848K from June 19 to June 26, 2019, a 12K increase in just one week. As a comparison, TBM jumped from 103K to 104K and Honey Dijon from 128K to 129K over that same period.

22. https://www.instagram.com/peggystshirts/

23. https://www.elle.com/uk/life-and-culture/a26793999/peggy-gou-interview/

24. https://www.michigandaily.com/section/music/peggy-gou-universal-dj

25. https://www.magneticmag.com/2020/12/peggy-gou-vs-daniel-wang-sorting-through-the-drama/

26. While all successful DJs are expected to navigate this terrain, women DJs often have a different set of rules and regulations to juggle especially given the fact that they do not have the same privileges as DJs and producers who are men (Farrugia 2012; Gavanas and Reitsamer 2013).

Chapter 3

Contemporary Dance Music Spaces and Their Dance Floors

A Snapshot

As described in the previous chapters, a serendipitous introduction to The Blessed Madonna in Shoreditch, London, on a late summer night in 2017 subsequently led to this research project and book. I remember telling friends that I hadn't quite danced like that since my early rave days. A house music scene was alive and well, I realized, especially if one was following The Blessed Madonna and her colleagues. From that night forward, my research shifted. Although I did not yet have a grasp on The Blessed Madonna's politics and social justice work, I knew there was something special about how she was contributing to dance music. Simply listening to and being present (as a dancer) at her shows, there was something happening that was not emotionless, that was healthily self-aware, and that, once again, harkened back to a PLUR/rave ethos. As Honey Dijon's quote below reflects, without ever uttering the word, a PLUR ethos seemed central to the contributions TBM and her colleagues continued to make:

[*Interviewer:*] Do you feel like the culture of dance music has shifted towards consumption?

[*Honey Dijon:*] *No one is bringing anything to the party! You go to the club and no one's wearing color, no one's bringing attitude. They're all standing there, wearing these bland clothes, looking at the DJ—who gives a fuck?* I remember when I started going out I actually had to have a look or an attitude to get into the party. *I was there because I was creating part of the atmosphere, not taking something away from it.* I wanted to contribute to this music and I wanted to contribute to this culture. *I come from that school of thought where art, music, fashion, clubbing, all of it was a cultural center. This was where people—I have a saying: meet, mate, and create.* (Wray 2017, my emphasis)[1]

In order to offer a snapshot of contemporary dance music spaces and the scene most connected to TBM and her colleagues' ongoing critiques and genre-bending sets, after my 2017 summer trip to London, I decided to follow her and other related DJs over the winter holiday.[2] This led to three whirlwind winter holiday research trips that primarily included following TBM directly before, during, and after the New Year.

Over the 2017/2018 winter holiday, I booked a three-week trip to London and proceeded to continue to check out the dance music scene in the city in addition to following TBM from one European city to another over a five-day period. Following her meant that my route started in Berlin, continued to Rotterdam, and ended in Manchester, leaving me completely exhausted after well over three full days without any good sleep. The following 2018/2019 winter holiday was also a whirlwind, although I was a bit more careful the second time around. TBM's tour schedule was similarly intense, yet also unclear where she would be when she was booked to play at multiple venues in one day. Therefore, I decided to also follow Honey Dijon to Edinburgh about a week before my NYE tour with TBM. Hedging my bets, I also made a risky choice to fly to Amsterdam to catch TBM at a show for which I had not yet purchased tickets (nor found a way to actually purchase tickets online), followed by a NYE party in Glasgow, featuring TBM as the head-liner. The third and final NYE 2019/2020 research trip is described at length in the Conclusion and preceded the pandemic shutdown that dance music experienced from March 2020 to Spring 2021 (TBM performed at her first "postpandemic" event on April 30, 2021).

While I will go into more detail about the specific patterns I found during these winter holiday/NYE trips and additional events I attended between the NYE trips,[3] in the following sections I describe what actually happened on these trips, how I was navigating through data collection, and some themes that immediately surfaced as I visited the spaces connected to TBM and her colleagues. While I didn't get to every single NYE event on TBM's tour schedule, I also describe my NYE trips in order to highlight how dizzying and taxing it is to follow a major DJ like TBM; making it in the dance music industry requires an incredible amount of travel and lack of sleep that is undoubtedly (given my experiences below) hard on the body.

NYE 2017/2018

For the first trip, I flew into Berlin and immediately started stressing out about how the heck I was going to get into an infamously difficult club, one where people in line are often turned away: The Berghain (Campbell 2020; Collin 2018).[4] I spent my first day in Berlin navigating the city and trying to sort out how I was going to miraculously get into this club, subject myself to the excruciatingly cold weather while standing in the long line to enter, and risk not getting in. During my second day in Berlin and before I was about to make my way to the club, I finally got access to the set list and realized that TBM wasn't actually playing until noon the following day, a set time that conflicted with my scheduled train to Rotterdam. So, instead, I decided to go to another dance music club, one not featuring TBM but, at the very least, offering a small snapshot of a similar dance music scene in Berlin.

It was already NYE morning the next day and I had a train ticket to Rotterdam for an all-night NYE event, with superstar DJs such as Nina Kraviz and, of course, TBM. Given the fact that it was NYE, trains weren't exactly running on time, which temporarily rerouted me to Amsterdam before I finally made it to Rotterdam, landing me there at about 3:00 a.m. on January 1, two hours before TBM's 5:00–7:00 a.m. set. Unlike anything I had seen since the 1990s, yet different in how thoroughly organized it was, the Rotterdam NYE party was massive with thousands of clubbers, many of them in cuddle puddles[5] throughout the venue, and huge warehouse-sized rooms with the DJs at the front and thousands of dancers on the dance floor. The event also had a token system that made it impossible to pay for anything with cash. Clubbers were required to buy tokens in order to buy anything in the venue, even access to the bathrooms.

While this party did not have the do-it-yourself (DIY) structure of 1990s raves I had attended in the San Francisco Bay Area (instead, this event was like a well-oiled machine), it felt more like a rave than any party I have attended during this research. Given Anderson's (2009a) analysis of what she calls modern-day corporate raves, a "variation of today's new branded EDM parties," this event certainly fit that description: "[w]hat distinguishes [corporate raves] from classic raves is their professionalized, organizational style" (36). The large warehouse rooms, the mass of people, the drug use (I estimated that about 90 percent or more of the people at the party were on some kind of drug and saw more people on Ecstasy in one single place than I had seen since the 1990s), and the light shows and music felt far more like a rave than a concert; yet, all of those features were also highly organized and professionalized. For example, given how thoroughly drugged everyone seemed to be, I was completely floored when, at 7:00 a.m. sharp, the lights flashed on, the music stopped, and the mass of people were herded out the front doors of the venue.[6] Additionally, there was a medical crew available in case anyone got sick. While there were taxis waiting outside, I followed a mass of people to public transportation that was entirely free and available to hundreds of clubbers who had just left this party. As a woman completely alone, I felt remarkably safe, though cautious, as I eventually made my way to the Amsterdam airport and my afternoon flight to Manchester.

Upon arriving in Manchester with only a few stolen moments of sleep[7] in the Amsterdam airport and on the plane, I made my way to the city and immediately looked for a restaurant to eat and relax. After multiple days without any good sleep, the "Closing Party" in Manchester was my last stop and my energy was fading fast. This final party started at 5:00 p.m. and ended 12 hours later; thus, staying awake until 5:00 a.m. felt Herculean but possible with the help of a good meal and a lot of caffeine. After resting for a couple hours in a café, I made my way to the party, entering the massive venue at about 6:45 p.m. It looked like an old armory, with dirty brick walls throughout, multiple rooms and dance floors, areas for resting, a large area in the back with portable toilets, and at least three areas where clubbers could buy drinks and snacks.

Not surprisingly, there were hardly any people at the venue when I showed up, with all of my belongings in one single, small travel bag. By 10:00 p.m., however, the party was completely packed. By 2:00 a.m., entrances into the main room overflowed with people, making it nearly impossible to move into the center of the front area of the dance floor. With all of the energy I had left, I managed to stay for Peggy Gou's earlier set and the end of TBM's 2:00–3:30 a.m. set, literally slapping my face, arms, and legs to stay awake as I finally made my way out of the venue.

NYE 2018/2019

For the second trip, I began the "NYE tour" with a Saturday night Honey Dijon performance in Edinburgh about a week before I started following TBM. Her performance was in a large theater and the event, itself, felt very heteronormative, much like what I had experienced at the "Closing Party" in Manchester during the last trip. This meant that gendered dress and behavior was the norm, typically positioning men as active participants and women as both active and passive but also very much on display. For example, most of the women wore far less clothing than the men, a pattern that seemed especially painful in the cold weather.[8] Much like Manchester, the crowd was also young (estimated median age = 21–23) and predominantly white.

By Friday, December 28, I made my way to *Geluk*, a club in Amsterdam, to see TBM perform a three-hour set at a venue that didn't allow clubbers to use their smartphones for pictures or videos, an issue I address in the sections below (also, see chapter 2). My final stop was the Glasgow NYE party with TBM as the headliner. Again, the event felt and looked very heteronormative and white—much like Manchester and Edinburgh—yet, as I had experienced in Rotterdam the year before, ringing in the New Year contributed to a notable increase in how clubbers interacted with one another. Instead of being distracted by smartphones or facing the DJ booth without interacting with each other, clubbers made a point of turning toward one another, exchanging love and appreciation for the moment with total strangers, a pattern that I also address in the sections below.

A POSTRAVE ERA: MAKING SENSE OF TODAY'S DANCE MUSIC SPACES

As Anderson (2009a) concludes in her book on rave culture in Philadelphia, the shifts that dance music continues to experience point to the current post-rave era. That is, while there are certainly features of today's scenes that overlap with the 1980s and 1990s rave scenes, we have entered another era, one far more commercial, legal, and organized than the early days. She describes this shift, writing:

> While the authenticity of raves has been and can still be debated, one conclusion from my work is that there are very few, if any, EDM parties in Philadelphia today that contain all of the cultural elements of the original raves in the 1980s and 1990s. I reviewed how my respondents and key informants characterized an "authentic" rave as having many cultural elements [such as: PLUR or intimate solidarity, leftist or progressive (antigovernment and anticorporate) politics, nonbusiness owners, secretive/underground marketing, unlicensed venues, transport sound and light show equipment, massive crowds, musical diversity by area, numerous rotating DJs (equity), extended/after hours, fashion such as parachute pants, props such as glow sticks, a shared language with regard to music or use of ecstasy, dancing, music appreciation, drug use, DJ worshiping, and cuddle puddles.] Of course, debate might persist over how many or which of these elements constitutes an authentic rave. *Still, the fact remains that there are very few unlicensed, illegal, massive indoor or outdoor all-night dance parties operating with a PLUR ethos and rave identity markers and behaviors today in Philadelphia or other U.S. cities. This is also the case in the United Kingdom and Europe. Thus, if we define raves by these cultural elements, then it is safe to say that we are in a post-rave era.* (Anderson 2009a, 32, 45; my emphasis)

In mapping out this shift, she utilizes a continuum between authentic raves and commercial club events with the following events listed from one side to the other: underground parties, corporate raves, music festivals, monthlies, weeklies, and superstar one-offs (Anderson 2009a, 31). In our postrave era, "[n]one [of the events listed above] boast completely authentic or completely commercial [cultural traits]. Instead, they possess gradations of rave authenticity and EDM or club culture commercialism" (Anderson 2009a, 46). My research is consistent with these findings, with the added analysis of how new technologies, social media platforms, and other unexpected changes have shifted dance music spaces over the last ten years and only exacerbated the ongoing presence of *both* rave authenticity *and* EDM/club culture commercialism. Smartphones and the use of *Instagram* and other social media platforms, for instance, were nonexistent or far less pervasive ten years ago. The following sections outline these new patterns by drawing our attention to the dance floors.

Using the dance floor as our starting point, I show how "gradations of rave authenticity and EDM or club culture commercialism" are present, how these gradations impact experiences of the dance floors, and how scene insiders (superstar DJs, for example) are turning our attention to what they see as lacking or fading on dance floors and in the larger dance music industry today. Bringing us down to the dance floors and utilizing autoethnography that takes embodied interactions seriously, I focus on the norms, behaviors, and activities one finds in these spaces, thus outlining these cultural components of dance music (Anderson 2009c). Taking up Anderson's (2009a) call for more research on "the important social and cultural space between authenticity and mainstream commercialism," (168) this chapter highlights how this social and cultural space in between is physically realized, negotiated, and often resisted on actual dance floors.

PLUR AND THE DANCE FLOOR: THEN AND NOW

The lyrics in "Ready to Freak—Disco Mix" (Soul Clap, Featuring Kathy Brown 2019) connect a number of PLUR and house music themes that consistently reemerge in DJs', fans', and clubbers' reflections of the past. First, these lyrics begin with a history lesson:

Now let me tell ya a little story tonight
It's a story way back when, huh!

Next, we learn how DJs acted as "priests" for the night (also, see Lawrence 2003, xi; Takahashi and Olaveson 2003, 86–87; Sylvan 2005, 112) and the legendary Frankie Knuckles is referenced:

When DJs took you to Church!
Like Frankie Knuckles used to say

Again, we are given a history lesson about house music, pointing to its philosophy:

A time when house wore many hats
And music was a unifying voice

Finally, its PLUR-ness is made clear:

That brought all races and cultures together
As one family . . .

And dancing—not standing and looking at the DJ booth or scrolling through a smartphone—was what happened on the dance floor:

When the dancers would sweat, groove, jump and sliiiiiiiiiiide
Ah, y'all know what I'm talkin' about

Once again, we're given another history lesson, with reference to dance music's roots (Lawrence 2003):

Do you remember The Shelter?
Do you remember The Paradise Garage?

And, finally, a bit of nostalgia to emphasize what has changed:

Do you remember The Sound Factory, boy?
They don't do it like they used tooooooooooo

But, tonight, those on the dance floor will get a little taste of what came before:

But tonight . . .
We're gonna bring it to you riiiiight . . .

Returning to TBM's quote from chapter 1, these lyrics paint a picture of idyllic house music dance floors, spaces where "music was a unifying force" (that facilitated crossing boundaries) and "ladies shakin' all through the night . . . keep it goin' 'til the mornin' light" (encouraging timelessness or rethinking our temporal dimensions) in addition to the other features TBM highlighted in her quote: slipping into another space and leaving better than we came. Lamenting the assumed loss of many of the features of old dance music scenes and spaces, "they don't do it like they used to" directly calls this out, reflecting what so many DJs and fans alike have to say about what dance music looks like now (see chapter 1). Its transparent commercialization (Conner 2015) has certainly contributed to these shifts at the same time that

other changes have occurred such as generational schism, cultural otherness/
deviance and self-destruction, social control, and genre-based scene fragmentation, changes that Anderson (2009a, 2009b) analyzed pre-2009.[9] Both TBM
and Honey Dijon have released remixes that address some of these changes,
patterns that are often occurring on dance floors. In TBM's collaboration
with Georgia titled, "About Work the Dancefloor—The Blessed Madonna
Remix," the following lyrics emphasize the ongoing importance of the dance
floor. Thus, the dance floor is an obvious place to both better understand what
has changed since the 1990s and think about what needs to shift, perhaps, for
a PLUR/rave ethos to remain present. These lyrics immediately invite us to
get on the dance floor with those we love:

[Chorus:] I was just thinking about work the dancefloor . . .
Here we go again, my love

Here is where timelessness can happen:

You've got so much time to spend . . .

And where money and material gifts should not matter:

'Cause I don't have much in terms of money now
I don't have material gifts for you

All that matters is for "me to stay a while" and "be in a moment with you":

You want me to stay a while, stay a while
To be in a moment with you[10]

In a *Pitchfork* review of the song, Michelle Kim (2019) highlights both the
obliqueness of the song's chorus and its slipperiness:

> "I don't have much in terms of money now/I don't have material gifts for you/
> You want me to stay a while/To be in a moment with you," she beckons, until
> she launches into the perplexing hook: "I was just thinking 'bout work the
> dancefloor." At first listen, it seems grammatically incorrect (is she talking about
> "work the dancefloor" as a concept, the function of a DJ to get people moving in
> a crowd?). But as she turns the phrase over and over in her mouth, the oblique-
> ness eventually disappears, like the slippery moment in the club when you stop
> *thinking* about the beats and just start letting the sounds flow through your
> body.[11] Nobody . . . quite knows what it means, but it's provocative. Georgia
> gets the people going. (Kim 2019)[12]

Georgia explains further:

> There was this band called *Cybertron* . . . A lot of the songs have vocoders guid-
> ing you through a trip. It's grammatically incorrect but it's all about rhythm....
> [I had this line:] "I just want to be able to dance on the dance floor." [Then] I
> thought let's do it like *Cybertron*. It was a rhythmic thing. It was another percus-
> sion element over the drums. (Murphy 2020)[13]

As Georgia explains, the lyrics undoubtedly aim to get dancers moving on the
dance floor, addressing both the importance of the dance floor and, beyond
that, the importance of a dance floor that allows dancers to "just be able to
dance on the dance floor"—it "gets the people going" (Georgia in Murphy
2020).

Returning to Honey Dijon's remix of Jayda G's "Stanley Get Down (No
Parking on the DF)," the lyrics also draw our attention to the dance floor,
encouraging dancers to get out of their phones and start groovin' (see also,
chapter 2). TBM and Honey Dijon's remixes emphasize themes they see
as relevant to the dance floor: coming together, dancing with one another,
even or especially with strangers; focusing on the dance floor and danc-
ing/groovin' rather than looking at one's smartphone and *Instagram*-ing;
temporarily losing any sense of time or obligation or truly experiencing
timelessness and flow while dancing; and experiencing dance floors as
community, not just as individual experiences to share out on one's social
media. Unfortunately, these themes are far less prominent on today's dance
floors.

My own experiences and fieldnotes reflect what has shifted on the dance
floor. In the mid-1990s, for example, I attended raves at a large warehouse
on Oakland's Hegenberger Road (described at the beginning of this book's
Introduction), where a few key dance floor themes were present: smartphones
did not exist and were, therefore, not present on any dance floors (pagers were
used but rarely, if ever, on the dance floors); dancers danced with one another
in small and large groups, formed dance circles where dancers performed
for larger groups, and/or dancers would find an area and dance on their own
(e.g., in a large warehouse space, I would typically leave my group and dance
with my shadow, a dance practice that was possible in large venues); the DJ
booth was not treated as central (in most cases, the DJ booth and staring up
at the DJ was far less important than getting on the dance floor and dancing);
and, finally, given the fact that the DJ booth was not central and "superstar/
celebrity DJs" had not yet fully emerged, dance floors rarely cleared out after
a DJ finished their set.

Typically, dance floor themes in contemporary dance music spaces paint
a different picture: unless a venue forbids the use of smartphones, they are

usually very present and have an impact on what people can accomplish on dance floors; dancers dance far less with each other, more on their own or with friends and often forgo dancing altogether (instead, clubbers often stand or sway back and forth, staring at the DJ booth, using their smartphones to capture the moment); as innumerable *Boiler Room* videos show, inventive, creative dancing that was so central to 1990s raves is largely absent at events today; usually, the DJ booth is central (this means that instead of clubbers turning toward one another to dance or mingle, clubbers are turned toward the DJ booth and away from each other, shoulder to shoulder, often swaying back and forth; see also Rietveld 2013, 92); this disconnection with other dancers/clubbers often results in a lot of pushing and shoving on the actual dance floors, usually to get a better look at the DJ booth; a DJ's celebrity status physically changes the dance floor (i.e., a dance floor will literally clear out if a popular DJ finishes their set or get crowded if a popular DJ is playing). Large spring and summer festivals, of course, have their own set of patterns, many also outlined above but not closely studied for this research (see Introduction for Methods Used and Data Collection). Honey Dijon draws us a picture:

> I always say that a great DJ has lived. The ear, the experience, the confidence, them allowing you to breathe, needs to be there for you to really experience the music. Now you go to hear 20 DJs in the course of a night and everyone is mixing so fast and trying to outplay the other DJ and bang, they want to be the superstar of the night. Festivals with massive DJ line-ups. How can you experience and know what an artist is even fucking about in 60 minutes? It is so quick. *That to me is not how a good night should be or how House Music, techno or disco should be experienced. That's speed-dating.* So, how is this lockdown [(in reference to the COVID-19 pandemic)] doing? In a way it's amazing that you can just stop and breathe. (Flynn 2020, my emphasis)

Dijon often references authenticity (what "should be") as she critiques what she sees as the detrimental effects of today's dance music culture industry (Conner 2015), an industry that is largely standardized, professionalized, and highly efficient. For Dijon, one of the many detrimental outcomes of the rationalization (Weber [1925] 1978; Ritzer 2019) of dance music is that it's more like "speed-dating" (an emphasis on quantity and competition among DJs) than longer, quality DJ sets, where "you [can] experience and know what an artist is even fucking about." The following sections outline many of these changes, locating how "gradations of rave authenticity and EDM or club culture commercialism" are present on today's dance floors.

CONNECTING ON THE DANCE FLOOR:
"GOD ISN'T SILENT. GOD IS LOUD"

In TBM's 2016 Artist of the Year *VICE News* article, she makes a number of connections between her own history, house music, and what the dance floor and dancing have meant to her:

> The connection between house music and gospel is well documented. Frankie Knuckles, for example, described Chicago nightclub The Warehouse as "church for people who have fallen from grace." *My heart, hungry for that feeling of transcendence and acceptance again, zoned in on this connection immediately. I loved everything about dancing. The records booming out of a speaker. For the next twenty years, I poured myself into dance music and discovered that for me, God isn't silent. God is loud.*
>
> *Going out to the club became a new kind of ritual, akin to attending mass as a child. There were so many analogs for my early spiritual life waiting for me on the dancefloor, including the simple, gentle act of turning to your neighbor and hugging them simply because you're having the same beautiful experience. Indeed, many of the most powerful experiences of spiritual connection have happened on a dancefloor. I am at my most in-tune—my best self—when the music lifts the whole room together, and all the separations between us dissolve for a little while.* (The Black Madonna 2016, my emphasis)[14]

To start, the "Ready to Freak—Disco Mix" lyrics capture the first point TBM makes:

When DJs took you to Church!
Like Frankie Knuckles used to say

As Maloney (2018) shows, all of these connections make sense and are historically connected to a PLUR/rave ethos:

> House allowed for the quasi-religious iconography within disco to become explicit and subversive in equal measure by drawing more directly from the Church, creating a new, expanded ideology that spread through the marrow of house music from its point of conception in disco. (236–237)

Describing her religious upbringing and especially her experiences with her church, TBM sets up the context for how house music and raves entered into her life and share similar qualities:

I grew up going to Holy Cross church in Jackson, Kentucky, and I loved everything about it. The rituals. The singing. The scholarly tradition within the church. The simple, gentle act of turning to your neighbor and saying, "Peace be with you." I became friends with a nun and dreamed secretly of wearing her habit someday myself. I was a bad student. Sister Wendy said it didn't matter if I could say the Ten Commandments as long as I knew that God loved me. And I did know it. I felt accepted, loved and a part of something much bigger. (The Black Madonna 2016)

As she describes it, "[g]oing to the club became a new kind of ritual, akin to attending mass as a child," an experience that made her feel "accepted, loved and a part of something much bigger."

Also, Honey Dijon often describes the church-like, spiritual import of clubbing and dancing:

LOVE[/Flynn]: When was the first moment you recognised nightclubs as a kind of church?
HD[Honey Dijon]: Well, growing up in Chicago I experienced club music at a .very early age. We had DJs at school dances and things of that nature. *My "a-ha" moment would have been a party thrown at the skating rink. I just got lost in the music. It was transcendental, spiritual, like I'd found myself.* I've had a lot of moments like that: at loft parties in Chicago, clubs in New York. I've been able to participate in a lot of different environments that had church-like moments (Flynn 2020, my emphasis).

Both acceptance (feeling loved and held) and transcendence enter into these descriptions, experiences that have certainly emerged in my fieldnotes, were similarly central to my experiences in the 1990s rave scene, and are supported by existing research (Malbon 1999; Hutson 1999; Hutson 2000; Takahashi and Olaveson 2003; Sylvan 2005; Anderson 2009a; Goulding and Shankar 2011; Redfield and Savard 2017; Collin 2018). In other words, the presence of acceptance and transcendence kept bringing me and many ravers back to the parties (St John 2001; Takahashi and Olaveson 2003); a PLUR/rave ethos coupled with "connectedness, [emotional] embodiment, [and] altered states of consciousness" (ibid., 72) realized on the dance floor, made the overall experience so blissful and fulfilling that returning to it was obvious. Alice Nicolov (2016) describes this well, writing:

What was it that made rave so popular, so transcendental when it came to colour, creed and social background? What brought people from every walk of life together?

Its euphoric, ecstasy-fuelled atmosphere where the predominant feeling was
love and happiness, rather than people getting drunk and fighting, appealed to
a broad cross-section of people. The clandestine, "no rules" nature of the raves
themselves kept it fresh. While anyone was welcome, in an age where internet
and mobiles were basically non-existent, you had to be in the know to get to
a rave, adding to its popularity and its "us against them" feeling. "Clubbing
culture is everyday now. Back then it was mystical, no one knew anything about
it. It was like nothing that had ever come before it or since," Uncle Dugs elabo-
rates. (Nicolov 2016, my emphasis)[15]

Anderson's (2009a) respondents also describe how transformative the
dance floors, the music, and the scene could be. Those who experienced either
social or personal marginalization or alienation as children and/or adolescents
often gravitated toward the scene (see also Conner 2015, 42; Wilson 2006)
and stayed because they found a place where they belonged:

This personal identity pathway was common among the respondents and key
informants, especially insiders who were once ravers. Themes related to this
trajectory helped define their personal identities and motivated them toward the
rave and EDM scene where they found a way to "fit their face and feelings to a
new social world[.]." (Anderson 2009a, 74)

While there are changes (see below) happening on dance music floors that are
certainly making connecting with others more difficult, during my research
there were multiple instances where connection happened, even momentarily.
Additionally, there were two events where connection happened almost from
the moment I arrived and continued until I left the venue: in Rotterdam (NYE
2017/18) and again in Glasgow (NYE 2018/19). For both of these events, the
NYE celebration contributed to connection, often giving people an excuse to
come closer together and share a hug and/or an appreciation for the moment
and each other.

WARM, LOVING INTERACTIONS WITH STRANGERS

Beautiful moments still happen on the dance floor. The following fieldnote excerpts highlight a number of those beautiful moments. When these
moments happen (and they typically happen multiple times throughout any
one event), they contribute to what I call a "love fog," one where exchanging a smile, wishing someone well, looking out for one another on the dance
floor, and sharing an appreciation for the music with a complete stranger are
normalized and often expected (see also Wilson 2006).[16]

At a daytime San Francisco party with Honey Dijon (also, see below), my partner and I were closer to the center of the large dance floor, kissing and dancing together. While I had exchanged warm smiles with multiple clubbers during Dijon's set, the loud music made it nearly impossible to carry on a conversation with any one clubber. Also, while there was a lot of dancing, most clubbers were packed close together on the dance floor (this left people with little room to actually move) and most of the people in the venue were turned toward the DJ booth rather than toward each other. Even with these possible barriers to connection with other dancers/clubbers, one single clubber insisted on connecting:

> My partner and I were kissing and a sweet Filipino man behind us exclaimed, "You guys are so cute!" as he pointed to us and smiled wide.

Similar, warm and loving connections happened with multiple strangers at the NYE parties I attended. As I described in chapter 1, the Glasgow NYE event, especially during the countdown, was notable for the love that clubbers shared with one another, even for a short moment. My fieldnotes highlight the warmth I felt throughout the night:

> I think this was the friendliest night I've had since I started this research: almost as soon as I got on the dance floor, other clubbers started talking and dancing with me; I made fast "friends" with two men (a white straight man and his best friend, a South Asian gay man) and proceeded to dance in and around them for most of the evening; additionally, these two men made a point of telling me how wonderful I looked and/or danced as we spent the evening together; and, also, during the New Year countdown, total strangers embraced me and wished me a Happy New Year.

Reflecting on how warm and loving these interactions actually felt, my fieldnotes included these reflections:

> Thinking about how beautiful it was on the dance floor, as the clock struck midnight, all these women kissing around me, is bringing up some heavy, teary emotions. It really was so beautiful, so free, where I want to be every NYE from this point forward.

While friendly interactions with strangers are often normalized in the context of dance music clubbing, it continues to feel novel and special because these practices are not typical, everyday practices that we are encouraged to engage in (Malbon 1999; Jackson 2004). In fact, most of the interactions between strangers I observed and experienced would be considered wholly inappropriate in everyday spaces and activities such as work, school, public transportation, and/or running errands.

Rotterdam's NYE 2017/2018 party also offered multiple examples of warm, loving interactions, particularly as I watched my new "friend," Carina (a queer, Dutch woman of color and stranger I met within an hour of arriving at the party), navigate the dance floor:

> She got ALONG with everyone! I didn't see ONE single negative exchange between her and everyone with whom she interacted.
>
> Let's go on her journey: So, we made our way from the back of the dance floor. She was leading the way and held my hand tight as she dragged me forward.
>
> I'm trying to keep up with Carina and then, as she makes her way to the front of the dance floor, she says something to literally every single person she passes (she was speaking Dutch so I didn't understand all of what she was saying but I wouldn't have heard all of it anyway, the music was so loud; when I could hear something, a number of people she passed also said Happy New Year in Dutch to me so it was pretty clear at that point that this is what she was saying to most people she passed).
>
> I frequently looked up toward the DJ booth and saw DJ Nina Kraviz, completely enthralled by how she was moving, dancing and performing to her set and for her audience. Nina was mesmerizing and SO was Carina. *She mesmerized and put smiles on nearly every person she passed.* She would lean into a new stranger, perhaps saying Happy New Year, and then she would smile wide and dance sweetly next to them, shifting her body back and forth with theirs as she raised her arms and moved mostly with her hips. I would dance with her too, finding even the smallest bit of room. She also playfully messed with men's masculinities, butting up next to men she passed[17] (chest to chest as she raised her arms, elbows bent) and aggressively dancing next to them, playfully trying to "start some shit" but not really going through with it. There was often laughter after this as she smiled wide at the man she was "trolling" but would leave and fall deeper into the crowd and often avoid anything that might have gotten heated between herself and this man. Notably, she did this at least 5 or more times in front of me and always GOT AWAY WITH IT. No man (or his group of man friends) ever tried to start a fight with her. He would simply smile wide too, smile playfully and laugh, or simply ignore her playful aggressiveness and keep dancing.
>
> Her behavior and presence was often treated as a temporary distraction from a dancer's current dancing, with this distraction often ending in a wide smile and friendly exchange. And this didn't just happen with men; Carina interacted with everyone she passed as we made our way to the front of the dance floor and closer to Nina Kraviz.

At one point, I got a little bit worried because I thought she actually pissed off one guy that she aggressively pushed up against. She quickly made her way further into the crowd, dragging me along as his friends (three men) looked to me to see what was up with my friend. I smiled devilishly and raised my shoulders and my hands as if to say, "I don't know? Sorry!" They laughed as I did this and as we quickly passed by all of them.

While Carina's behavior and presence was exceptional, what stood out to me was how she was able to accomplish these warm and loving interactions with complete strangers throughout the entire evening, even if some of her behavior was read as aggressive. That is, warm and loving behavior was the norm and Carina simply took advantage of those opportunities. She took complete advantage of the PLUR-ness that permeated the dance floor and I simply came along for the ride.

Friendliness, "'connectedness,' 'unity,' or simply 'love'" (Takahashi and Olaveson 2003, 77) in "rave" spaces are running themes. Even Angela McRobbie's (1994) often-quoted chapter, "Shut Up and Dance: Youth Culture and Changing Modes of Femininity" makes this point when she considers changing masculinities: "laddishness has been replaced by friendliness" (418). While she attributes these changes to the use of Ecstasy, drug use can certainly play a part but is not the entire story. As research over the last few decades shows (Malbon 1999; Jackson 2004; Takahashi and Olaveson 2004; Anderson 2009a), what I call a "love fog" and the friendly interactions that clubbers often experience on dance floors points to a much larger set of expectations for how to behave. Jackson's (2004) research comes to the same conclusion:

> I came across this style of social interaction again and again and it always felt radically different from the social frameworks I encountered in the everyday world. These social practices have often been overlooked in examinations of clubbing. They have been seen as a side effect of Ecstasy, *rather than as a series of bodily techniques, which people learn and take away from the clubs.* (175, my emphasis)

That is, Ecstasy does not necessarily have to be present or used widely for a "love fog" to permeate the dance floor. Normalized bodily techniques such as exchanging a smile with another dancer or dancing in unison with the music are learned and honed in any given night or across multiple nights.

Returning to my journey with Carina, the love fog we entered also reconfigured and "disarticulated" masculinities and femininities (Pini 2001, 195) and the relationship between the two. She was able to playfully and aggressively maneuver through the crowd, often dancing with a group of men without stirring up anything beyond a lot of laughter, smiling, and more dancing. Like many of my own interactions with clubbers, the fact that she was read as a woman probably gave her more flexibility with other men; that is, if she had been read as a man, the same groups of men might have responded very differently. While constraining gender relations are never entirely absent (Pini 2001), "[t]he non-confrontational, consciously open attitude that many clubbers suggest forms one of the most attractive aspects of clubbing" (Malbon 1999, 127) certainly has an impact on the love fog that permeates its dance floors. Nonetheless, even with these new configurations of gender that are realized in this fog, sexual harassment is not entirely absent (Pini 2001; Hutton 2006).

LEAVING BETTER THAN WE CAME

Curbing Harassment on the Dance Floor

How Subtle and Covert Harassment Operates

There are a number of patterns, both historically and in current spaces, that aim to make TBM's quote a reality: "When it's all over and the world comes back, we can say good morning and leave better than we came." To start, in clubs throughout London, signage such as the following were common:

IF IT'S
UNWANTED,
IT'S
HARASSMENT.

PLEASE SPEAK OUT AND NOTIFY OUR STAFF
IMMEDIATELY OF ANY ISSUES YOU ENCOUNTER
AND LET US DEAL WITH IT FOR YOU.
YOUR SAFETY AND ENJOYMENT COMES FIRST.

Coupled with various degrees of a PLUR/rave ethos at house music events, simply having the signs present seemed to curb harassment on the dance floors. For example, in all of the venues I attended, I did not witness anything even remotely close to the defensive and strategic dancing that women often have to engage in to curb sexual harassment on dance floors in the heteronormative spaces sociologists Grazian (2008) and Wade (2017) studied.[18] Unlike Kavanaugh (2015), I did not observe anything close to "female bartenders doing shots with patrons . . . [sometimes hopping] atop the bar with bottles [to] give anyone free shots of liquor, poured directly into their open mouths" (249). Instead of "venue-sponsored rituals . . . to sexualize the event, objectify women, as well as normalize heavy alcohol use" (ibid.), the venues and crowds/clubbers typically featured only muted examples of these dynamics (heavy alcohol use); venue-sponsored rituals like those described by Kavanaugh (2015) did not dominate any one space. For instance, clubbers hitting on one another served as an anomaly; it happened but it was very infrequent, often awkward and/or sneaky, and ended almost as soon as it started.[19] Like Hutton's (2006) research on underground club spaces, harassment was more covert and subtle, often forcing those who were harassed to delicately navigate their way out of the interaction. The following fieldnote excerpt largely reflects this pattern:

> My partner (a cisgender, white man) Clark and I were at a daytime Honey Dijon show in San Francisco [also, see above]. We were dancing in an area to the left of the larger dance floor in front of the raised DJ booth. After about twenty minutes in this area, a tall Black man wearing a rainbow tank top approached Clark and said (after he leaned in and tried to make out with Clark), "if you want to play video games or hang out sometime, I'd be ok with that." Clark smiled and told him he wasn't interested, closing off any further interactions.

Sharing all of the elements listed above, nothing else like this occurred at all throughout the entire daytime party, it was exceptionally awkward and sneaky (especially the attempted "make-out" and the actual pick-up line), and it ended immediately after Clark turned the man down. Nonetheless, harassment (though subtle and covert) did ultimately happen, requiring Clark to carefully assess the situation and respond without upsetting the man who harassed him.

Again, while these interactions stood out because they were so infrequent, they usually happened when I was alone and ended almost as soon as they started. In one single night, two fairly intense harassment interactions occurred at the Shoreditch club (ironically, one of the clubs with "Anti-Harassment" signage). Two intense occurrences in one night was especially odd and, for the first and only time, it made me regret not reaching out to staff about the second occurrence, in particular:

> Dancing on a raised platform to the right of the larger dance floor, a South Asian man dancing to my left put out his hand and nudged me a little, indicating to me that he wanted me to dance with him. Immediately after he touched me, I looked at him and said extremely clearly, "NOPE!" and then continued dancing. As he left the area, he moved close to my face and said, "Have a nice life."

> And then, when I was walking from the crowded dance floor to the bar for water, a white man with a sweaty white t-shirt on ran his hand down my back. The first time he did it, I thought it might have been a mistake but then he did it a second time. As soon as he did it again, I turned around and stared at him hard. I was about to yell at him before I saw how smiley he was and realized how drunk he seemed. Upon realizing what state he was in, I decided that I wanted to get as far away from him as possible.

These two incidents were subtle and covert, thus forcing me to carefully navigate how to get out of the interactions and engage in actual work, disrupting any good feelings I was having about the night and raising my heartbeat. Their subtlety also impacted how I dealt with them, unfortunately; instead of charging up to the bar and reporting the incidents, they seemed so minor at the time, that I held back and failed to report anything. While these two interactions were decidedly unnerving and scary, especially given the fact that I was at the club alone, they did not constitute a typical experience at any one of the clubs I attended; they were not typical or normalized cross- or same-gender practices that I witnessed or experienced over the course of my research.

As a final example, less intense exchanges occurred in Rotterdam. Over the course of the entire evening, I was hit on twice (by men), briefly on the dance floor and again near the token-purchasing area:

> While I was over at the token area waiting for Carina, two white men started flirting with me. They both spoke Dutch but also a little English. One of the white men with dark hair (in his early 20s) said, "I love your tattoo! Spinster! What does it mean, Spinster?!" "Oh, thank you," I smiled sweetly with my lips closed a bit, "it means old maid . . . you know, like a never married woman . . ." "Oh," he seemed a little perplexed and then his friend said, "Oh, it's a religion!" "No!" I laughed . . . "it just means I'm not married and not interested." But this entire conversation shifted because Carina chimed in and said, "oh, she's with me . . . she's my girlfriend" "Oh, she is?" the first guy asked. "Yes, she's with me!" Carina exclaimed again and grabbed me by the arm. The first guy kind of backed away but slowly and stopped flirting but glanced my way a few more times before he left the area.

Like the other occurrences, I certainly wasn't getting hit on all night, the flirting was a little awkward, and the man flirting with me backed away as soon as Carina cut him off. While this exchange lasted longer than other typical exchanges, it shut down as soon as the person pursuing me became aware of his inability to continue doing so. Again, however, some covert behavior persisted as the man stole a few glances my way a few times before we left the area.

Overall, there was never a relentless quality to harassment. Instead, it would happen and be done within a few minutes. Reflecting a gradation of PLUR-ness, infrequent or no sexual harassment at events with house music DJs makes sense and is consistent with Anderson's (2009a) research on rave culture:

> "If you're *looking* for a typical good-looking girl, like all done up, like you're not at a rave. You know what I mean." That raves did not value sexual court-ing and conquest is logical with the PLUR ethos but is yet another factor that rendered them somewhat strange to mainstream "socializing" venues of both the past and present. (Anderson 2009a, 29)

While the events I attended did not, by any stretch of the imagination, feel like an old school rave (except Rotterdam, described above with Carina), a PLUR/rave quality that flourished was respect and especially respect for other clubbers' sexual and intimate desires. Additionally, however, these harassment patterns meant that it often went "underground" (Hutton 2006) or was sometimes hard to locate or make sense of; it wasn't "in your face" harassment but rather subtle and covert. That subtlety meant that harassers often got away with their harassment and, in the process, made those they were harassing do the extra work of figuring out what was actually going on, getting rid of them and/or figuring out what to do next.

How Alcohol and Harassment Operates

Experiences with harassment often intersected with the presence and/or con-sumption of alcohol, a pattern that Hutton (2006) identified in her research[20]: "Female clubbers stated that alcohol produced more risky behaviour both in others and in themselves. It is the consumption of alcohol within club spaces that makes the use of drugs and the pursuit of pleasure more risky, as it is a contradiction of the early 'luved up' atmosphere" (111).[21] Returning to Clark's interaction with the man who hit on him, while I can't definitively say that he was drinking alcohol, he certainly was not sober and eventually fell asleep in a seat next to the dance floor, prompting those of us near him and club security to check in on him.

The use of alcohol also intersected with one of the most intense, aggres-sive interactions I had with another clubber, a white woman who completely caught me off guard:

> Before I left for the night (at about 1:00 am), I was making my way through the crowd and had to get up on one of the raised platforms at the back of the dance floor to make my way close to the exit. This is when I ran into a woman

named Becky who was VERY drunk, managed to grab me and immediately pull me into her as we started dancing together. I tried to go with the flow as she smiled wide and said, "YOU ARE SOOOOO BUUUUUUTIFUL!" looking me up and down and pulling on my waist. She accidentally dropped her almost-empty can of fruity beer, picked it back up and drank the last bit before she returned to us and wouldn't let me get away. Before she dropped her beer, she had grabbed onto me pretty aggressively; she kept pulling on me and trying to dance (although, admittedly, she was falling into me A LOT; once again, she was extremely drunk and could hardly stand up straight). As we danced together, she moved into me multiple times and said, "If I could, I would FUCK YOU SIDEWAYS!"

At one point, she grabbed me from the front, pushed me up against the brick wall behind us and kissed me passionately but also drunkenly; in other words, she stuck her tongue down my throat. She said how much she wanted to fuck me again but then followed it with, "BUT I'm on my period!" and frowned hard before dancing up against me again.

At one point in this back and forth with her, she said she wanted my information because she wanted to get together with me before I left London: "we should go for a cup of coffee, at least, before you leave," she exclaimed. She was shorter than me (about 5'3") with very blonde shoulder-length hair and huge, wide eyes that looked at me lustfully from the moment I entered her space until I left again (to steal away for some water; I never saw her again after this encounter). At one point before I left, she said, "Are you EEEven gay?!?" she asked as I replied, "Yes! I am definitely gay," I smiled wide.[22]

Although Becky was extremely drunk, the fact that she felt safe enough to dance with and kiss another woman on the dance floor without threat of harassment from other clubbers reflects how heteronormativity was often challenged or largely absent in some of these spaces.[23] However, her behavior remained problematic because she did it (especially the unexpected kiss) without my consent; that is, this points to how less heteronormative dance floors are also occasionally disrupted by aggressive, nonconsensual behavior that often intersects with alcohol. Even more "luved up," less heteronormative club spaces are not devoid of harassment (Hutton 2006, 105) and reflect an ongoing tug of war between a PLUR/rave ethos and practices such as harassment that one tends to experience in more mainstream spaces. That is, dance floors and club spaces often reflected this tug of war, an ongoing battle between features inherent to rave authenticity (connectedness, respect, etc.) and EDM/club culture commercialism (disconnectedness, harassment, etc.) that became more pronounced as the night progressed and alcohol continued to flow.

Dancing into Timelessness

Returning to the title of this section, "Leaving Better Than We Came," so much of this idea connects to losing oneself on the dance floor, engaging in timelessness and truly being present for the dance floor experience, whatever that may look like. In Anderson's (2009a) review of ravers' norms and behaviors, she emphasizes how important dancing was to the culture, writing:

> Most ravers I spoke with told me dancing to electronically produced music was the primary activity at a rave and that identity markers (clothes and props) centered on it . . . ravers danced individually but in unison with others around them. Their dancing simultaneously embodied the values of independence and connection, running consistent with raves' collective identity. (Anderson 2009a, 29)

At the same time and given my research now, a clubber's—particularly a woman's—ability to get lost in the moment, on the dance floor, where she can be completely present for the dancing experience is only made more accessible by the effective use of anti-harassment policies and the consensual behavior of clubbers. That is, if harassment behavior is rampant and ignored, those being harassed (typically women) are immediately brought back into their bodies, unable to lose themselves in a timeless experience of the dance-music-transcendent moment; whether or not drugs are involved, harassment cuts off one's access to a "peak moment" (Pini 2001), jouissance (Gilbert and Pearson 1999),[24] oceanic experience or flow (Malbon 1999, 107).[25] Instead, they are forced out of timelessness and into a mental space that requires them to be on alert. For example, Hutton's (2006) research directly challenges work that emphasizes only "luved up," happy environments in club spaces without also addressing how clubbing experiences for women often include harassment and inequality.

The signage that so many clubs in London post on their walls, "Your safety and enjoyment comes first," can speak volumes if those messages are actually connected to actions. If the club is actually putting every clubbers' safety and enjoyment first, experiencing timelessness and bliss on the dance floor will continue to remain accessible and possible for clubbers who are usually harassed, touched, or otherwise bothered by clubbers in other venues. For example, Hutton's (2006) work points to the ongoing import of *undergrounds* or nonmainstream club spaces: "Female clubbers feel safer, more relaxed and at ease in *undergrounds* where they can explore their identities, take risks, have fun and feel part of a (sub)culture in which they are surrounded by like minded people" (105). As I show again in the Conclusion, *Geluk* (the Amsterdam club described above) would be considered more *underground*, a nonmainstream club for a number of reasons, such as their posted policies that clearly outline their PLUR-like ethos and the anti-harassment, consensual behavior that they encouraged in their club. Of course, while accessing peak experiences can certainly happen in a club that is more mainstream and less committed to anti-harassment policies, there is typically more work or strategizing involved (especially for women) if they want to "lose it" on the dance floor.

Complicating this access to peak experiences/dancing into timelessness even further, Pini (2001) makes the following point: "Ravers themselves . . . very often indicate that a quite rigorous self-regulation, monitoring and management is an integral part of raving" (175). That is, accessing peak experiences is always accompanied by the work that must happen in order to get there, what Pini describes as "the production and maintenance of the 'peak' state" (176). Given what we know about women's experiences in dance music, the production and maintenance of their "peak state" always intersects with hierarchical gender relations and gendered expectations, in general. While Malbon (1999) does not focus specifically on women clubbers on the dance floor, he makes a similar point about the work that any clubber must negotiate as they're navigating the dance floor, work that is not simply about learning the game of clubbing but can be as subtle as exchanging a furtive glance at the right moment or how one is wearing clothing:

> It takes so much more than knowing the rules of a game to be able to play it effectively—practices are about more than 'knowing how'. Clubbing is constituted through the skills, competencies and shared knowledges which only repeated participation can instil. Clubbing is not just about wearing specific clothing, but also the way that clothing is worn; not just about presence within a space at a certain time, but also the way in which this space is inhabited through one's use of the body; not just about dancing in an acceptable way, but also about dancing in an acceptable space at the right time and possibly with the right people. (Malbon 1999, 184–185)

Thus, simply navigating a club requires an impressive amount of time, attention, and practical consciousness (Giddens 1984, 375)[26]—embodied work— that is certainly made more intense when a clubber is also forced to negotiate and navigate harassment of any kind. Further, Malbon's quote above also highlights the ongoing practices or spatiotemporal, embodied processes that clubbers must constantly negotiate; given these negotiations, this is precisely why I used my particular ethnographic method as I conducted fieldwork. This method allowed me to pick up on these subtleties, embodied negotiations that clubbers are acutely, though not always consciously, aware of.

In sum, if a PLUR/rave ethos is even marginally present, it often contributes to less or no harassment in the venue and on the dance floors.[27] For Hutton's (2006) "female" clubbers, *attitude* or social rules (109) ultimately defined who belonged in which spaces. Given the following definition, the "right *attitude*" looks quite a lot like a PLUR ethos: "The 'right' attitude as defined by female clubbers was one that included appropriate behaviour towards women such as the absence of sexual harassment, tolerance of different sexualities and tolerance of expressions of female identities" (106). I return to this issue again in the Conclusion, thus analyzing when a PLUR/ rave ethos or, in Hutton's case, the "right *attitude*" is not really present and the outcomes of that nonpresence. Finally, "increasing commercialization seems to reinforce gender difference" (Gavanas and Reitsamer 2013, 60), a pattern that I certainly found on dance floors across venues and as I followed DJs' activities online, an issue that I return to in the following chapters.

LESS OR NO CONNECTION ON THE DANCE FLOOR

Returning to TBM's *VICE News* article, she continues to describe how dance music has played out in her life:

> You might expect that dance music would completely replace my complicated relationship with Catholicism. But I found that—in spite of my firmly held disagreements with the church—the ritual, contemplation, and allegory of my faith continued to provide guidance and comfort to me. Whereas nightlife can be joyful yet transitory, my faith keeps me tied to more permanent traditions and to my family. (The Black Madonna 2016)

While TBM certainly captures how acceptance (unity, respect, and love) and transcendence (peace and timelessness)—dance music themes so closely connected to PLUR—are still felt and experienced by her and many people on dance music floors, nightlife is, nonetheless, "joyful yet transitory" and often experienced as lacking PLUR-related practices. In the following sections, I locate a number of current practices that are contributing to less or no connection with other clubbers and/or with oneself (disrupting one's access to a flow state, for instance) on today's dance floors.[28]

New Technologies: Smartphones On and Off the Dance Floor

The use of smartphones on dance floors is so pervasive today that clubs have to constantly remind patrons to refrain from using them. At the Shoreditch club where I initially discovered TBM, a framed sign (posted throughout the club and in its bathrooms) read:

PHOTOS & VIDEOS
ARE NOT PERMITTED
OUR DANCEFLOOR IS FOR DANCING
THANK YOU

While smartphone use was not policed at this club, clubbers typically used their smartphones less than they did in other venues where smartphones were pervasive. Other clubs had strict smartphone policies. As I entered the Amsterdam club, *Geluk*, in December 2018, I had the following conversation with a staff member at the front of the line:

Staff: "So, have you ever been here before?"
Me: "No."
Staff: "What do you know about this event?"
Me: "Definitely here to see The Bl[essed] Madonna and HAAi . . . .I've seen The Bl[essed] Madonna all over the world . . ."
Staff: "Ok . . . great . . . for this event, there are no pictures or videos allowed."
Me: "Ok, can I have my phone with me at all? For texts?"
Staff: "Yes, you can. That's fine if you want to keep it with you. Just don't use it for any pictures."
Me: "Ok, got it. Thank you."
Staff: "Enjoy"
Me: "Thank you"

While our exchange was friendly, she was clearly screening me for knowledge of the club and its event[29] and, perhaps most importantly, stating some club behavior rules and regulations, particularly with regard to smartphone use. Upon entering the club's security line and to further curb the use of my phone, a security guard put a red circular sticker directly on the camera of my phone. This happened at a number of clubs over the course of my research and especially at smaller, more intimate clubs with hundreds rather than thousands of clubbers. Also, if the club covered my phone camera, it happened throughout Europe and the UK and never happened in the United States.

Smartphone policing did not simply start and end with staff. A couple hours later, I was approached by an actual clubber who directly policed my smartphone use:

Standing at the other end of the main room, at the back of the dance floor, I was more than fifty feet away from the DJ booth, in an area that hardly had any dancers. I was searching the internet (for the song that Gideon (the current DJ) was playing in his set) and a tall white man got really close to my face and said, "turn your screen light down!" I thought I was getting in trouble by someone working in the club (only to realize later that this was a tall man who had been dancing close to me for at least an hour and had reprimanded me for my bright screen). Since I thought staff was upset with me for the screen and didn't want to get kicked out, I quickly said, "oh, of course! I will!" I exclaimed as clearly as I could and fumbled to turn down the screen light. I only realized a couple minutes later that I probably got scolded by another clubber, not someone working the event.

When smartphone use is not monitored, clubbers usually use their phones a lot, especially if most of the people on the dance floor are focused on the DJ booth (watching a DJ play their set). At Honey Dijon's December 2018 performance in Edinburgh, for example, every single time she dropped a beat or played a song that resulted in audience cheering, hundreds of clubbers would raise their phones and start recording the moment, often ceasing their dancing altogether.[30]

Returning to TBM's quote and the feeling of timelessness/losing oneself in the moment, looking at or using one's phone draws one out of the moment and into their phones. Therefore, when clubbers stop what they're doing on the dance floor to look at or use their phones, they turn away from the present moment, often pulling away from whatever is happening on the dance floor. Timelessness, on the other hand, is all about being present and fully in the moment (not thinking about what's ahead, what you might want to post to your social media, or how best to capture a picture or video of the current moment): "[t]he scene is at its best when the entire room is active, participating and locked into the moment" (Heath 2019). Like harassment and other disruptive forces, the blue screen of a smartphone often cuts off access to this flow state; if one is constantly looking at their phone, it's highly unlikely they're going to engage in creative, present, joyful, collective dancing. Instead, dance floors with a proliferation of smartphones often include clubbers shifting back and forth, one hand holding up their phone and the other hand twirling or pumping to the beat, their eyes fixed on what their phone is capturing, "reasserting the ego's wish to document, record, and share" (Heath 2019) and "genuinely kill[ing] the vibe" (ibid.) in the process. In contrast, 1990s raves were never like this. While dancers certainly took a break and shifted back and forth, this nearly static type of dancing was not the norm; instead, a full range of dance styles were represented on the dance floor and throughout a party. This full range of dancing is atypical now and, in fact, dancers who are especially creative and in a state of flow tend to stand out because there are so few of them on dance floors today.[31] This finding is consistent with Conner (2015) who found that "[i]t has become increasingly rare to see people dancing at contemporary EDM events" (136).

Extending and revising Malbon's (1999) conceptualization of clubbing as experiential consuming, "a form of consuming in which nothing material is 'taken home,' but which can nevertheless produce important memories, emotional experiences and imaginaries" (183), the use of smartphones on the dance floor means that digital, intangible though consequential memories are being made and often used to engage in brand-building (via social media sharing) on the part of clubbers. When a smartphone is used to capture digital memories and/or share out those memories from dance floors, while "nothing material is 'taken home,'" something digital is certainly being collected and often being shared across social media platforms.[32] While future digital research is needed in this area, perhaps something more like "experiential branding" is happening on today's dance floors, especially dance floors where smartphone use is ubiquitous.

This dance floor pattern—parking on the DF and using your phone—has not gone unnoticed, generating "stay in the moment" policies that clubs and events have continued posting. In an advertisement for their September 11, 2021, party at *fabric* in London, @he.she.they listed two justifications for their policy: "you can focus on actually having fun and interacting with the people around you and the music" and "you don't have to worry about being a sweaty mess or dressing how you want to and it showing up on insta when you don't want it too [*sic*]" (@he.she.they, June 28, 2021).[33] As clubs, promoters, and clubbers are realizing, smartphones on the dance floor make connecting with other clubbers, feeling free to "lose it," and privacy that much more difficult to access.

Privacy issues for DJs and clubbers have also led to smartphone restrictions at clubs. As Collin (2018) astutely highlights, when smartphones are out, everyone in the club is increasingly more visible: "Not for the first time, Berghain's [(see above)] sternly enforced no-photos rule seemed to make a lot of sense, guaranteeing a temporary privacy from the all-seeing eye of the smartphone. In most venues by the 2010s, clubbers and DJs had to assume that they were potentially under some kind of surveillance—either official or amateur—pretty much all the time" (121). Again, when smartphones are readily available and used to take videos and pictures that are often shared on social media accounts, this reality changes how the dance floor looks and feels. While future research is required to systematically study the impact of smartphones on clubbers' confidence and creativity on the dance floor, there was a discernible difference between dance floors with a lot of smartphones out and dance floors with restrictive smartphone policies. Typically, far more dancing and socializing (exchanging appreciative smiles and glances with other clubbers, making room for each other, complimenting one another, etc.) occurred when smartphones were largely absent from the dance floor. That is, the "love fog" I described above happened far more frequently and often permeated the entire club when smartphone use was restricted.

Smartphone use does not always have to be curbed or policed, however. Over the course of my research, there were a few events where clubbers—particularly queer audiences—danced with each other and hardly used their phones at all (even without a strict phone policy), such as a queer-friendly San Francisco party featuring a b2b set with Eris Drew and Octo Octa, another queer-friendly San Francisco pool party featuring TBM as the headliner, the queer-friendly San Francisco day party with Honey Dijon as the headliner (mentioned above), and another "underground"/less mainstream London club near Elephant & Castle.

Finally, in addition to how smartphones can often shift clubbers away from the present moment, the celebrity status of DJs is also changing clubbers' behavior in and around the dance floor.

Celebrity DJs and the Dance Floor

TBM highlights how celebrity status impacts the scene and her role in it:

> [Interviewer:] How do you feel about being as well known as you are?
>
> It feels so weird to talk about it, to be honest. It's very surreal. Two years ago I can remember trying to strike up a conversation with certain people in clubs and just being completely rejected. I was completely outside the circle.
>
> It's been a pretty disorienting shift, going from private to public in a short period of time. Recently I did a set at a festival and afterwards, my agent and I were walking around, and a large crowd of people began to applaud spontaneously when we passed by. That was [a] very, very strange experience. I turned around to see if they were clapping for someone else. The social part is something I'm still adjusting to. (Arkenbout 2015)[34]

The dance floors literally reflect this behavior—treating DJs as celebrities.

Unlike early raves where dancing often happened regardless of which DJ was playing any one set, the celebrity status of the "spectacular DJ" (Rietveld 2013, 91) and where they're located in the club has an impact on what is actually happening on the dance floor. Conner (2015) highlights this spatial shift: "At early EDM events, DJs were often placed in dimly lit corners or off to the side—in marked contrast to today's multi-million dollar spectacles where they are placed at the center of attention. This meant the focus was more on the DJs skill and ability as a performer" (68). Given my research, across all of the nightclubs and events (both smaller venues and massive warehouses), DJs were positioned in front of the dance floor and never off to the side. For clubbers, facing the DJ booth tended to be the default dance floor behavior across all of the spaces. That is, in spaces without smartphone restrictions, their widespread use meant that the vast majority of clubbers would often turn toward the DJ booth and stop dancing (or sway back and forth) as they used their smartphones to take pictures or videos. When less or no smartphones were present, most clubbers still faced the DJ booth but often danced by themselves or in groups, thus focusing on the dance floor rather than what they might capture on their phones.

In Conner's (2015) analysis of the transitions that occurred in dance music from 1995 to 2003, he writes: "Indeed, many participants in the early EDM scene noted that they often had no clue as to who was playing. Once EDM events started being produced in legitimate spaces, this changed. DJs became featured on the ads and placed front and center like a live band. By putting DJs on top of a well-lit stage, it changed the interaction between DJs and the audience" (104). My research shows that the interaction between DJs and the audience has, indeed, changed and continues to change with the use of new technologies and the varying ways that celebrity DJs interact with their fans both online and in physical spaces. Even the way that academics talk about DJs contributes to their ongoing allure: "By creating unique (re)combinations of musical elements in response to the dancers on the floor, the successful club and party DJ can take on a magical role in a culture of industrial reproduction and alienating globalization" (Rietveld 2013, 7). Additionally, whether or not a stage is well-lit, placing DJs "front and center like a live band" physically impacts the dance floor. For example, even at *Geluk*, where the smokey, dark dance floor made it impossible to see anything beyond a few dancers immediately next to you, clubbers faced the DJ booth positioned in front of the dance floor.

Treating DJs as celebrities both changes how people move and interact on the dance floor and—spatiotemporally—what the dance floor actually looks like at any given time. At the Glasgow 2018/19 NYE party, within a few minutes of TBM finishing her countdown set, the entire front area (near the DJ booth) of the dance floor cleared out. Clubbers literally left a gaping hole right at the front of the dance floor and under the DJs' booth as soon as she stopped playing. As I captured in photos and videos, clubbers continued filing out of the main room for the first 20 to 30 minutes after she left the DJ booth; this means that there was a massive hole directly in front of the DJ booth and as the next two DJs started playing their b2b set. Similarly, clubbers will flood a dance floor and cheer as soon as the headlining DJ steps up to the DJ booth. Much like a concert where the opening act gets far less attention from the audience than the headlining band, clubbers now do this with DJs. For example, at the Rotterdam 2018 NYE party, TBM was not a headlining DJ in the main room; instead, she played her 5-7a set in the second, smaller room. While she closed out the party (with another DJ in the main room), the fact that she was not in the main room had an impact on her actual dance floor. Unlike the massive main room (Hal 1) with thousands of people, the second room (Hal 2) had considerably less people, a less impressive light show, and felt completely cleared out in comparison to the main room. In fact, it was so cleared out that my new friend, Carina, eventually lost interest and convinced me to go back to the main room. Circling back to PLUR-ness, leaving a gaping hole in front of a DJ's booth (after another DJ just finished their set) is a clear sign of disrespect that is treated as acceptable and normal in most dance music spaces today and was certainly treated as such at the Glasgow NYE party. This is just one example of how an awareness of a PLUR/rave ethos coupled with PLUR-like cultural components (norms, behaviors, and activities) is often lacking.

Yet, there is a both/and quality to the dance floors I studied; *both* "love fogs" *and* moments of disconnection and disrespect can happen at the same time or within moments of one another. As the fieldnote excerpts above show, clubbers were embracing and sharing love and affection during the New Year countdown only moments before that same group of clubbers decided to clear out the dance floor as soon as TBM left the DJ booth. Thus, whatever good feelings I had after embracing other clubbers quickly faded away as I watched them collectively contribute to a gaping hole at the front of the dance floor.

CONCLUSIONS

Beginning this chapter with the NYE trips that primarily included following TBM from one venue and European city to the next over multiple days, the dance floor is used as the starting point for making sense of social patterns that now govern dance music spaces. While dancing and dance floors remain central to dance music culture, the cultural components (norms, behaviors, and activities) that are actually happening on dance floors have certainly changed since the 1990s rave era. DJs such as Honey Dijon are speaking up about these changes, calling out clubbers for pulling up *Instagram* on dance floors or just standing, wearing bland clothes, and staring at the DJ. My research shows that Honey Dijon's frustration is warranted at the same time that connection, timelessness, and bliss still have a place on the dance floor. In other words, there is a *both/and* quality to dance floors now; they are *both* blissful *and* alienating, sometimes at the same time or separated by a few minutes, depending on what else is happening in the space.

Locating "the important social and cultural space between authenticity and mainstream commercialism," (Anderson 2009a, 168) on actual dance floors, it's clear that both extremes are present. A PLUR/rave ethos remains present and is realized in the following ways: via a "love fog" that permeates dance floors and club spaces, encouraging friendliness, connecting with strangers, and a reconfiguration of masculinities and femininities; anti-harassment policies that are posted in venues and impact how clubbers interact; and smartphone restrictions that encourage clubbers to get out of their phones and dance. In this way, PLUR-ness has become institutionalized, especially as its ethos is used to dictate and monitor clubbers' behavior.

Problematic, anti-PLUR practices have also emerged, some more subtle than others: if harassment does occur, it tends to be subtle and covert, often requiring those who are harassed to do an extra amount of mental and physical work to get out of the interaction; and harassment often intersects with the use of alcohol, especially when it is extreme or intensified. Additionally, less or no connection on the dance floors is exacerbated by the widespread use of smartphones and the treatment of "DJs as celebrities/superstars"; clubbers are increasingly encouraged to focus on their phones and/or face the DJ booth during an entire event instead of focusing specifically on coming together and dancing with other clubbers or accessing their own "peak moment"/ timelessness. While the "the production and maintenance of a 'peak state'" (Pini 2001, 175) was certainly a challenge before the age of smartphones and celebrity DJs, these disruptions aren't making it any easier for clubbers to "lose it" and come together as a community.

Building upon these analyses and returning to the section in chapter 1, titled "Where the Dance Music Scene Fails," chapter 4 and the Conclusion interrogate commercial, less PLUR, patterns in the industry. How does commercialism and corporatization impact dance music's dance floors, social media activity, the current role of DJs, and other recent patterns that dance music must navigate? Since gradations of PLUR-ness remain present and are still highlighted by DJs and fans alike, larger questions about how this ethos can continue to flourish are needed. The book's Conclusion offers some suggestions for how to keep peace, love, unity, and respect present on the dance floors and beyond.

NOTES

1. https://www.ssense.com/en-us/editorial/music/meet-mate-and-create-the-life -of-honey-dijon

2. In future research, I plan to do similar research trips, mapping out how much has changed since the pandemic.

3. For example, from 2017 to 2020, I completed fieldwork at venues in major cities throughout the United States, Europe, and the United Kingdom, featuring TBM, Honey Dijon, and Peggy Gou and a full range of other DJs such as Nina Kraviz,

Hunee, Eris Drew, Octo Octa, Tzusing, Mark Farina, Derrick Carter and Bicep, to name only a few.

4. https://www.telegraph.co.uk/travel/destinations/europe/germany/berlin/articles/Berghain-how-to-get-into-Berlins-most-exclusive-nightclub/

5. Olaveson (2004) captures this behavior well, writing, "I have no doubt that some ravers actually taste each other in cuddle puddles and other masses of half-clothed, sweaty bodies" (269).

6. This abrupt transition from a dark dance floor, a light show, and thousands of clubbers dancing to loud, pulsating music to a suddenly brightly lit warehouse without music or dancing clubbers is a perfect example of the timelessness that I described in chapter 1. There is a notable feeling of pleasure, escape, and release when one experiences timelessness on the dance floor primarily because "the pleasures of the present may temporarily obliterate the concerns of life before, beyond and outside the clubbing experience" (Malbon 1999, 102). Thus, Malbon (1999) articulates exactly what I experienced when the lights flashed on: "a very common feature of the end of a club night is the palpable sense of disbelief that the night might actually be over, despite the inevitability of this moment" (102). This "palpable sense of disbelief" is a common theme, one that is often only magnified by an other-worldly night on the dance floor (see also Jackson 2004, 20).

7. When on tour, TBM often talks about how she falls asleep without even realizing it, often sitting upright. Given how many times this happened to me in the Amsterdam airport and on the flight to Manchester, while it was unnerving, it also gave me an embodied glimpse into what touring feels like for global DJs; as I finished the mini tour, I could hardly imagine touring like that on a regular basis.

8. In this book's Conclusion, I address how heteronormative spaces impacted clubbers' behavior and the degree of PLUR-ness present on the dance floor. Also, as I outlined in the Introduction, the spaces I studied often shared more or less features of both *mainstreams* and *undergrounds* (Hutton 2006), again representing *a combination* of rave authenticity *and* EDM or club culture commercialism in any given space (Anderson 2009a).

9. Given how much has changed—once again (Conner 2015)—since Anderson (2009a) published her book, future research that revisits and updates the forces she located to "explain the alteration and decline of the rave scene from its high point in the mid to late 1990s to its diminished and fragmented state" in 2009 (Anderson 2009b, 307) is needed.

10. This is the music video, with the original (not remixed) song: https://www.youtube.com/watch?v=A4Y9V07wry4

11. Once again, this describes flow or timelessness, a state of being that brings one into the present and often encourages bliss and transcendence (see chapter 1).

12. https://pitchfork.com/reviews/tracks/georgia-about-work-the-dancefloor/

13. https://theinterns.net/2020/01/07/georgia-wants-feel-dancefloor/

14. https://www.vice.com/en_us/article/kb5pkn/artist-of-the-year-the-black-madonna-catholic-faith-essay

15. https://www.dazeddigital.com/music/article/29976/1/thirty-years-later-and-rave-still-hasn-t-left-the-dancefloor

16. Wilson (2006) and other research on raving and/or clubbing is consistent with this finding: "The PLUR philosophy manifested itself in various ways at raves that I attended. At no time did I feel physically threatened at a rave. Often people would smile or offer me a cigarette. When people would bump into me accidentally, they would often say "sorry" and smile—a contrast to the macho norms of many nightclubs" (79–80).

17. All of these men were white, usually with a group of about three to seven people; sometimes a couple of white women were also in the group.

18. This is also consistent with Anderson's (2009a) and Wilson's (2006) research. In discussing what made the EDM scene appealing, Anderson's interviewees "appreciated the relative absence of a sexualized environment and preferred dancing in an individual and nonsexualized style" (Anderson 2009a, 76). In Wilson's (2006) interviews, "ravers talked about the differences between the 'pick-up culture' of bars and the more friendship-oriented relationships at the rave" (117). Additionally, ravers described interactions at rave parties as much more in line with the love fog I described above: interactions were described as "'sensual as opposed to sexual,' since hugging and massaging are central parts of the culture for many ravers" (118). While hugging and massaging were typical practices during my 1990s rave days, this is no longer typical. Instead, friendliness—without touching—permeates the dance floors and surrounding areas.

19. Hutton's (2006) research on what she calls *undergrounds* or underground (not mainstream) clubs is consistent with this finding: "Some of the more aggressive men might try intimidating behavior such as staring or following people round the club, but it usually goes no further" (31).

20. This pattern is also consistent with Palamar and Griffin's (2020) research on nonconsensual sexual contact at electronic dance music parties in New York City.

21. Gilbert and Pearson (1999) made the following point over 20 years ago: "If Ecstasy and house music have even slightly displaced drunkenness and violence as the common culture of young men in Britain, then Britain can only be a better place for it" (182). While my research shows that violence is largely absent from dance music events I studied, drunkenness is certainly present (especially at large (hundreds to thousands of people), heteronormative spaces), a reality that often intersects with clubbers of any gender behaving badly.

22. Given the state that Becky was in, I decided that this was not the best time to have a lengthy discussion about my queer (not gay) identity.

23. As Hutton's (2006) research in club spaces shows: "It was seen as unacceptable to display same sex affection if the women concerned did not conform to stereotypical images of femininity" (99). The fact that we both presented ourselves as "stereotypically feminine" almost certainly had an impact on how we were treated in this space.

24. Given its definition, *jouissance* is appropriate here: "a pleasure which can never be adequately described precisely because it is pre-linguistic, pre-subjective—can be experienced in situations in which *our normal relation to the symbolic order is disrupted* . . . .[it is] excessive and unmasterable pleasure which spills over the boundaries of sense" (Gilbert and Pearson 1999, 65, my emphasis).

25. While scholars use a number of varied terms, temporary moments of pure bliss (discussed in chapter 1) captures both the temporal and ecstatic dimension of these moments. Additionally, when dancers describe these moments, they often describe timelessness or losing track of time; that is, they become so fully immersed in the activity that they access a flow state: "[w]hen we experience timelessness, we are creative" (Berg and Seeber 2016, 27) and often joyful. This is precisely what I mean when I talk about creative, joyful dancing that can certainly happen when one accesses a flow state or what Malbon (1999) describes as an "extreme flow" (141) experience. Building upon and quoting Csikszentmihalyi ([1975] 2000), he writes, "[d]uring these extreme flow experiences . . . those 'going with the flow' might: [C]oncentrate their attention on a limited stimulus field, forget personal problems, lose their sense of time and of themselves, feel competent and in control, and have a sense of harmony and union with their surroundings . . . some people emphasize the move-ment of their bodies; others try to maximize emotional communication; still others respond to the social dimensions of activity" (Malbon 1999, 141).

26. Giddens (1984) defines practical consciousness as the following: "What actors know (believe) about social conditions, including especially the conditions of their own action, but cannot express discursively" (375).

27. Given the ongoing import of curbing harassment in clubs and dance music venues, I return to the importance of club policies, the actual enactment of those poli-cies, and the behavior of clubbers in this book's Conclusion.

28. As I show in the following sections, there are a number of forces that inhibit or disrupt a dancer's flow. Malbon (1999, 143) highlights disruptions that predated smartphones and treating DJs as celebrities, such as: feeling self-conscious while dancing, especially if the feedback a dancer is getting from the crowd feels negative or judgmental and/or dancing on the edge of the dance floor and thus feeling judged and on display in the presence of nondancing clubbers. Of course, on the other end of flow is an elevated feeling of competence and thus extreme flow if certain spatial and/or musical arrangements work in a dancer's favor: "the edges of the dance floor can also provide opportunities for overtly staged displays of skill, dancing styles and self-control—a static audience is also a captive audience" (Malbon 1999, 143). It's worth stating that these moments often fluctuate throughout the night, especially as a dancer interacts with a DJ's set; that is, while a set of beats might push a dancer into extreme flow for a few minutes, a new set of beats could just as easily break her dancing flow.

29. In Anderson's (2009a) interviews with scene insiders, they identified a cat-egory of outsiders they called "clubbers" or people who were invested in "going out late at night to socialize, drink, and dance" (66) but not deeply invested in dance music. For example, clubbers (as defined and analyzed by Anderson) might like a musical genre but "at a more general level than insiders" (Anderson 2009a, 67). She explains: "I ran into lots of people who liked dance music parties but did not necessar-ily care who the DJ was or what subgenre was being featured" (Anderson 2009a, 67). As my interaction with *Geluk*'s staff elucidates, their screening questions indicated that they were trying to avoid letting people in who were more like outsiders than insiders.

30. Zak "DVS1" Khutoretsky highlights how the music, itself, is changing because of the rampant use of smartphones on dance floors: "People are literally making and performing music unconsciously to create moments for the fucking camera now, because it's really obvious when you go hear a set and you start to hear this epic breakdown every couple of tracks and you hear the snare roll—you know it's a 'moment' and people throw their cameras up and they're ready to capture it and it becomes this thing of having moments. This is why I love 'adventure' DJ sets, loopy techno stuff, because there is no obvious moment, when it happens, it just happens" (Heath 2019).

31. As an example, I remember wondering why clubbers were stopping and watching me as I "lost it" dancing to TBM's set that first night and realized later that dancing like this—really getting into the groove and flowing with the music—was pretty uncommon and therefore stuck out on the dance floor. Additionally, this became a pattern as I followed TBM and other DJs; I would start getting into it and fairly quickly find myself on display.

32. Future digital research in this area is needed. For example, what are clubbers sharing out on their social media platforms? Given how disruptive this behavior is on dance floors, how are clubbers branding themselves or what picture, video, and/or caption is worth "killing the vibe" on dance floors?

33. https://www.instagram.com/p/CQsVfaRg9mB/

34. https://www.vice.com/en_us/article/pg8g3k/the-black-madonna-clubs-are -dangerous-for-women

Chapter 4

"We Still Believe. *Do You?*"

Navigating and Challenging the Business of Contemporary Dance Music

What do you desire?
Love or material things?

These lyrics in Seth Troxler's set are direct and unapologetic, coupling a critique of consumerism with pleasure:

I can take you higher (!) than you've ever been!
Meet me at the club.[1]

Raves can be magical. In my early rave days, a big part of the allure was entering into another dimension, one that literally transported me to a space far removed from my everyday life. I would arrive as late as midnight and dance until the sun came up. As so many of us walked out of the venue, we often felt like vampires, assaulted by the early-morning sun.[2] Transitioning from the rave's cocoon to the "real world" felt dramatic and stark, another piece of evidence that the rave we had just experienced was something special. Capturing some of this "magic," TBM's *Instagram* picture and caption offers a glimpse into how raves can feel:

> I am remembering the morning this picture was taken. [DJ] Servito and I had just played our first back to back in a warehouse in California. *Everyone was running around hugging each other the way you do after one of those perfect, impossible nights, when somehow against all odds, you play the right records and the cops don't come and the spirit of dance descends on the room and gets all the way in everyone's bones for a while [sic]. We continued into the morning, well past the hours that rational people do much of anything. I remember realizing that a skylight was turning grey and thinking holy hell it's daytime. . . . It was a set*

theblessedmadonna • Following   ...

theblessedmadonna ⦿ I am remembering the morning this picture was taken.
Servito and I had just played our first back to back in a warehouse in California. Everyone was running around hugging each other the way you do after one of those perfect, impossible nights, when somehow against all the odds, you play the right records and the cops don't come and the spirit of dance descends on the room and gets all the way in everyone's bones for a while.
We continued into the morning, well past the hours that rational people do much of anything. I remember realizing that a skylight was turning

Liked by **leiferoonie** and **1,615 others**

AUGUST 30, 2017

Add a comment...

Figure 4.1   The Blessed Madonna's *Instagram* Post.

of emotions I hadn't felt in a long time. *American dance music has waxed and waned over the years, but there simply is no other experience like an American rave in full bloom.* Since that morning, I've relocated to London and been on tour in Europe since April. *It's been a grueling, amazing, body destroying, soul saving, perfect, terrifying dash around the world.* I found myself one day DJing on a raft in a quarry inside a former Soviet gulag and the next in a Welsh manor, complete with peacocks guarding the property. But now it's time to come home. I will spend the next two months touring the Americas largely and continuing studio work. And as I write to all of you from an airplane, 35,000 feet over the earth, it is with high hopes that when I land in America that together we can recapture a little of the magic I remember from that picture and that morning. From our nation's capital to the twin poles of dance, Detroit and Chicago, we need that magic now more than ever. Let's go together. I'll be somewhere by the left front speaker.

We still believe,
TBM (@theblessedmadonna, August 30, 2017, my emphasis)

I begin with this description because it so wholly captures both the beauty and magic of attending some dance music parties or "raves" at the same time that it also captures the whirlwind, dizzying, relentless dance music entertainment machine that exists today.[3] In many ways, The Blessed Madonna, Honey Dijon, and Peggy Gou are squarely in the center of this dizzying display of dance music, sorting out what works best for them as they navigate their careers and publicly addressing issues that they want to see change or challenged within and beyond the scenes they occupy.

Summarizing her dance music philosophy, The Blessed Madonna's "We Still Believe" radio show begins with the following intro:

We believe in love.
We believe in togetherness.
We believe in disco.
We believe in house and our house music.
We believe in techno.
We believe in dance.
We still believe.
Do you?

TBM's philosophy clearly draws from a PLUR/rave ethos at the same time that it offers new and creative ways to navigate increasingly corporatized dance music. Considering how TBM, Honey Dijon, and Peggy Gou accomplish their work as DJs, how do each one of them individually or collectively address any problems that commercialization and corporatization have introduced? How are they navigating and changing dance music and what might some of these changes mean for its future?

In Brian Wilson's (2006) *Fight, Flight, or Chill: Subcultures, Youth, and Rave into the Twenty-First Century*, he argues "that rave, while embodying the *potential* for transcendent connections among its members, has become (with notable exceptions) a business that exploits glorified and nostalgic images in order to "sell" the dance party to youth" (Wilson 2006, 158–159). Relatedly, my research shows that "gradations of rave authenticity and EDM or club culture commercialism" (Anderson 2009a, 49) are constantly present; that is, in virtually every contemporary dance music context (on its dance floors, via social media, in magazine articles featuring (global) DJs, etc.), "rave authenticity and EDM or club culture commercialism" are constantly in conversation. This chapter continues to address that conversation, paying particular attention to how The Blessed Madonna, Honey Dijon, and Peggy Gou navigate it, directly challenge or succumb to the commercial end of it, and, in some cases, offer new and creative ways of engaging it. As stakeholders (Anderson 2009a) or scene insiders, they are squarely in the center of the conversation and often tasked with *both* challenging *and* upholding the commercialization of dance music.[4] Relatedly, when scene insiders categorize other people (DJs, promoters, clubbers, etc.) and/or social and cultural practices as either authentic or commercial, they are defining the ongoing and often contradictory rules and regulations (Anderson 2009a, 171) attached to those concepts. Thus, the DJs I followed are actively engaged in *both* proving their ongoing legitimacy via a set of strategies I call *authenticity maneuvering* (which I expand upon below) and, in the process, adding to a proliferation of authenticity (and commercial) discourse (Foucault 1978) in dance music. In other words, as they navigate their own brands,[5] they simultaneously contribute to the ongoing debates about what constitutes authenticity[6] and what needs to change in dance music. Also, of course, as they add to the proliferation of dance music discourse, they may also reproduce hierarchies as much as they aim to work against them (Gilbert and Pearson 1999, 159), a contradiction that requires carefully teasing out the multilayered outcomes of their contributions.

NAVIGATING THE BUSINESS OF CONTEMPORARY DANCE MUSIC

How Social Media Transformed Club Culture

While technology has certainly shifted how people interact on dance floors (see chapter 3), it has also impacted virtually everything else that goes into dance music culture (e.g., how events are promoted, DJs manage their careers, clubbers experience the scenes, music is distributed and played). In an article titled "Honey Dijon on whether dance music can save us" (Abraham 2019), she talks about how much technology has shifted the overall dance music scene and, specifically, what DJs like herself have to contend with as they manage their careers:

Honey Dijon: I think the biggest challenge for me is that *we've gone from community to entertainment. Now with the visibility of social media, DJs have to be more like performers than artists.* Now the biggest challenge is clubs or festivals won't book you unless you're a certain number of followers or more. I think that's such a mistake. One thing I was really happy with was when Resident Advisor got rid of the top 100 DJs because this is not a comparison game! Everyone is doing something truly unique and different. Just because someone has 1 million followers doesn't make them a quality artist, in my opinion.

So I think the biggest challenge is that it was always the music business but now it's less about the quality than the quantity . . . there might be some really wicked local DJs who are good or deserve an opportunity to play big lineups *but they don't have the visibility on social media.* I'm glad they're getting rid of the likes on social media because it's not good for young people, it gives them anxiety. And it's the same for DJs; *"what should I post?" etcetera . . . that's a lot of work now*, and it takes away from the music, which is what it should fucking be about in the first place! (Abraham 2019, my emphasis)

Much like the "Celebrity DJs and the Dance Floor" section in chapter 3, the fact that "DJs have to be more like performers than artists" is not only literally changing dance floors but also changing what DJs can accomplish and what they are expected to do, thus changing their actual labor.

DJs can get swept up in the current dance music entertainment machine, one that is far more focused on the bottom line (making money) than producing "quality" content and creating PLUR-like experiences for those in the scene (see Conner 2015). Peggy Gou, for example, posts far more *Instagram* stories than Honey Dijon and TBM combined (especially from summer 2017 to fall 2019), thus highlighting how much time, energy, and work she dedicates to her social media presence and, relatedly, how much she values that presence. In other words, she is keenly aware of how important her social media presence is and how it continues to impact her meteoric rise to DJ superstardom. On August 23, 2019, for example, the fact that she hit 1 million *Instagram* followers was not lost on her. Before she hit this mark, she posted an *Instagram* story with the following video announcement: "I'm trying to act cool but my follower [*sic*] is 999[K]. It makes me feel like aaaaaaaaaaahhhhhh!"[7] As Honey Dijon explained above, "the biggest challenge is that it was always the music business but now it's less about the quality than the quantity." DJs like Peggy Gou are, in many respects, completely swept up by and increasingly enmeshed in this quantity over quality music business practice. A quick search of article headlines featuring Peggy Gou illustrates how her fan base and near-constant social media presence are, in fact, having a direct impact on her career:

"Just Gou It: How Peggy Gou Became the World's Hippest DJ" (Cliff 2019)[8]

"Peggy Gou Is Kicking Her Electronic Music Career to the Next Level" (Bromwich 2019)[9]

"Techno Queen Peggy Gou Shows Us Her Camera Roll" (Macias 2019)[10]

While Gou is undoubtedly talented, "[s]he has [also] benefited from an ability to forge useful connections—the celebrity designer Virgil Abloh is a friend—and *a nose for branding*" (Bromwich 2019, my emphasis). In other words, she knows how to play by dance music's current rules and regulations, business practices that deeply intersect with making the right connections, selling one's brand, and playing the quantity over quality game, especially via social media.

George Ritzer's (2019) *The McDonaldization of Society: Into the Digital Age* recognizes how our "McDonaldized" society, one that values quantity over quality is "both 'enabling' and 'constraining' . . . a 'double-edged' phenomenon" (Ritzer 2019, 8). It has enabled us to do things we never imagined before (such as the access that DJs now have to their massive fan base on social media) at the same time that it constrains us in new and often unexpected ways (how social media also requires DJs to engage in new forms of labor[11] to constantly perform and connect to their fan base). A close analysis of how TBM, Honey Dijon, and Peggy Gou navigate and manage their social media presence and branding reveals some stark differences. TBM and Honey Dijon publicly engage in far more self-reflection than Peggy Gou at the same time that they critically think about dance music legacies and their place in those stories, often challenging the commercialization of dance music either in social media posts or interviews; in the process, they have cultivated brands that are much more activist-oriented and aligned with a PLUR/rave ethos. As I show below, TBM and Honey Dijon's *branding practices* are almost entirely wrapped up in reflecting on, performing and re-educating fans about a rave ethos, so the commercial or economic imperative inherent to branding is often made invisible or less obvious. Peggy Gou, on the other hand, engages in far less public displays of self-reflection or overall critiques of dance music and is much less inclined to challenge any form of commercialism. Her *branding practices*, therefore, are often far more visible as commercial/business-oriented because she does not do the extra rave ethos (referencing it, using it, performing it) work that TBM and Dijon have adopted. Therefore, Gou often appears fully caught up in the commercialization of her brand, a risky strategy to employ in scenes that often criticize DJs (especially women DJs[12]) for "selling out" (see Haidari 2019; see also Anderson 2009a, 172).[13]

In fact, Gou's social media posts are so focused on feel-good displays of her brand that anything that counters this particular DJ performance stands out. After posting a "montage" of *Instagram* stories featuring pictures of her fans enthusiastically sitting on one another's shoulders at one of her shows, she posted two *Instagram* story videos reprimanding "haters" who subsequently criticized her fans:

> If you have a problem with the video that I just post[ed] . . . people screaming: "Worst crowd! I can't listen to that anymore! Uuuuuuuhhhh, the screaming! Stop this bullshit."
>
> Get the fuck outta here. They're just having a fucking good time and if you have a problem, stop watching the video!
>
> You know, I don't really engage with haters. They can give me shit as much as they want [and] I'm like, "Talk to my hand." But if they start giving shit to the

crowd *that I love*, they need to get the fuck outta here. (@peggygou_, August 4, 2019, my emphasis)[14]

This post stands out because Gou typically avoids difficult conversations and/ or conflict via her branding, a tactic that TBM and Dijon often employ. Yet, like TBM and Dijon, when she wants to make a statement or disrupt (as she does here), she also uses emotionality and authenticity (the fans "that I love") to get her point across, a tactic that drives her point home and, of course, allows her to continue performing the intimate connection she is expected to have with her fans and continues to positively impact her branding.

Even a cursory review of Gou's social media feeds highlights how busy she is building her brand; that is, her followers usually see her playing one of her packed shows, promoting her new music video, attending a party for the release of her new fashion line, selling tickets for her own dance music party, or any number of brand-building ventures she's engaged in. Thus, while the post above certainly feeds into the building of her brand, the authenticity imperative—loving her fans—also allowed her to criticize "haters." However, Gou's post was not activist-oriented or critical of commercial practices; instead, her counterattack was directed toward "haters" who had criticized and "attacked" her fans. So, unlike TBM and Honey Dijon's activism in and beyond dance music, Gou's post still appeared to feed into the dance music entertainment machine; in other words, there was no direct critique of the dance music industry. Instead, there was an emphasis on taste (Thornton 1996); if "haters" online didn't have a taste for how her fans acted, then they could "[g]et the fuck outta here!"[15] Once again, while TBM and Dijon are also in today's dance music entertainment machine, their branding tactics often make it less obvious that they're just as embedded as Gou is. Nonetheless, Gou's branding strategies are rarely at the expense of her profit-growth, a finding that points to her ongoing indoctrination; for TBM and Dijon, they're embedded at the same time that they're ongoing ambivalence (and/or discomfort) with dance music's entertainment machine points to *both* their resistance to *and* engagement with it.

DJs' Branding: Making Money on Fame

While all three DJs are wholly engaged in building their brands, TBM's brand-building usually connects to her social justice activism (described in the "Making the World that I Am Advocating For" section below); for example, she often engages in "giving back" to dance music, a practice that positions her as authentically dedicated to the scene. DJs such as TBM often engage in these authenticity practices via a process I call *authenticity maneuvering*. Conceptualized as an ongoing social practice, *authenticity maneuvering* is the enactment of strategies to gain and maintain legitimacy—the maneuvering one does to project authenticity.[16] Scene insiders are especially adept at utilizing this practice because they are also creating the norms and behaviors that constitute authenticity.[17]

My conceptualization of *authenticity maneuvering* differs from Schaap and Berkers's (2020) use of the same term. In their research, authenticity maneuvering was "[t]he act of attempting to change the hegemonic form of authenticity of a configuration [or the music genre they studied]" (Schaap and Berkers 2020, 419); in other words, their definition means messing with the authenticity status quo. In my analysis, *authenticity maneuvering* is not the act of attempting to change the hegemonic form of authenticity in dance music. Instead, it is the act of attempting to position oneself as authentic or legitimate within a scene, a genre, and/or an industry; it's the act of navigating the hegemonic form of authenticity (in this case, rave authenticity and everything that attaches to that authenticity), not attempting to change it. In this way, it intersects with *discursive authenticity*, defined as "one's fit with a sociocultural configuration and its discourse [that] establishes (in)authentic participation" (Schaap and Berkers 2020, 419). Also, as scene insiders, TBM, Dijon, and Gou engage in *authenticity maneuvering* at the same time that they're actively creating discourse around what is or is not authentic in dance music (a moving target, to be sure). Given its history and how it's consistently used in the present, a PLUR/rave ethos is undoubtedly wrapped up in rave authenticity discourse and used here as a starting point.

Authenticity maneuvering also aims to capture the *authenticity imperative*,[18] an expectation that DJs and other key actors in dance music must, at the very least, perform acceptable authenticity practices as they interact with the industry. Since there is such a fine line that DJs must walk to continue earning a living in the scene while at the same time supporting (or at least appearing to support) its culture and collective identity (Anderson 2009a, 63), *authenticity maneuvering* helps DJs—especially house music DJs—accomplish that ongoing goal. Some examples of *authenticity maneuvering* are: name-dropping (encyclopedic knowledge of music is especially valued); telling "back in the day" stories; utilizing a PLUR-like ethos; calling other DJs out for being inauthentic and/or "selling out"; and reflecting on and educating people about dance music's history.[19] As Jaimangal-Jones's (2018) research shows, *authenticity maneuvering* intersects with the media discourses surrounding DJs as authentic performers and artists. These media discourses emphasize a number of authenticity imperatives that DJs feel compelled to engage and somehow navigate in order to stay in the game (authenticity measures such as time served as a DJ, positioning some DJs as "gods, masters and pioneers" (232), etc.).

While some DJs use *authenticity maneuvering* constantly and explicitly (TBM and Seth Troxler, for example), Gou and Dijon tend to use it implicitly while also engaging in near-constant brand-building. Their new fashion lines are a case in point. Marking Gou's fashion venture as decidedly global, she launched a September 2019 "City Tour" of her fashion line—*KIRIN*—that landed in Seoul, Hong Kong, Moscow, London, and Paris, all events that were heavily documented and archived on her social media accounts and via KIRIN's own *Instagram* account. A KIRIN description reads:

Peggy Gou Has Dropped Kirin
  We've been (impatiently) waiting since it was announced that Peggy Gou would be taking the reins to design her own high-octane streetwear collection in partnership with the New Guards Group. A ready-to-wear debut, that we are ready to see.
  Mixing fashion and club culture (and named after her spirit animal the giraffe), this collection channels the energy of the DJ's on stage presence with her cooler-than-cool style. This is a fusion of standout colour-blocking, Korean mythological iconography and classic club culture graphics that will make you turn heads for all the right reasons.
  Enough said. Mic drop![20]

This description couples her building fame and "cool-ness" with some muted *authenticity maneuvering*. First, Peggy Gou's meteoric rise in dance music is certainly rare; in other words, she is the only South Korean cisgender woman DJ with her level of fame and success. Thus, the description capitalizes on how special her rise has been while at the same time highlighting her difference (clothes with "Korean mythological iconography," much like the "K House" or Korean House she's introduced to the industry). Just as Gou has done with her music, she is also mixing "Korean mythological iconography and classic club culture graphics," introducing imagery and style that directly challenges Eurocentric depictions of dance music. Second, while PLUR isn't directly mentioned, Gou is building upon this ethos by "mixing fashion and club culture,"[21] thus subtly *authenticity maneuvering* with this indirect, though consequential reference. While the description above does not explicitly address any social or political issues, there are implicit social and political themes present and an emphasis on how Gou is "giving back" to and honoring "classic club culture," a move that positions her, even indirectly, as legitimate.

  Also launching a fashion line, Honey Dijon posted previews and a new *Instagram* account for her new venture—titled *Honey Fucking Dijon*—before its October 5, 2019, launch.[22] *Honey Fucking Dijon* is an extension of her DJ brand and the fashion line is the commodification of that brand. The name of her fashion line directly builds upon her fame, visibility, and "cool-ness" in addition to the garments and other merchandise displayed in her preview posts: for example, she posted photos of multicolored T-shirts with "Honey Fucking Dijon" in bold, rainbow-colored lettering in addition to wallets and bags with the Honey Fucking Dijon logo. It's worth mentioning that these commodities are expensive: cotton T-shirts are as high as £70 (or ~$100), hoodies are £160 (or ~$226), and a Honey Fucking Dijon embossed leather "bumbag" is £430 (or ~$609). When Peggy Gou talks about why she decided to launch a fashion line, she often recounts her initial foray into fashion design as a student before she dropped out of school and started working on her DJ career. For Gou, this is one more money-making and creative project she wanted to launch as her career takes off, a project that further contributes to her visibility as an artist (and her unique contributions) but does not directly take on any social or political issues. As described above, for Gou, any challenges to commercialization are largely absent; in fact, she is extremely adept at and committed to monetizing her brand and less adept at making that monetization less visible with aggressive *authenticity maneuvering*. Further, when Gou challenges the homogeneity of dance music, those challenges are implicit rather than explicit. Honey Dijon, on the other hand, often describes how central fashion has and continues to be in club culture and dance music, *authenticity maneuvering* in the process:

> *For me, there's never been a difference between fashion, art, music, and nightlife.* Growing up in Chicago at the beginning of house music culture, in order for other people to know that you were into this music, there was a dress code. A lot of that had to do with recreating images that you saw in *Vogue*. That's how I discovered Jean-Paul Gaultier, Claude Montana, and Versace. All these inner-city black kids mopping—mopping is stealing—these clothes. Not all inner-city kids stole, a lot of them worked to pay for it, but my introduction to fashion was just seeing kids on the street. It mirrors today with Off-White and Dior and Alyx. These kids are wearing codes to talk to each other. That doesn't change over time. In New York, you couldn't get into a club unless you had a personality or a look. I met most of the people in fashion just DJing in clubs or when I got asked to do after-parties. *Nightlife, for me, has always been about meeting, making, creating, and participating, and that informs what I do today.* I don't believe in aspirational fashion. *I believe in engaging with fashion and using it to express who you are and to speak to your tribe. It's not about money, it's about creativity. Nightlife is always going to be my inspiration for how I do anything and everything.* (Dijon 2020, my emphasis)[23]

Given how closely she connects the history of club culture to her own political and social statements about race, class, gender and sexuality, the launch of her own fashion line highlights her continued focus on visibility (she is the only trans woman of color DJ with her level of fame and success), "giving back" to the scene, and creating art: "It's not about money, it's about creativity." Thus, her quote above is a quintessential example of *authenticity maneuvering* because she uses her own personal history, connection to "house music culture," and politics to justify her new business venture. For her, fashion has always been present in club culture and should reflect active engagement—"to express who you are and to speak to your tribe." Thus, she often constructs this new venture as an individual dream that is finally coming true (@honeydijon, 8/29/2019),[24] one that allows her to finally be visible and, as she often describes, opens up space for other trans girls and women of color to see themselves in her artistic contributions, too. TBM, on the other hand, is not as interested in the same business ventures as Dijon and Gou for a number of reasons:

> I'm kind of in a weird position because it's been a really good year but at the same time *I'm a thirty-eight-year-old woman who looks like someone's mom.* I'm way outside the cool, fashion part of this world and I don't think I'll ever be good at it. . . .
>
> [Interviewer]: Right. So, despite all the recent success you've had you still feel like an outsider?
>
> In a sense yeah, in as much as generally I'd prefer to be at home watching *Downton Abbey* than doing all the pool-party stuff. You know I'm a lot older than some of the people who've just started touring. I'm not interested in fashion or drugs or any of that stuff for the most part. I don't really party, so in some ways I'm a little outside of our peer group. (Trax Magazine 2016, my emphasis)

For both Dijon and Gou, they often frame their new business ventures—ventures that build upon their growing fame—as more opportunities for visibility in a dance music industry that typically features white, cisgender men as superstar DJs. TBM, on the other hand, is certainly building her career but in a way that is far more aligned with her age (as she describes it),[25] interests, and abilities; in other words, she often positions herself as "way outside the cool, fashion part of this world," and has a loyal fan base that recognizes and adores her difference (Trax Magazine 2016). In fact, given the vitriol that women DJs often receive when they're perceived as "selling out," TBM's statements above are actually another way for her to engage in *authenticity maneuvering*, thus inadvertently positioning herself as a "different kind of DJ" who isn't into the partying, drugs, and fashion; instead, she's in it for the music, her fans, and dance music cultural spaces (dance floors, for example). Nonetheless, in order to "do DJing" today, TBM, like Dijon and Gou, has to remain active on social media platforms like *Instagram*; even though she's "a little outside of our peer group," she still has to play the current dance music entertainment machine game, especially as it plays out on social media (see Kale 2018).

"WE STILL BELIEVE. *DO YOU?*": CHALLENGING THE BUSINESS OF CONTEMPORARY DANCE MUSIC

Authenticity Maneuvering in Practice

"Fighting for the Freedom to Escape"

In an interview, Honey Dijon insists that any degree of release and escape on the dance floor must go hand in hand with fighting "for the freedom to escape" (Abraham 2019):

> [Interviewer:] Do you agree that in such an awful climate for young liberal people or queer people, music and losing yourself . . . feel important for celebration or respite?
>
> Honey Dijon: I do, but I really think we need to realise that while we're escaping we need to fight for the freedom to escape. You can't really have one without the other, you know? I just find it impossible not to live in the world today and be a part of some kind of activism while we are just fighting for the right to *be* (ibid.).

In her interviews, social media presence, and contributions to dance music, TBM follows the same philosophy. For example, how she promotes and talks about her "We Still Believe" tour constantly returns to this question: "How do we love ourselves and one another not just on the dance floor but beyond?" She directly addresses this question in a tweet, asking, "How can you hear Can U Feel It even once, or Love Is the Message, and not want to stand in love and defense of the people around you, no matter who they are? Are you not moved?" (TBM Tweet, 8/17/2019).[26] A TBM bio further explains the origins of "We Still Believe":

> In some ways, the story of The Black Madonna begins with three magic words, scrawled in shoe polish on a broken-down box and hung with Christmas lights on the wall at a small sweaty party: We Still Believe.
>
> "I think you have to give up completely to really understand what hope is. We didn't have any decorations, so I took a box and wrote, 'We Still Believe' on it. I needed to believe that something better was possible and that's how it started. If you don't have any hope, then write some up and hang it on the wall."
>
> (TBM Bio posted for "The Black Madonna w/support from David Harness." Day Party Sunday 9/22/2019 @ Phoenix Hotel, in San Francisco).

TBM's tweets above and her quote about the origins of her "We Still Believe" tour, though not directly stated, draw upon a PLUR/rave ethos and thus offer additional examples of how she utilizes *authenticity maneuvering* in nearly everything she does in dance music. In a cover story for *Exposed* magazine ("Sheffield's Ultimate Entertainment Guide"), TBM is pictured with the following headline, "The Black Madonna: Fighting for Change from the Dancefloor Up," again highlighting how she approaches her work. Her dance music philosophy—a message of hope, connection, and resilience—is integral to her work as a DJ. Like Honey Dijon (yet more explicitly), she remains razor-focused on connecting this philosophy to virtually everything she does. Whereas Gou typically promotes her own personal brand and her music, TBM often promotes herself in the service of a cause, thus employing *authenticity maneuvering* in a much more explicit way than both Dijon and Gou.

DJs Using Their Platform for Activism, Personal Empowerment, and Love: "Making the World that I Am Advocating For"

TBM is directly making moves that reflect what she hopes to see in the dance music industry, on her dance floors, and in the world:

> In the dance and electronic-music world, where women are not just few but also routinely overlooked, Ms. Stamper has become a de facto activist whose call to arms for dance music involved a demand for, among other things, riot grrrls, "women over the age of 40," and "poor people and people who don't have the right shoes to get into the club."
>
> "The internet gives people a great chance to talk the talk, *but I am most interested in using any leverage I have over my own shows and projects to go ahead and make the world that I am advocating for*" (Vincentelli 2017; my emphasis).

In a video posted on all of her social media feeds, TBM talked about the shirt that she often wears—a black T-shirt with "Choose LOVE" in bold, white lettering—before she described her role as an ambassador for "a global organization called *Help Refugees*, which does amazing work with people seeking asylum or migrating around the world" (@theblessedmadonna, September 26, 2019). She explained that she wanted to get more involved and decided that she would announce a tour:

> Called "We Still Believe, The Choose Love Tour" . . . [set to] raise money, awareness, and help fund all kinds of amazing projects that the *Help Refugees* organization does, especially with a group in London called *Say It Loud*, which helps support queer, LGBTQI+++ refugees as they try to find a better place to live.

Thus, as a DJ who has "transform[ed], barely overnight, from hometown hero into one of the most sought after and respected DJs on the planet" (TBM bio for Phoenix Hotel party, 9/22/2019),[27] TBM is using her platform to actively advocate for a better, more loving world. "Love is the message," the mantra that so closely connects to a PLUR/rave ethos and serves as the starting point for TBM's work, is completely wrapped up in her branding. Yet, it does not simply serve as a starting point for making money and building her brand indefinitely. Instead, while TBM is certainly building her brand and interested in making money via her own branding, she is engaging in these dance music business practices in service of a cause, in service of a world she hopes to see. Thus, TBM's branding practices reflect another example of the ongoing connections between *both* rave authenticity *and* EDM/club culture commercialism; via her *authenticity maneuvering*, she utilizes the social media requirements expected of working DJs to *both* build her brand *and*—in the case above—launch a fundraiser for an issue she cares deeply about. This is a practice she utilizes frequently, using her social media platforms (*Instagram* and *Twitter*, in particular) to post about social and political issues such as the COVID-19 pandemic, #blacklivesmatter, the Trump administration, and #metoo in dance music and beyond, to name only a few topics she takes on. While Honey Dijon's current fashion line is not as explicitly utilizing her fame for a social or political cause, she is, however, making similar authenticity/commercialism moves, particularly via her social media presence and interviews.

Love Yourself and Each Other

In considering how she uses her "platform for activism" (Abraham 2019), Honey Dijon prefaces her answer with a history lesson, thus also engaging in *authenticity maneuvering* to talk about her contributions to dance music:

> [H]ouse music and techno were created by queer people of colour from marginalised communities that weren't allowed in white spaces or straight spaces. These people made art out of pain and marginalisation. And I feel that even though I am playing in arenas where people can . . . lose themselves it's very important not to lose touch with where this came from and to help people to remember that. To remind people that even though someone is still telling those kinds of people that they're not worth anything, see what can happen, see what art can come out of . . . being left out of the conversation. (Abraham 2019)

She goes on to explain how she does activism and how important her role is:

It's about telling people your life does have value and purpose and you can create something that inspires millions of people around the world and make people dance and celebrate and love. *So I don't take my role lightly at all.* There are many ways to be an activist; some people run for office, some people march in a protest and art can also bring consciousness to people. *I want my art to inspire other people and make them have less fear about being themselves.* (Abraham 2019, my emphasis)

Like TBM, Honey Dijon sees the work that she does as a privilege and a space for her to "inspire other people [in order to] make them have less fear about being themselves." Her social media posts typically emphasize both her political and social justice views and experiences, in addition to personal empowerment advice. For example, some typical personal empowerment posts read:

Comparison is
the thief of joy
(@honeydijon, 4/18/19)

Worry less about
getting things done.
Worry more about
things worth doing.
Worry less about
being a great artist.
Worry more about
being a good human
being who makes art.
Worry less about
making a mark. Worry
more about leaving
things better that you
found them.
(@honeydijon, 6/4/19)

"Get the
inside right.
The outside
will
fall into
place."
(@honeydijon, 3/4/19)

what if
you just
turned
your magic
ALL
the way on?
(@honeydijon, 2/23/19)

This last *Instagram* post was coupled with her own set of questions and advice: "What if you let go of fear? What if you let go of insecurity? . . . What if you stopped looking for people to make you feel ok about yourself? *What if you were completely yourself?* . . . What if you believed in your dreams? What if you stopped judging others? What if you really loved you for you? What if you didn't need validation from others to do things that make you fulfilled? Be yourself. Everyone else is taken. #livewhileyouarealive" (@ honeydijon, February 23, 2019, my emphasis). In a podcast interview, she is adamant about how she approaches her life: "I really believe investing in yourself and *also giving back* are two of the best things that you can do and then everything else sort of unfolds from there" (Dijon 2021, my emphasis).[28] The themes that pepper Dijon's posts and interviews intersect with a PLUR/ rave ethos without actually making any direct references to PLUR. For example, loving yourself and others is often highlighted, in addition to self-respect, "being yourself," respecting one another and gratitude, all themes that Honey Dijon posts multiple times per week; additionally, her posts often emphasize peace and calming down, sometimes directly challenging her followers to put their phones down in order to cultivate some inner peace. Also, Dijon often references unity and connection in her posts, especially when she talks about social justice and political issues. Much like TBM and Peggy Gou (to a certain extent), she often talks about "giving back," a theme that runs through dance music's history.[29]

Approaching authenticity from a slightly different angle, Dijon's *Instagram* caption above reads, "Be yourself. Everyone else is taken," a theme that inadvertently aligns with social media branding practices, in general. As Berg's (2021) research on porn work shows, using social media can be both enabling and constraining; social media can be enabling in that (creative) workers can market themselves and access their own revenue streams via their fan base (as we have seen in the case of Dijon and Gou's fashion lines and other merchandise, for example) and constraining when managers and consumers expect "authenticity" via their social media activity and related performances at work and/or offline (67). Dijon's caption above feeds right back into this authenticity imperative where DJs online are increasingly expected to reveal more of their own "real" lives and "real" thoughts, among others, to do the work of DJing, an imperative that certainly requires work, time, and attention (Kale 2018). Thus, *authenticity maneuvering* is used by DJs to gain status and legitimacy and, at the same time, often intersects with a more generalized *authenticity imperative* that has become cultural, especially on social media (e.g., this idea that people get more attention and "likes" when they're "just being themselves").

Additionally, DJs often use a PLUR/rave ethos to describe what they do, emphasizing taste or their love for the music, scene, and/or fans. Utilizing her tastes to accomplish *authenticity maneuvering,* Peggy Gou references love and an ineffable desire as she describes music.

"Music, For Me, Is Like Love"

While Peggy Gou often uncritically adopts the commercialization of dance music, she nonetheless uses a PLUR ethos to talk about how music impacts her: "Music, for me, is like love. Sometime[s] you cannot describe it, you just feel it. It's very hard to rationalize it so when I listen to acid music I'm just like . . . Fuuuuuck!" (*Instagram* story post).[30] To her, music can often have an ineffable quality, one not easily explained. Gou describes an enchanting, unquantifiable quality to music, a quality that brings up emotions—"you just feel it"—and directly challenges any attempts to rationalize one's experience with it.

Furthermore, in an interview with SceneNoise (SceneNoise Team 2018),[31] she draws a distinction between EDM and house or techno:

> I like to share my vision, I like to share my taste. I guess this is one of the reasons why I try to *express my tastes* and preferences, although some people might not like it.
>
> [Interviewer:] They might not like it, but surely this is good for the crowds you play to, right?
>
> Exactly. For example, I just played in Korea recently, where the EDM scene is still bigger [than house or techno]. *And I decided to play exactly the same kind of sets that I'd play in Europe.* They need to hear it, otherwise they won't know because a lot of Asia is a little bit behind in music. So yeah, in a way it is educating, but who am I to educate anyways? But if I can be somebody who can influence other people on new music, then yes, I'll take that responsibility. (SceneNoise team 2018, my emphasis)

Much like TBM's genre-bending approach to her sets, Gou's description above highlights her love of music and willingness to venture into areas that her audience might not necessarily understand or appreciate without some coaxing. Once again, however, while the quotes above make clear PLUR-like connections between Gou's work and her love of music, they remain focused on her individual tastes: "I like to share my vision, I like to share my taste." While "quantity over quality" is challenged here—especially as she describes the feeling of music—connecting this challenge to a broader critical discussion about the state of the world or the dance music business is typically missing.

This is primarily how Gou engages in *authenticity maneuvering*; rather than focusing on activism or directly critiquing problems she sees in the scene, she tends to focus on her taste. Her love of music and dedication to her fans constitute her main contributions and thus exemplify a muted version of *authenticity maneuvering*, one that falls closer to the right side of the continuum from rave authenticity to EDM commercialism. Notably, she is able to get away with using taste because dance music cultures are still largely "taste cultures" (Thornton 1996). Dance music culture and its clubs "facilitate the congregation of people with like tastes—be they musical, sartorial or sexual" (Thornton 1996, 22) and Gou simply uses those taste discourses to justify her "less tasteful" business practices.

Taking Breaks and Paying Attention to Mental Health

As chapter 1 outlined, Avicii was completely immersed in the dance music entertainment machine and came up against a lot of resistance when he tried to retire. Since his death, while the machine still exists, how DJs navigate it has started to change. TBM and Honey Dijon often talk about taking much-needed breaks. Also described in chapter 1, TBM published an article about how she takes care of herself. Given the grueling tour schedules that successful DJs must navigate, getting sick and burned out is common, especially if any one DJ fails to find their own healthy way of navigating the larger dance music business (for early discussions of DJs' mental health, see Brownbill 2016).[32] Over summer 2019, for example, Peggy Gou was forced to cancel some appearances and slow down, writing two posts to her fans:

everyone knows how
much I love italy [*sic*] and I
was so looking fwd to
come back [to] kappa [the event she had to miss] this
year but I'm now stuck
in an [*sic*] hospital at the
moment without being
able to catch my flight
is simply killing me.
Since last night i'v [*sic*]
been dealing with food
poisoning since 4am

I'm suffering and i [*sic*]
won't unfortunately be
able to be in Turin
today. I'll be back in
Turin the soonest, [*sic*] so
gutted I won't be able
to see you today I was
so looking forward to
be back to this festival.
My heart's broken,
please forgive me[.]
(@peggygou_, July 7, 2019)[33]

I noticed my immune system got low recently from crazy schedule and it's right time for me to take some holiday[.] Lots of vitamin D, healthy food, exercise, sleep enough for next 10 days, bye[.] (@peggygou_, July 9, 2019)

In a video about TBM, she describes her self-care practices and directly connects those practices to the pressures of her job:

Anxiety and depression are an epidemic in DJs. Being tired thins the walls between you and any kind of pre-existing mental stuff. You find out really quickly that if you don't get serious about what you're doing to your body on tour that all kinds of problems will manifest—psychological, physical, everything. (Resident Advisor YouTube video titled "Between the Beats: The Black Madonna" 2016)[34]

In a Peggy Gou interview with *Hypebeast*, this issue comes up again:

[Interviewer:] You're very busy traveling the world. How do you cope with the mental and physical stress?

That's a question I'm asking myself every day, really. I tell myself, "You know what? I need to find a solution to meditate, both physically and mentally." I'm doing all of this because I like to keep myself busy. Whenever I have a day off at home, I'm still always doing something or finding something to do. I guess that's just my personality. *But of course, I'm still trying to figure out how I can meditate to cope with all the mental stress. Recently, I noticed that because I'm stressed and don't have much time for myself, I'm becoming more sensitive easily. I'm thinking of trying meditation or looking into counseling.* (Li 2019, my emphasis)[35]

In the podcast interview described above, Honey Dijon said that she treats herself like an athlete when she's on the road; this means that she stopped drinking alcohol, sleeps "as much as humanly possible" when she can, eats healthy food, stays hydrated, regularly exercises, and surrounds herself with people who are good for her (Dijon 2021). Peggy Gou has made similar remarks, citing the pandemic as a wake-up call that encouraged her to take stock of her life: "I thought a lot of stuff was ok to neglect, but it really wasn't—especially my health. My body was sending me signs, but I chose to ignore them."[36]

Returning to the social media discussion above, DJs have also been vocal about how debilitating social media activity can be on their mental health. In a *Mixmag* article titled, "Social Media is Dangerously Affecting DJs' Mental Health," both HAAi and TBM talk about the "levels of hate" they received online as soon as their careers took off. TBM took action, calling "on YouTube to delete their comment section": "It's damaging," she wrote in a Twitter thread. "I straight up went to therapy over this shit. It was like being whacked with a shovel" (Kale 2018). Like touring, social media activity is a requirement for any up-and-coming and successful DJ these days; since we know how hard these two activities are on one's mental health, ongoing discussions about how to better support DJs going forward are needed.

While the current dance music business has not significantly changed since Avicii's death and, in fact, technology and the "DJ as performer rather than artist" appears to be intensifying for DJs like TBM, Honey Dijon, and Peggy Gou, ongoing discussions about mental health and slowing down are also present. Many key actors in dance music see the post-pandemic return to physical dance music spaces as a potential restart, one that will directly take on some of these problems. Pre-pandemic discussions about slowing down centered primarily around individual DJs taking care of themselves rather than a larger discussion about how the dance music business, itself, should address and take action that supports the mental health of its DJs. Now these discussions are always connected to the pandemic, thus opening up space for DJs and other key actors to talk more openly about rethinking the entire industry (not just the individual practices of DJs).[37] The pandemic has encouraged those in the industry to seriously consider what needs to change in dance music in order for the culture to thrive creatively, challenge corporate practices that are depleting and self-defeating, and open up opportunities for marginal groups.[38]

CONCLUSIONS

TBM makes clear what those lucky enough to have a career in "underground dance music" should be in service to:

Any of us that are lucky enough to be a part of underground dance music, we do have a responsibility to share certain values about race, class, gender, economic equality, everything. *All of those things are built into dance music.* I believe that strongly and you know the great thing about having all kinds of people participating in house music now is that there are all these songs that we used to miss out on. Can you imagine if movies only had men in them? Like what if movies only had 2 percent women? It would make for a completely strange story and right now when you look at these festival lineups that have almost exclusively men participating that means we're missing out on all those songs. Whatever we can do to get women into the process of making music. That's going to change things and the song is going to change and I'm really looking forward to what the next few years look like when those songs come to be. (Resident Advisor 2016, my emphasis)

So much has happened since TBM made this statement in 2016 at the same time that so much still needs to change, and all three of these DJs are squarely in the center of these changes. Taking a closer look at how TBM, Honey Dijon, and Peggy Gou accomplish their work as DJs, this chapter outlined additional examples of how "rave authenticity and EDM or club culture commercialism" are in constant conversation. In some cases, these DJs use commercialism and their social media presence to explicitly address political and social issues they believe in. In other cases, they engage in the commercialization of their work with political and social goals that are more implicit or less direct. All of this work is wrapped up in their branding.

On a continuum from explicit to implicit and/or rave authenticity to EDM commercialism, TBM falls on the more explicit/rave authenticity end,[39] Honey Dijon falls somewhere in between, and Peggy Gou typically engages in implicit forms of activism and muted forms of *authenticity maneuvering*, thus falling closer to the EDM commercialism end of the continuum.[40] In fact, Gou typically uses taste as a way to talk about her engagement in dance music, often refusing to engage with the political ramifications of her work entirely. Since her *authenticity maneuvering* is muted, the way that she's "selling herself" and her brand tends to stand out; she's unable to make her business practices less visible because her *authenticity maneuvering* is so subtle. TBM and Honey Dijon, on the other hand, "go there"—their brand-building is totally wrapped up in their politics, and they're often willing to have difficult conversations about race, class, gender, and sexuality. Thus, their *authenticity maneuvering* both raises their profiles and—given how skillfully they deploy it—allows them to engage in a number of business practices that are often made invisible by the authenticity work that they're doing.

All three DJs have to constantly navigate and contend with "EDM and club culture commercialism" in order to continue playing by the rules and regulations of contemporary dance music; thus, their *authenticity maneuvering* reflects the ongoing dance they have to engage in to *both* make a living *and* avoid undermining dance music culture and its collective identity (or at least avoid appearing as if they're undermining the culture).

In the Conclusion, I return to dance floors on one final NYE trip while also considering what the DJs' ongoing work means for the future of dance music. Admittedly, it remains to be seen what the future holds, especially given how disruptive the pandemic has been to our lives and dance music, in particular. Nevertheless, I end the book with some hopeful reflections, highlighting what "movers and shakers" in dance music are currently doing to shake things up.

NOTES

1. Lyrics in Seth Troxler's set, Circoloco—BPM Festival, Mexico—16.01.15, on *Soundcloud*; https://soundcloud.com/sethtroxler/new-add-circoloco-bpm-festival -mexico-160115

2. Again, this connects to clubbers' experiences of timelessness in and around the dance floor (see Malbon 1999, 102). When the party suddenly ends and clubbers are forced to leave the venue, it feels like a shock to one's system. This "palpable sense of disbelief" (Malbon 1999, 102) that the party is actually over is something I vividly remember from my early rave days. Unlike clubbing now (that often ends before the sun comes up), every single rave I attended in the 1990s went all night long. This meant that I often left the venue as early as 6:00 or 7:00 a.m., literally assaulted by the early-morning sun.

3. Given its detailed description with multiple rave culture identity markers, it also captures TBM's status as a scene insider, a theme I analyze throughout this chapter.

4. In Anderson's (2009a) research, she defines stakeholders as scene insiders who are "the scene's professionals, seeking to make a living from or earning income in it . . . [m]ost are loyalists, but their professional stakes in the scene have the potential to either shore up or undermine their commitment to the EDM culture and collective identity" (60). Given this definition, TBM, Honey Dijon, and Peggy Gou are stakeholders, "movers and shakers in the scene" (Anderson 2009a, 60) who have to carefully navigate making a living in it without undermining their commitment to its culture and collective identity.

5. I use Banet-Weiser's (2012) definition of brand here ("the intersecting relationship between marketing, a product, and consumers" (4)) as I focus on the *branding practices* DJs are expected to engage in, thus treating their brand-building as an ongoing negotiation that requires careful curation, *authenticity maneuvering*, and finding creative ways to connect marketing (what they do on social media, for example) + their products (themselves, their music, etc.) + their consumers (fans). Also, see Whitmer (2019) for an examination of "the social construction of authentic self-brands, how branding the self on social media impacts the process of

self-presentation, and how workers [(particularly in creative industries)] experience the imperative to self-brand" (1).

6. While authenticity discourses can certainly create hierarchies, rules, and regulations for what constitutes authentic or inauthentic behavior, I am primarily interested in what DJs actually do or accomplish as they're *authenticity maneuvering*.

7. Citation is in *Instagram* story post and no longer available; included in data archive.

8. https://www.theguardian.com/music/2019/aug/08/freedom-fashion-and-being-scouted-on-facebook-how-peggy-gou-became-the-worlds-coolest-dj

9. https://www.nytimes.com/2019/07/03/arts/music/peggy-gou-dj-kicks.html

10. https://www.interviewmagazine.com/culture/techno-queen-peggy-gou-shows-us-her-camera-roll

11. There is no doubt that this is a requirement of "doing DJing" today, as HAAi and others describe in "Social Media is Dangerously Affecting DJs' Mental Health" (Kale 2018), https://mixmag.net/feature/social-media-is-dangerously-affecting-artists-mental-health

12. I am fully aware of the sexist double standard in which women DJs are often criticized for the same marketing practices that men DJs have been adopting for years; this is much like the sexist double standard women DJs have to navigate regarding how they look (Gavanas and Reitsamer 2013). In order to avoid recreating this double standard, I analyze Gou's branding practices against all of the DJs in this book, paying particular attention to the gendered constraints inherent in any form of branding today.

13. https://mixmag.net/feature/what-the-hell-is-business-techno

14. Citation is in *Instagram* story post and no longer available; included in data archive.

15. See the Conclusion for more on how taste is used as a gaslighting tactic by Peggy Gou and other DJs.

16. While *authenticity maneuvering* intersects with Thornton's (1996) subcultural capital, it aims to capture the dynamic, ongoing processes one engages in to appear legitimate, "in the know," and/or aware of and capable of understanding and practicing a PLUR/rave ethos.

17. As Thornton (1996) argues, industry professionals such as DJs and promoters "often enjoy a lot of respect not only because of their high volume of subcultural capital, but also from their role in defining and creating it" (12).

18. McLeod's (2001) work on subgenres in electronic/dance music scenes captures how both authenticity and commercialism are at work: "[e]xperimentation with new styles is highly valued" within dance music communities at the same time that "this cultural urge is compatible with the logic of consumer culture and planned obsolescence" (70–71).

19. *Authenticity maneuvering* is also important for clubbers and fans. As I reflected on my research process and contacted interviewees (other clubbers) for my next dance music project, I quickly realized how often clubbers (myself included!) use this practice to legitimate their connection to dance music culture.

20. Citation is in *Instagram* story post and no longer available; included in data archive.

21. Relatedly, Honey Dijon often describes early club culture as a place where people came together to meet, mate, create, elevate, and participate (Flynn 2020). The Kirin description captures some of that essence.

22. https://www.instagram.com/honeyfuckingdijon/

23. https://www.interviewmagazine.com/culture/honey-dijon-and-kim-jones-dior -air-jordan

24. https://www.instagram.com/p/B1vur-WCQ9F/

25. The fact that TBM mentions her age here is notable. Men DJs rarely talk about their age because their DJing is not contingent upon how they look and certainly less so than for women DJs (Farrugia 2012). In Gavanas and Reitsamer's (2013) research with women DJs, "some interviewees pointed out that as they aged they could no longer rely on their looks as marketing strategy" (68). In fact, one of their interviewees felt empowered by that transition, describing those gigs that were based on her looks as less enjoyable "because the people didn't appreciate my music as much as they do now" (68). TBM often talks about how she doesn't look like a typical DJ, thus disrupting the marketing strategies that are often used for women DJs and freeing her up to rewrite some of the rules and regulations that usually dictate a woman DJ's career and how they embody any dance music space (Farrugia 2012).

26. Tweet no longer available; included in data archive.

27. https://dothebay.com/events/2019/9/22/the-black-madonna-tickets

28. Honey Dijon, "What I Learned From Honey Dijon About Living a Creative Life," interview by Georg Stuby, *Portal to Creation Podcast,* May 10, 2021, audio, 50:07, https://open.spotify.com/episode/3ZABhFxhGOk6EQ905KGy33?si=QhL Nq3FvROmSWnLnTs2gqA&nd=1

29. See Wilson (2006) for an analysis of this theme: "Many ravers I spoke with contributed to the rave community by volunteering in a variety of ways . . . [thus,] 'giving back' to the scene is applauded by rave culture idealists, while avoiding life's responsibilities through raving is condemned" (122–123). This "giving back" theme re-emerges throughout dance music today (and has been especially pervasive during the pandemic), thus it certainly qualifies as another example of how DJs engage in *authenticity maneuvering.* Additionally, I would argue that simply talking about "giving back" qualifies as an example of *authenticity maneuvering.*

30. Citation is in *Instagram* story post and no longer available; included in data archive.

31. https://scenenoise.com/Interviews/noise-101-peggy-gou

32. https://mixmag.net/feature/mind-dimension-djs-are-finally-opening-up-about -mental-health

33. Citation is in *Instagram* story post and no longer available; included in data archive.

34. https://www.residentadvisor.net/features/2793

35. https://hypebeast.com/2019/9/peggy-gou-dj-kirin-fashion-launch-interview

36. https://www.gqmiddleeast.com/Peggy-Gou

37. Jaguar's new podcast, *Utopia Talks,* reflects this trend. She describes it as "a springboard for further conversation . . . [about creating] a more inclusive and equal world in dance music and beyond" (Jaguar 2021; https://open.spotify.com/

episode/1UPq39AIAWhtAj7OnKhnM5?si=-OVWp5Y4TYOAmWNsSwlq-Q&context=spotify%3Ashow%3A3JJDwKDjajLeSE01byNl8O&dl_branch=1&nd=1).

38. In some 2021 *Mixmag* articles, for example, a number of DJs reflect on the pandemic and what they hope to see and experience in post-pandemic dance music culture (see Dowling's (2021) interview with Baby Weight, Olufemi's (2021) interview with TAAHLIAH, and Moore's (2021) interview with Jayda G).

39. Given the overall whiteness of dance music culture today, the fact that TBM is white definitely plays a role here, one that I plan to interrogate in future research and one that I hope other dance music researchers will take up as well.

40. TBM and Gou do not fall on the extreme ends (authenticity or commercialism) of the continuum, an approach that would fail to capture the ongoing negotiations they have to make; instead, the continuum is used as a sensitizing device to analyze their ongoing, often contradictory practices.

Conclusion

Future Possibilities for Dance Music: "Never for Money, Always for Love" and Other Challenges

In dance music today, rave authenticity and EDM/club culture commercialism are constantly present and more or less fraught depending upon the context. DJs like Seth Troxler express their contempt for the profit-driven motives of EDM, while EDM DJ Steve Aoki uses taste to justify his commercial practices, often ignoring his critics altogether. Troxler rarely minces his words:

> That's the conversation I'm trying to bring to the table against EDM. We're part of a dance culture that is making music based on an idea that is completely authentic, whereas they're making music that is based on profit. (Khawaja 2015)[1]

As Troxler alludes to above and TBM summarizes below, these dual processes—authenticity and commercialism—are constantly in motion, both enabling and constraining the cultural components (norms, behaviors, and activities) that happen in and through the industry:

> *One upshot of the internet's impact on dance music is the collapse of geographic and cultural distances.* SoundCloud exposes small town teens to new sounds and subcultures, file-sharing facilitates collaboration between beatmakers from disparate worlds who may never meet face-to-face. *It's a utopian standpoint, but rave culture has been drenched in rhetorical idealism since dial-up was a desired commodity, and even in today's increasingly individualistic world, the only good artists are only doing it because there's no alternative.* To Marea Stamper, A.K.A. The Bl[essed] Madonna, *being a good DJ is still an ongoing quest for the collective experience of ecstasy . . .* Stamper's world is an imperfect one by nature—"Dance music has always been fucked up, and it will always be

fucked up, and I will always be fucked up!" she laughs—but it's a world where anyone is welcome as long as they also Still Believe in it.

(Ongley 2019, my emphasis)[2]

The Internet and new technologies continue to impact dance music in new and unexpected ways that have been both extremely productive and revolutionary (in many cases) and extremely problematic and worth thinking critically about and resisting. TBM, Honey Dijon, and Peggy Gou have firsthand experience with these positive and negative dynamics and utilize their own either explicit or implicit strategies for navigating the scene as it connects to their own careers, values, and goals for the future of dance music. If we place TBM, Honey Dijon, and Peggy Gou on a rave authenticity to EDM/club culture commercialism continuum, TBM would fall close to the explicit end, Honey Dijon would land somewhere in the middle and Peggy Gou would fall at the implicit end.[3] TBM and Honey Dijon (usually) explicitly challenge what they see as problematic and often use new technologies to address social and political issues they care about. On the other hand, Peggy Gou and, to a certain extent, Honey Dijon implicitly address issues they care about at the same time that they remain razor-focused on monetizing and building their brands.[4] In Gou's case, she is constantly monetizing her brand, particularly via social media such as *Instagram*. Their strategies for navigating the scene and their own careers reflect both the disruptive possibilities of dance music and its ongoing problems. In order to make sense of how *both* rave authenticity *and* EDM/club commercialism are accomplished, negotiated, and resisted in physical and digital dance music spaces, this chapter continues to connect their stories to my on-the-ground research, thus revealing the ongoing authenticity/commercialism tensions that permeate dance music today.

FROM SOCIAL JUSTICE TO SPECTACLE

Steve Aoki's Cake-ing

In her actions and reflections, TBM explicitly connects dance music to social justice: "All of those things are built into dance music. I believe that strongly." Similarly, Honey Dijon sees her DJing as her form of activism, often framing her work as not simply about selling her new fashion line or releasing her next single; she is also actively engaged in challenging the status quo and particularly the dance music status quo—*authenticity maneuvering* that heavily draws on a rave ethos *and* pays the bills. On the opposite end of the authenticity to commercialism continuum, there is superstar EDM DJ/producer Steve Aoki. In the Netflix documentary about Aoki, titled *I'll Sleep*

When I'm Dead (Krook 2016), the film begins with a montage of his performances and reflections on his persona, described by other DJs, producers, and musicians as the following:

Tiësto (DJ/Producer): "You can't compare Steve to any other DJs. He has his own role in the DJ world."

Afrojack (DJ/Producer): "He's one of the first entertainers that took DJing to a different spot."

Pete Tong (DJ/BBC Radio 1 Host): "I think Steve is like a force of nature. That's what made him stand out, he's a larger-than-life character."

Diplo (DJ/Producer): "Dance music doesn't really have a personality. Steve has an overabundance of personality."

Travis Barker (Drummer/Blink 182): "It's very much elements of punk rock shows. But he's flipped them and made them his own."

Diplo: "If you don't know Steve personally, you're gonna have a perception of him right away."

Jason Bentley (DJ/KCRW Music Director): "I don't know how he can be in a rowboat in the middle of a crowd and be a DJ."

Felix Cartal (Former Dim Mak Artist): "If you're doing something that people are afraid of or against, I think you're doing something right."

Jason Bentley: "That's what EDM is now, it's more of a big spectacle show."

Pete Tong: "Everybody asks the question, 'Where is it going?' And I think the evolution of the scene will be more about characters and personalities. Steve was always more than a DJ."

Reflecting the patterns I have seen on the dance floor, Pete Tong's quote above ("the evolution of the scene will be more about characters and personalities") highlights how EDM DJs like Aoki and the events in which he performs typically display extreme versions of the patterns I found. Conner and Katz (2020) use the concept of pseudo-individualization to help us make sense of these patterns: "As EDM subculture moved toward becoming a culture industry the minor semblances of resistance that made it once attractive became what Horkheimer and Adorno ([1944] 1972) referred to as pseudo-individualization—which are the superficial features that provide consumers with an 'authentic' experience" (460). Steve Aoki is deeply committed to today's dance music culture industry/EDM commercialism and pseudo-individualizes himself on a regular basis. For example, treating DJs like celebrities is taken to the ultimate extreme in the case of Steve Aoki's shows and his following (as of January 19, 2021, he has 8.7 million *Instagram* followers); also, thousands of fans at Aoki's shows are all facing him and watching his performance (typically, they're not dancing with or facing one another), getting "caked" by him if they're close enough (he is famous for throwing large cakes at cheering audience members (Rettig 2014),[5]) pulling out their smartphones to record videos or take pictures that they share out on social media, and crowd-surfing in and around inflatable rafts, to name just a few examples of the "big spectacle show" that is experienced at events like Aoki's. In fact, Aoki is fully aware of his branding and the importance of the spectacle, from multiple angles. In a *Grammy Awards* interview, he describes how the Aoki brand is produced via an ongoing set of strategies captured in his documentary:

> Justin's the director and I travel with him a lot . . . I travel with someone that films and someone that takes photographs and we've been uploading and making video content for the YouTubers out there that follow me that don't get to see the shows but they get to see the shows through the YouTube. . . . It's all controlled around the shows and the pace and the adventures and the people I meet on the road and it's fun and it's like, *it's what the Steve Aoki brand is all about.* (Krook 2016, my emphasis)[6]

In many ways, Aoki's branding is a masterclass in "building an affective, authentic *relationship* with a consumer, one based . . . on the accumulation of memories, emotions, personal narratives, and expectations" (Banet-Weiser 2012, 8); as he describes above and his cake-ing describes below, he creates memories for his fans, a branding strategy that has served him well. Yet, like Gou, he often fails at adequately *authenticity maneuvering* by engaging in the spectacle of his EDM performances, a set of performance practices that do not align with a PLUR/rave ethos. For example, Jason Bentley's comment about how Aoki "does DJing" ("I don't know how he can be in a rowboat in the middle of a crowd and be a DJ") largely reflects the ongoing critiques leveled at Aoki for the kind of DJing he engages in. Critics ask, how does he do the typical labor of DJing (e.g., playing music for an audience) if he's running around in front of the DJ booth, throwing cakes at audience members and encouraging call and response audience participation?

Aoki talked back to his "haters," and "electronic music purists" (Aoki 2017)[7] in an article he wrote for the *Daily Beast*. In it, he provides some answers for why he started incorporating rafts and cakes in his performances. Notably, all of his answers center around entertainment, making people happy ("I realized how happy it made people and how happy it made me"), selling music (exploding cakes in an *Autoérotique* (an artist on Aoki's *Dim Mak* label) music video morphed into throwing cakes at people while playing his song: "I literally woke up with the idea of caking someone while playing that song to help promote the video"), and building his brand ("The cake had gone viral"). In order to capture his interpretation of his work, I quote him at length here, thus allowing him to speak for himself:

In the end, all these props are tools of expression. When the average person sees someone getting caked they probably think "Wow, that looks horrible" or, "That is so rude and uncalled for. How could you cake your fans that love you? That is just mean and cruel." I always do my best to try and avoid anyone that does not want the cake . . . I pick . . . who shows me the most energy and is screaming for it. *The cake is about celebration. It's something to be experienced in person. When you see fans begging to be caked and how happy they are afterwards, it's like scoring a touchdown. The whole place erupts and joins in that happiness.*

I know it sounds really cheesy, but . . . that's the whole point. These tools of expression are meant to create and amplify energy. It doesn't necessarily have to be a cake . . . [or] a raft. It can be anything that entertains and amplifies that happiness and energy . . . *my goal as a DJ is to make people feel something significant, something that they will remember.*

The common complaint though is that when I'm caking or rafting, I'm placing the entertainment over the music. But if you're going to come to a Steve Aoki show and you don't care about my music, you're not going to want to get the cake or ride in the raft anyways. There's some emotional energy that takes place for you to sit up on someone's shoulder and beg for a cake. Without that bond between myself and my fans there would be no entertainment. It only makes sense if the people there are there for your music or . . . have a positive inclination towards your music. Can you imagine someone spending money on a ticket to my show, muscling their way to [*sic*] in front of the stage all while disliking my music but still wanting to be [*sic*] get caked? It makes no sense. That affinity has to come from somewhere besides just the entertainment value. But people on the outside, that don't like or know me or my music, will automatically say, "Well, a Steve Aoki show is all about cakes and rafts. It's all entertainment, not music."

. . . This is my expression. This is my way. So the question is, do I sacrifice all that? . . . *When I see the person who was begging for the cake then get covered in frosting as the crowd roars, smiling from ear to ear, it's a unique and incredibly exciting feeling for myself, for them and for the crowd.* I love being part of that energy, being part of that feeling. The haters and Internet trolls don't get it. There is no context because they don't understand where I'm coming from.

So this is why I wrote this. I wanted to give context to what I do . . . [and] share my feelings with my fans and my haters . . . I plan on caking people as long as people want it. My choice is to cake. (Aoki 2017, my emphasis)

While Aoki is certainly using PLUR-like language here such as amplifying "happiness and energy," "mak[ing] people feel something significant, something that they will remember," what is missing in his actual performances and in his decision-making as a DJ is an ability to actually engage in a robust form of *authenticity maneuvering*. Unlike TBM and Honey Dijon, he is unable or unwilling to draw upon a PLUR/rave ethos to talk about the work that he does and couple that work with activist-oriented practices that reflect that ethos. Instead, nearly everything he does (especially on social media) entails selling his brand, his clothing, and anything else that he has monetized. He is expertly playing the culture industry game: "[i]n an attempt to distinguish, or 'pseudo-individualize' themselves, [some] DJ[s] now put on spectacular stage productions consisting of massive laser light shows, fireworks and other pyrotechnics, dance troupes, animated projections produced on LED screens, incredible stage designs, and by wearing wild costumes" (Conner 2015, 135). Cake-ing screaming fans and running around the stage in front of his DJ booth are quintessential examples of pseudo-individualization. Once again, the cake-ing idea came to be because he wanted to sell one of his artist's songs. He can say all day that he believes he is building something special for his fans (and given his successful branding, he probably is) but that does not address or take away the fact that he continues to make other decisions as a DJ/producer that should be considered critically, decisions that are totally aligned with a dance music culture industry. On the continuum that runs from authenticity to commercialism, Aoki represents an extreme version of commercialism and, like Gou, engages in a muted form of *authenticity maneuvering*, a strategy that uses taste ("haters and Internet trolls don't get it" and "they just don't like me") to avoid any difficult conversations about the business practices he engages in.

Similar critiques have also been leveled at Peggy Gou, though the criticism tends to center around her branding practices rather than her music and performance style. In a long comment thread that followed a meme[8] of her (because she performed in Saudi Arabia, an issue I take up below), people in the thread had some cutting remarks about her (and others') ongoing practices as a DJ, all reflecting various gradations of rave authenticity:

"Dance music Hypocrisy at an all time high these days . . . "

"ya that's why the music is a celebrity based movement spewing out garbage while real artists continue to struggle and create."

"I just can't with these people . . . if only they could just live on an island by themselves . . . this influencer thing is one of the worst things that has happened to society."

"You know, there are lots of hardworking cool groovy female DJs out there, and even if they look dreadful, no one here cares or would criticize—because they're real DJs."[9]

Authenticity is a running theme in the quotes above, reflecting the ongoing imperative to engage in *authenticity maneuvering* as a DJ/producer; for instance, there are references to "real artists," "real DJs," "hardworking cool groovy female DJs," and a clear distaste for "this influencer thing" and "music as a celebrity based movement." Honey Dijon speaks to this frustration when she insists that music "is what it should be fucking about in the first place!" (Abraham 2019), indirectly calling out performances by DJs like Aoki that are far more focused on the spectacle—throwing cakes at audience members—than the actual music he is playing for that audience. Aoki, of course, resists this interpretation, arguing instead that his music informs and is informed by his caking and rafting during his performance. Yet, the fact that he literally moves away from the DJ booth and runs around the stage in front of it for extended periods of time highlights how he has, without any doubt, shifted the DJ landscape (for better or worse), summarized in Afrojack's quote: "He's one of the first entertainers that took DJing to a different spot." In this case (and so many others), "DJs have to be more like performers than artists" (Honey Dijon in Abraham 2019) and every single DJ—even DJs who are not completely swept up in dance music's entertainment machine—are feeling this shift and trying to make it work for them.

The Spectacle and Influencers

"For-Hire Human Billboards" and the MDL Beast Festival in Riyadh

Influencers are certainly impacting dance music, but they are also coming under fire for practices that are wholly based on making a dollar and conveniently ignore how they are complicit. Returning to the Gou meme above, it was in reference to "a massive festival called MDL Beast, which recently recruited supermodels Alessandra Ambrosio, Jourdan Dunn, Halima Aden, Irina Shayk, and Elsa Housk to party in the city of Riyadh" (Gordon 2019; see also Thebault and Mettler 2019).[10] As Gordon's (2019) article explains, this festival was part of an "ongoing attempt to modernize the country and maintain its lucrative relationships with other nations while distracting from the country's history of violence" (Gordon 2019) where "[m]any attendees apparently received '6-figure sums' or offers as high as 8 figures in exchange for their presence and social media posts" (ibid.). An *Arabian Business/Lifestyle* article describes the area where headliners, such as Peggy Gou, performed: "One of the main highlights of the festival is the Big Beast stage, which will shine a spotlight on top performers. As the festival's largest stage, it can accommodate more than 45,000 people" (Bridge 2019).[11] Some famous models and other celebrities flatly declined an invitation to the festival, including model Teddy Quinlivan who "made her opposition public, putting things a bit more bluntly" (Gordon 2019):

> If you're an influencer and you're promoting tourism to a place to [*sic*] openly kills journalists and LGBTQ people as well as a list of other horrible and archaic

laws and politics: "You're a f*cking SELL OUT," she wrote. After receiving backlash, she quipped on Instagram: "I've been called a sl*t and a wh*re more times in the last 24 hours by Saudi Arabian trolls and bots than I have in my entire life. (Gordon 2019)

Karen Attiah, a journalist and friend of assassinated Saudi Arabian dissident Jamal Khashoggi, added, "[t]he dark side of influencer culture is that it really is the ultimate expression of capitalism. Money over human lives. What is your platform if you overlook Saudi regime's murder and torture for a few bucks? *These influencers are just for-hire human billboards*" (Gordon 2019, my emphasis). Gordon ends the article by asking: "When is art separate from politics, or is it ever? Are influencers and advertisers separate from politics?" (Gordon 2019). Further reflecting on these questions, she writes:

> In a situation where artists and influencers' positive PR is literally purchased by the state, it's hard to say that these people can or should separate themselves from the political implications of their actions. While music and performance can create a bridge across political and ideological differences, in today's political theatre—when public personas are inextricable from their political contexts—musicians and content creators are increasingly obligated to actively align themselves with human rights, or face the Internet's ire. However, in a world where influencers still flock to Saudi raves, one question that remains is: At what point does an apolitical stance become indistinguishable from taking the position of the oppressor? (ibid.)

This is precisely the point of so much criticism, clearly encapsulated in "the Internet's ire" and, of course in Gou's case, the ire of house and dance music fans, far and wide. In response to widespread criticism for performing at *MDL Beast*, Gou posted a *Tik Tok* video on *Instagram*, lip-synching @rickythompson as she said (wearing a bright orange t-shirt that read "MY LIFE IS MY LIFE"):

> Attention! Attention! To all you opinionated-ass bitch-ass. Listen up! I don't care! Which means I don't care for the common tirade. Ok? Which means I don't care for the opinions! Ok? You're over here running your mouth to this person and that person, too! Over here saying what I can and cannot do but the real question is. Do I even know you?! FUCK NO! So, therefore, shut up, girlfriend! Shut up! And let me do me! This is my life. Not yours! So sit the FUCK BACK! Bitch! MY LIFE! (@peggygou_, January 6, 2020)

While Gou generally received support for her video post in the thousands of comments posted under it, a few critical comments were not deleted, including one that spoke to exactly why she continues to receive criticism in the dance music community; @audiomorph91 posted:

Just shows every one You['re] out of touch with reality starlight! Hopeless!!!

In other words, widespread criticism is not simply a personal attack on her; it's a critique of the decisions she is making in dance music culture that puts money, wealth, and fame over good behavior, social, and political awareness. These are all PLUR-related philosophies that house music purists and others in dance music are quick to hold up, especially if DJs who call themselves house music DJs are doing things that absolutely counter these philosophies.

Gou responded to her widespread criticism in an article titled "Peggy Gou discusses online criticism and her resolutions for 2020" (Loiseau 2020):[12]

When I ask about her recent gig at Saudi Arabia's controversial MDL Beast festi-val, Peggy looks hesitant. Since drawing to a close a few weeks back, the inaugural edition of the three-day music event (reportedly organised by Saudi's entertain-ment authority) has been under fire . . . "You know what?" Peggy says eventually, "I'm going to talk about it." Having shared a lineup with the likes of David Guetta and Steve Aoki, she deplores the storm of online criticism she's received in which people called her a "sell-out," since posting a video from the festival to her 1.3m followers. "Influencers are a different story," she protests, highlighting the fact that she was the only female headliner at a festival which she believes can help trans-form the local music scene. "*I went there to play music for fans*," she clarifies. This may seem a reasonable position, but it isn't one shared by everybody. Just last sum-mer, Nicki Minaj pulled out of a gig at Saudi's Jeddah World Fest over concerns about women's rights, lgbt+ rights and freedom of expression, a move endorsed by the New York-based Human Rights Foundation. But since previously facing backlash for cancelling a set at DGTL Tel Aviv in 2018 (she later apologized for the announcement she posted online), self-described "naturally selective" Peggy explains that she has learned her lesson, *now preferring to stay out of politics*. "It doesn't matter if it's Israel or North Korea," she concludes, after admitting that her Saudi stint involved a substantial paycheck. "If there's people who want to hear my music, I will go. I don't give a fuck." (Loiseau 2020, my emphasis)

Gou says that her decision not to pull out of this festival for moral reasons (as she did with DGTL Tel Aviv in 2018) rests on the fact that she "went there to play music for fans" and is "preferring to stay out of politics"; in short: "If there's people who want to hear my music, I will go. I don't give a fuck" (ibid.). Returning to Gordon's quote above: "However, in a world where influencers still flock to Saudi raves, one question that remains is: At what point does an apolitical stance become indistinguishable from taking the position of the oppressor?" (Gordon 2019). Whether or not she thinks she was acting apolitically, Gou did, in fact, take a political position when she decided to perform at *MDL Beast* and collect a hefty paycheck for that performance. Given what we know about Saudi Arabia's government and their ongoing human rights abuses, she "took the position of the oppressor" in agreeing to perform at *MDL Beast Festival* and has unsuccessfully attempted to explain away her controversial decisions by reframing her behavior as simply "for her fans," "apolitical," and because "she was the only female headliner at a festival which she believes can help transform the local music scene" (Loiseau 2020). As I take up again below, these arguments are a form of gaslighting that reframes house music and dance music, in general, as a way to bring community together and "transform the local music scene" while conveniently ignoring the problematic political and social context in which a music scene is happening and the fact that large payouts were so central to why DJs and influencers were there to begin with. Money was the central motivator for how and why the festival happened. No amount of reframing by Gou or others affiliated with the festival can explain that away.

The Spectacle and Peggy Gou's Superstardom

Peggy Gou is the quintessential example of a DJ who is intimately connected to and promotes herself as a house music and/or non-EDM DJ at the same time that her meteoric rise over the last couple of years continues to place her in a precarious position vis-à-vis dance music spaces and rave authenticity. In other words, her popularity, overall success, business decisions and fanbase—her career trajectory—is starting to look quite a lot like other superstar DJs, particularly DJs like Steve Aoki. Yet, Gou is definitely not identifying herself as an EDM DJ nor is she playing EDM-like sets at her shows. In fact, returning to her *SceneNoise* (2018) interview (see chapter 4), she often engages in role distancing (Goffman 1961) when discussing EDM. Additionally, she and others often call her Korean-language dance music, "K-House," further distancing herself from EDM while at the same time emphasizing her Korean contributions to dance music (see *Oxford Union* 2020; Fatsoma 2020).

Returning to DJs' *authenticity maneuvering*, Gou's role distancing makes perfect sense, especially given the ongoing critiques of EDM that house music purists and fans have been engaged in for years. Much like the quotes from Aoki's documentary above, commercialized EDM scenes and spaces continue to receive severe criticism because they are often constructed as less serious, less in touch with dance music history, and far more focused on the spectacle and money-making—thus, inauthentic, fake, or cheesy. A raucous, "frat party"-like atmosphere (referred to as *rager* instead of rave culture) is often how EDM is described and experienced rather than PLUR-related themes such as building safe, inclusive spaces for audiences and performing DJs (Matos 2015; Conner 2015).

Gou's massive following and ongoing rise contains a complicated set of features that she continues to navigate: she is both fully engaged in her own monetization at the same time that she must carefully navigate that monetization as a house music/non-EDM DJ. Also, constructing herself as a house music and/or non-EDM DJ requires distancing herself from the EDM-like, corporate practices that are often bitterly criticized by house music purists and others who lament the loss of a rave ethos (see Heath 2019). She has to walk a fine line between those two disparate camps, both online and during her shows.

"NEVER FOR MONEY, ALWAYS FOR LOVE" AND OTHER CHALLENGES

In an *Instagram* post by @edkarney, he describes a club that is much like *Geluk* (and its philosophy put into practice; see chapters 1 and 3), that I want to talk about as I end this book. He writes:

I took these pictures at around 11:00 a.m. on the Sunday morning of the closing of Trouw in Amsterdam exactly five years ago today. So many things have happened in the last five years, and yet in some respects it still feels like yesterday. You weren't supposed to take photos in Trouw (for all the right reasons) and this had been rigorously enforced during the five years I'd been going to the club. Up until this point I'd been completely respectful and not taken a single photo even though I'd been flying over to Amsterdam every other month to go to Trouw, which meant that [I] had nothing but memories to remind myself of my favourite nightclub. The thought of Trouw closing forever and not having one single visual prompt to remind me of exactly how good it was spurred me to sneak out my phone four hours before the music stopped and take a few furtive pictures, then immediately feel guilty for doing so and hide my phone away again. Now, in retrospect I'm really glad that I did. People always ask me why Trouw was so special and it's actually quite a hard question to answer as so many elements came together seamlessly to make one very perfect whole. Yes it was the location in an old printing press complete with shower rooms and the insane Verdeeping beneath the main room; yes it was the excellent restaurant in the club; yes it was the fact that you could dance on the stage behind the DJ booth; yes it was the tight and dickhead-free door policy[13]; obviously it had a lot to do with the residencies of some of the world['s] best DJs etc etc etc. However what it really came down to was the people who ran the club and their total passion to push themselves to create at a very high level *without the promise of easy profits. Written into the original business plan for Trouw is a line from The Talking Heads song "This Must Be The Place" that goes "never for money, always for love"* . . . *something that every company could learn from.*

Amen to that and RIP Trouw.

PS I just saw that @olafboswijk posted one of these pics earlier which makes me feel a little less guilty for having taken it in the first place as he wrote the rules that I chose to break;)

#trouwamsterdam #rip (@edkarney, January 4, 2020, my emphasis)[14]

I quote @edkarney at length here because his tribute beautifully captures themes and conclusions that I want to focus on as I close this book.

Making Sense of Dance Music Today

I spent months thinking about and experiencing writer's block in the process of finishing this manuscript, primarily because I was still searching for some clarity about the current state of dance music spaces. A final 2019/2020 NYE research trip to London and Amsterdam was absolutely revelatory for a number of reasons and one of the main reasons is perfectly encapsulated in *The Talking Heads* song lyrics, "never for money, always for love." I use these lyrics as a guide for analyzing how the three DJs I followed are navigating dance music culture, who stays true to house music's history and/or a PLUR/rave ethos, and why and how they and other key actors and nightclub spaces choose love over money or vice versa. What does choosing "love over money" accomplish even or especially in the face of a dance music culture industry? Also, these lyrics helped me better understand and make sense of nightclub spaces, DJs and key actors who are *not* necessarily staying true to a PLUR/rave ethos, often using rave ethos markers and language without actually engaging in practices or providing spaces where this ethos is realized.

"Never for Money, Always for Love" in Practice

Over the NYE 2019/2020 season, TBM took a break from touring, Honey Dijon was in Bali and Australia and Peggy Gou headlined her own NYE party in Bali, called *GOU Year's Eve*. Therefore, I also took a break from following the three DJs discussed in this book and decided to focus on spaces in London and Amsterdam where one or more of these DJs has performed (at some point since Summer 2017, the season I started collecting data) in order to get a sense of how these spaces operate. I started with a NYE party at a fairly large club in London (that hosted a party called

Pleasure[15]) with headlining DJ Hunee and Eris Drew, DJs that certainly speak the same dance music language as TBM and Honey Dijon. On January 1, I made my way to another large party at a fairly new massive London club, called *Massive* for our purposes, a space that I had to see as it consistently hosts events with well-known DJs like Peggy Gou and up-and-coming DJs like HAAi (@haaihaaihaai). By Saturday, January 4, I was back at the club in Amsterdam called *Geluk* (I attended this club and saw TBM's set the previous year, NYE 2018/2019). *Geluk* was such a sharp contrast to *Pleasure* and *Massive* that it immediately put a number of patterns into focus and helped me clarify what was so desperately missing from the NYE and NYD events in London and what was so clearly present at this space in Amsterdam. In other words, the clarity solidified patterns analyzed in the previous chapters.

A Model for Creating a "Positive Environment"

To start, throughout the night in Amsterdam, I saw two sets of signs at *Geluk*, one posted near the entrance of the club and the other posted in an area for making out and having sex:

Near the entrance:
Welcome to [*Geluk*].
Feel free to let loose, experiment
and seek out new experiences as
long as your enjoyment doesn't
infringe upon a fellow dancer's
space.

Take responsibility for the energy
you bring with you, take care of
yourself and others, and together
we can create a positive
environment. Our staff is always
here to help if you have any
concerns or need support.

In the make-out/sex space:
if something makes you feel unsafe
do not hesitate to talk to our staff.
they are trained to handle these
situations with care.
feel welcome to hang and make

out.
consent is key, so please make sure
you know what others are
comfortable with.
sex is more fun when it is safe, so
condoms are available for free.

Breaking down these rules and regulations for the club, the space, its ambience, and clubbers' behavior will outline a starting point for a philosophy that
intentionally positions love, connection, respect, and inclusion (all PLUR-
related themes) as central to its goals. Further, we can think about how I
broke down TBM's quote in chapter 1 to emphasize what "love over money"
might actually look and feel like in any one space.

First, the statement opens up space for a clubber to "feel free to let loose"
or, for example, lose themselves on the dance floor, slipping into another
space (even temporarily), and leaving time behind for a little while. This is
a space that is often inaccessible and hard to reach in a world largely run by
late capitalism, forcing most of us to navigate our everyday lives in a way
that values work and the long hours we dedicate to that work above virtually
everything else in our lives. *Geluk* offers some relief from those expectations
and, perhaps most importantly, gives clubbers permission to explore that
relief on their dance floor, with DJs who are also committed to this principle.
To further emphasize their commitment to this principle, they add, "as long
as your enjoyment doesn't infringe upon a fellow dancer's space," further
clarifying for the clubber that their enjoyment does not and should not trump
the enjoyment of everyone on the dance floor. In short, dancers should be
engaged in a collective, not simply individual, effort to "let loose, experiment and seek out new experiences"; this principle is meant to be accessible
to everybody, not just a few "beautiful" dancers or cisgender white men who
(given my data) typically take up more space than most other people on the
dance floor.[16]

While everything I read in these posted statements reminded me of TBM's
quote and PLUR-related themes, the statement that read "take responsibility
for the energy you bring with you" was especially compelling. That is, this
club was not accepting all of the responsibility for its overall vibe. Instead
(and as my research consistently showed), the vibe is largely dependent upon
how clubbers are actually behaving in the club, itself. Even with all of the
tactics *Geluk* used to make sure clubbers put these principles into practice,
there was always going to be some group or some individual person who was
just not getting it. This statement put the onus on every individual clubber,
asking them to take responsibility for their own behavior, remaining vigilant
and honest about behavior that was not going to serve themselves or those

around them. The sentence continues with "take care of yourself and others, and together we can create a positive environment." Again, clubbers are reminded of the role they always play in creating community, contributing to transformative and/or simply pleasurable experiences on the dance floor, and making sure that they are not the only individuals having those experiences. Thus, every statement reframes individualistic thinking, instead encouraging clubbers to always act *both* for themselves *and* those around them; an act for oneself should always be accompanied by kind acts for others. Collective experiences that are pleasurable and positive are emphasized. Finally, they end their "Welcome" posting with a reference to their staff, writing: "Our staff is always here to help if you have any concerns or need support," offering their ongoing support for clubbers navigating a space that other clubbers might not fully understand. This final statement highlights their ongoing commitment to their principles. Notably, these principles were actually realized and experienced on *Geluk*'s dance floors: clubbers usually looked out for each other by making space on the dance floor, policing the use of other clubbers' smartphones (see chapter 3), and generating an atmosphere that centered around the music, dancing, and chilling out when needed over and above pushing and shoving, drinking excessively, and/or using smartphones in and around the dance floor. While bad behavior was not completely absent from *Geluk*, PLUR-like practices were far more frequent than anti-PLUR practices.

My partner, Clark, and I stumbled upon the second sign and its accompanying area. We stepped away from the foggy dance floor for a bit and explored, soon finding this closed off area to the left middle side of the dance floor.[17] There were about three "stalls" set up back to front, in an S shape where clubbers could find a free stall and make out or have sex. When we initially stumbled upon the stalls, we had not yet seen the sign before Clark peaked into one of the stalls and jumped back a little as he realized that there were people doing sexy things in the stall's nook.

Sexy parties are certainly not foreign to me but this space was different, outlined clearly in their statement. First, the statement emphasizes the support clubbers have to be free and safe in this space and all areas of the club: "if something makes you feel unsafe do not hesitate to talk to our staff. They are trained to handle these situations with care." Not only are hired staff here to support, but they're also trained to actually offer support and care if it's needed. Next, the statement gives clubbers permission to "feel welcome to hang out and make out." While we were not yet certain if this included more than making out, the final statement in this posted policy made that fairly clear: "sex is more fun when it is safe, so condoms are available for free." Like free earplugs and tap water at virtually every single club I attended over the course of this research, this was the first and only club that gave out free condoms and, to the best of my knowledge, provided clubbers with a safe and private space to use those condoms. In addition to this novel approach, the posted policy also emphasized consent: "consent is key, so please make sure you know what others are comfortable with." Like the other statement outlined above, this policy encouraged clubbers to take responsibility for their own behavior, and, given the training of their support staff, reach out to staff if they experienced something uncomfortable or unwanted at the club.

While there were "consent" or #AskAngela (see figure C.1) postings like this in other clubs such as the Shoreditch club and *Massive* in London, what was clearly missing were actual physical spaces where clubbers could engage in private sexual interactions with one or more people. Further, the statements always said something about reaching out to staff to defuse uncomfortable situations without ever mentioning whether or not support staff were adequately trained to handle these situations with care. This is one of the main reasons why I did not, in fact, reach out to staff at the Shoreditch club when I was clearly touched and assaulted by a very drunk cisgender white man on the dance floor (see chapter 3), even though the following sign was posted near the dance floor and in the women's bathrooms:

Figure C.1   Anti-Harassment Sign Posted Near the Dance Floor and in the Women's Bathrooms at the Shoreditch Club. *Source*: Picture taken by the author.

"Money, Not Love" in Practice

A Model for Failing to Create a Positive Environment:
Selling House Music and Other Problems

As further evidence of the ongoing commercialization of house and dance music, in general, what is happening on social media (via hashtags, advertisements, and selling merchandise, for example) is also happening in actual physical spaces. At the London New Year's Day party put on by *Massive*, I was struck by how the promoters were quite literally selling house music and using PLUR-like messages to make money without actually attending to practices that would have truly promoted safety, community, and love. In other words, *Massive* had a model that often failed to create a positive environment while at the same time "performing house music philosophy" or engaging in pseudo-individualization via the following: "*Instagram*-able" and "hashtag-able" signage throughout the club and especially near sitting areas, picture-taking areas (one area with a large bus that also advertised an upcoming Fall 2020 festival put on by the same promoters[18]), and an ongoing light show above the main stage and behind the DJ booth. The following images capture some of these branding practices:

Figure C.2   House Music Branding at *Massive*.

Figure C.3 The Author and Her Partner Pose for an *"Instagram*-able" Picture at *Massive*. *Source*: Anonymous clubber.

Unlike my NYE research trips in the prior two years, during the NYE 2019/2020 season I attended these events with my partner, Clark, a decision that helped me make sense of what I was experiencing and recording and confirmed patterns I had seen as far back as the Manchester party (NYE 2017/2018). We were both struck by how performative the commercial use of house music was. For example, large signs that read "In Our House We Are All Equal" ran completely counter to how people acted at these parties (aggressively, e.g., especially as they got increasingly intoxicated), conflicted with what house music actually means and how clearly absent house music philosophies/a PLUR/rave ethos was at these parties and in these spaces. In other words, "money-making"/anti-PLUR practices, rather than actually bringing community together for the love of the music, dancing, and the scene (PLUR practices), appeared to reign supreme. Conner's (2015) research offers a possible explanation for why these branding practices seemed so contrived and shallow. At the 2012 EDMbiz conference, festival promoters and other dance music professionals "talked about making the fan the experience . . . [in order to] get attendees to create memories and meaning, thereby generating a sense of authenticity" (Conner 2015, 130). *Massive* had adopted this commercial tactic ("the fan is the experience"), a tactic also used by corporate EDM festivals to strategically mask how totally inauthentic (or at the very least, anti-PLUR) and commercial the event was to begin with.

House was simply being used as a way to sell the party rather than as a set of practices and policies that clubbers were asked to be aware of or risk being kicked out. The messaging looked good on paper, but it would be a stretch to say that the same messaging was actually, truly being put to practice. In short, the dance music philosophy and club practices and policies that were present and fiercely protected at *Geluk* were not present at *Pleasure* and *Massive*.[19] Like the Shoreditch club where I was harassed multiple times throughout one night (see chapter 3) and on other occasions, there was harassment signage located in a space that was devoid of an actual feeling of safety because an environment that would actually protect clubbers' safety and comfort was notably absent. The following image captures one of those signs at *Massive*:

Figure C.4   Ask For "Angela" Sign at *Massive*.

Given how thoroughly different these parties were from *Geluk*, how clearly they missed the mark, seeing house music messages and consent signage in the club seemed almost absurd, a comical and offensive performance rather than an authentic representation of what was actually going on. As someone who had intimately experienced PLUR-like spaces, events, and community both in the 1990s and, to a certain extent, in more than a few spaces and moments over the course of this research, I remember getting angry at what I was seeing, turning to Clark and often laughing out loud as I reflected on what we were observing and experiencing over the course of this final research trip.

To emphasize this difference further, the hostility, aggressive displays of (hetero)masculinity, emphasized (hetero)femininity, and bad behavior, in general, were and continued to be present throughout the night and especially as clubbers got increasingly more intoxicated. Anti-PLUR practices were ubiquitous and unrelenting. Given the fact that I had experienced so many of these spaces over the course of my research, I was somewhat normalized to it until Clark joined me during this final research trip. His shock and dismay at how the hostility, lack of community, and obvious toxic heteronormativity[20] impacted our experience at the event and permeated the entire feeling of the club forced me to reflect. Over the course of my research, I had found similar patterns at the Manchester NYE 2017/2018 NYD event, the Edinburgh club during the NYE 2018/2019 season, multiple events at the Shoreditch club, and clubs in San Francisco, featuring house music DJs. Frustration permeates my fieldnotes as I describe being constantly pushed in large crowds of people—usually cisgender white men taking up space and treating myself and other women they're not interested in as if we were invisible. Women (typically white) also engaged in this behavior, often pushing their way through a crowd, stepping hard on my or someone else's feet as they danced or pushed through the crowd. Notably, all of the spaces with crowds like this (displaying aggressive heteromasculinity coupled with emphasized heterofemininity and bad behavior such as pushing and out-of-control intoxication) became increasingly more intense as the night wore on.

Pleasure was no exception and Clark's disgust and growing impatience with the entire scene only highlighted what was going on. While pushing, elbowing, and aggressive dancing simply persisted throughout the night, with clubbers constantly bumping into and pushing Clark and I on the dance floor and in hallways and resting areas throughout the rest of the club (at one point, a POC/(person of color) man simply sat on half of Clark's leg as we were sitting and resting in a seated area), we saw at least 10 or more very (eyes rolling in the back of their heads) drunk cisgender white men over the course of the evening. One man, in particular, was so intoxicated, hanging haphazardly on another woman, that I was certain he was going to fall into Clark and me. As we passed and to avoid his large body falling into us, I put up my hand and propped him upright from the back. While I thought I had simply repositioned him (perhaps helping him and avoiding his weight), Clark observed a bit more than I had. After I propped him up and continued walking away, Clark observed him fling his head around, twisting his unstable body in my direction and furiously glaring back at me. Given how he looked at me, perhaps, if I hadn't been a small woman, he would have confronted me.

Additionally, men simply took up space, often standing directly in front of me (treating me as if I were invisible) even if there was plenty of room in the area for both of us to observe or dance. For example, as I waited for Clark to use the bathroom, I stood in the back of the main room, near the wall to the right side of the dance floor. As I continued standing, observing, and swaying back and forth to the music, a man proceeded to stand directly in front of me, nearly stepping on my feet at the same time that he had at least 10 feet of free dancing space in front of him; in other words, he was pushing me against the wall behind me for no apparent reason. Finally, I had enough and simply said, "give me some room." He looked back at me—surprised—then apologized and stepped away from me, clearly unaware of how he was using space in this area of the dance floor and treating a smaller woman as if she were invisible. Notably, most of the men (especially white men) and some women remained razor-focused on using the dance floor in a way that only served themselves or their friends. That is, unlike *Geluk*'s posted policy and the subsequent clubber behavior I experienced on its dance floors (people usually making room for one another, an absence of aggressive dancing and/or hitting on other dancers, clubbers looking out for other clubbers in and around the dance floor, exchanging smiles with other clubbers when there was a shared appreciation for the music and the space, itself), clubber behavior at *Pleasure* lacked anything that even remotely reflected the *Geluk* policy: "take care of yourself and others, and together we can create a positive environment."

My fieldnotes further describe how this overall club and its crowd felt:

By the end of the night, I was telling Clark that I thought the crowd was just "awful." So, the ongoing hostility, overall bad behavior, and unorganized venue had finally gotten to me. And it was a total "mess" in terms of how everything was organized. For example, it took us at least 35-45 minutes to get our bag and coats checked because the first coat check we found wasn't accepting any additional coats and said they were only taking cash (even though they visibly had a working card machine) and the second coat check was really only taking cash but wouldn't take our bag. Later, when Clark ordered food (lettuce and fries), the food service was completely thrown together, with a very small space for ordering food and one single Black man serving an entire event with at least 3000 or more clubbers at any one time.

In others words, how the event was organized wasn't even remotely close to the well-oiled machine at *Massive* (see figures C.2–C.4) or the Manchester NYD 2017/2018 party or Rotterdam NYE 2017/2018 or the Shoreditch club or virtually any other club (of this scale and size) that I had attended over the course of the research; yet, at the same time, what *Pleasure* shared with these clubs (except Rotterdam) that it did not share with *Geluk* was a general lack of care—lack of care for those in the club and lack of care for a positive, safe, and welcoming environment. As a final example of this venue's lack of care, Clark's description of the state of the men's bathroom was "unlike anything I'd ever seen before." There was a short, confused line with some people waiting for stalls and others waiting for urinals and, mysteriously, the four urinals were almost entirely open. The bathroom attendant was pleading with people to stop using at least three of the four urinals because they were overflowing with urine, creating urine waterfalls that formed a urine pond with the help of a dam—in the form of many rags—that the attendant had created to keep the urine somehow contained. He was pleading with clubbers to "use your eyes!" because people were still walking up and urinating into the already overflowing, yellow urinals.

Although *Pleasure* was a mess as compared to the other clubs and events, what was similar was the hostility, toxic heteronormativity, and far less safe spaces or a general feeling of less safety. These patterns overlapped with my experiences at Manchester NYD 2017/2018, Edinburgh NYE season 2018/2019, the Shoreditch club, and a few clubs in San Francisco, particularly clubs that headlined big acts like Bicep and Nightmares on Wax. Notably, all of these clubs did not have a strict door policy, did not post anything even remotely close to the *Geluk* postings outlined above, and did not restrict cell phone use, instead encouraging clubbers to share out photos and videos of the performances and its dance floors. Additionally, all of these clubs had a predominantly heteronormative audience, with some heterogender displays more intense and rampant than heterogender displays at other venues. Conner's (2015) research found similar patterns. Older participants in dance music have expressed concerns about emerging cultures at some of these events, describing "the newer male fans as part of what they derisively referred to as the "bro' culture" (Conner 2015, 146). In fact, Conner (2015) met several fans who actually described themselves as "bros"—a masculinized and sexist self-image. As I have shown, these "bro culture" patterns were certainly present at some of the events I attended, particularly in how men actually used space in the venue and on the dance floors.[21]

Once again reflecting how virtually every physical and digital space in dance music incorporates *both* rave authenticity *and* EDM/club culture commercialism, while *Pleasure*'s dance floors and the crowd were inundated with anti-PLUR practices, the lineup was not completely devoid of PLUR-ness. For example, Clark and I stumbled upon Eris Drew for the first time at this event, a DJ who continues to challenge the commercialization of dance music in the music she produces, activism she engages in, events she organizes and attends, and in her ongoing work as a DJ. In fact, I remember wondering out loud why this amazing DJ playing actual records was performing at this particular event as she seemed so out of place. As I realized later, the presence of *both* authenticity *and* commercialism in dance music today is precisely why Eris Drew ended up at an event as disjointed and "rager" as *Pleasure*.

Selling Out in Riyadh and Elsewhere: "Taste" as an Explanation for Choosing Money Over Love

One of the common ways that DJs such as Aoki and Gou attempt to counter their critics is to focus on their own, individual decision-making (e.g., Gou's "MY LIFE IS MY LIFE" *Tik Tok* video) or they emphasize and promote how all music and musical tastes should be supported. A typical "musical taste" caption might look something like Aoki's December 2, 2019, post that shows him standing with other DJs and reads:

> We may come from different cultures of sound but we all share the same purpose to make u feel something special and bring happiness to everyone. Music is music! The division is superficial @camelphatmusic @kolschofficial @dirty south.
>
> (@steveaoki, December 2, 2019)

I was feeling confused and somehow convinced by their arguments until the sociologist in me stood its ground; that is, red flags went up as I continued to follow Gou's social media presence (especially the ongoing commercialization of her brand), experienced decidedly unsafe dance music spaces in clubs that claimed to follow house music's philosophies (see above), and, finally, discovered that Aoki, Gou, and many other DJs had willingly decided to accept Saudi Arabia's money and perform at the highly controversial and decidedly problematic *MDL Beast Festival* in Riyadh. As a sociologist interested and trained in studying what people actually do, I was less interested in personal empowerment (on the part of DJs, for example) and far more interested in their actual behavior. Thus, I immediately gained some clarity when I stopped listening to arguments about taste (musical taste, performance style, etc.) and started paying closer attention to what DJs and other actors in dance music were *actually doing*, regardless of their music, performance styles, fanbase, among others. When my analysis shifted to actions and actual contributions made to dance music, it soon became very clear that money is primarily making decisions for DJs like Gou, Aoki, and so many others, including promoters who put on some of the biggest parties and festivals in the world. As I watched money dictate actors' practices, I also witnessed how they—in their ongoing actions—were choosing money over love and actual PLUR practices, again and again and again.

Similarly, when these actors were challenged by those in the industry who read their actions as actually hurting dance music culture and putting money over all else, they often engaged in gaslighting tactics, making claims such as "You do you. I'll do me. Don't judge," instead of actually stopping and reflecting on how their actions might be problematic, unethical, and tone deaf. Further, I also witnessed these actors, essentially, rebranding PLUR-like philosophies to serve their own needs and, in the case of the *Massive* NYD 2020 party, for example, literally re-branding house music to serve their brand and the almighty dollar. Conner's (2015) work on EDM as culture industry helps us better understand how DJs who fully engage in commercial practices are able to get away with it without hurting their careers. While Gou has to be especially careful because of her non-EDM status and Aoki is often confronted with harsh criticism, the fact that dance music is more or less a culture industry means that DJs that are riding the commercial train have an entire industry that backs up those actions.

THE FUTURE OF DANCE MUSIC: PRODUCTIVE POSSIBILITIES AND ONGOING CHALLENGES

To somehow combat dance music trends such as commercialization, an emphasis on quantity over quality, and what many simply call greed or a love of money over all else, DJs and other key actors talk about and promote love. Yet, as I have shown, only talking about love and using love and/or PLUR-related themes and phrases to promote a party or boost a DJ's career or describe a song that gets the dance floor groovin' is not going to get us very far and often works in such a way that this talk ultimately serves capitalism and a few people at the top of the dance music entertainment machine only. Furthermore, when "love" talk is used to make money only, these money-driven practices ripple throughout entire dance music scenes, impact what music is actually being released and who is getting played, permeates, and leaves a mark on how a party actually happens and is experienced, and continues all the way down to the thousands of face-to-face interactions actually happening in these parties. That is, "money over love" is *felt* and weaves its way into all areas of dance music.

In a dance music documentary titled *What We Started* (Marcus and Saidi 2017), Seth Troxler sums up what he sees as the current state of dance music: "Underground dance music is about art, where *EDM is show business. And there is still some of the same shared aesthetics of unity, and expression, and people opening up,* you know. *But they are two different things*" (ibid., my emphasis). For Troxler, "underground" (a contested term at best; see Gilbert and Pearson 1999) dance music and EDM "are two different things"; yet, at the same time, they share *both* rave authenticity *and* EDM/club culture commercialism features, a pattern that has been normalized and largely institutionalized across the industry. Troxler and DJ Paul Oakenfold go on to explain how this "EDM [as] show business" component of dance music is playing out. In reference to an eighteen-year-old EDM DJ, Martin Garrix, who was set to headline Miami's *Ultra Music Festival,* "one of the largest music festivals in the world, with 165,000 attendees," for the first time, Troxler is completely flabbergasted, exclaiming, "How is a 17-year-old kid the fucking face of dance music?!? What the fuck?!? You know?" Oakenfold concurs: "A 16, 17-year-old kid makes a record, he's never . . . he has got no experience ever, playing in front of a crowd. And they book him. Why?" Troxler continues: "You know, a 17-year-old kid, who has no context of the greater history of anything he's doing. He made some track for teenage kids. Like, it's not music, 'cause it's just a way, for . . . to sell music to teenagers" (ibid).

In other words, "EDM as show business" positions money and the related features of the culture industry over virtually everything else; so it makes sense that an inexperienced 17-year-old DJ without any real understanding of the history of dance music (according to Troxler's comment above) would be asked to headline a massive EDM-centric dance music festival. Sure, he might have released a record-breaking EP that many young people are listening to but, as Troxler explains, this track is for teenage kids, a moneymaker that put him on the map and plants him firmly in the "EDM as show business" camp. Returning to Conner (2015), "EDM as show business" is another way of describing how dance music is now a culture industry that is realized in a number of different ways: quantity is valued over quality; branding is normalized and expected (particularly via social media); professionalization, standardization, efficiency, uniformity, and predictability are key features of the industry; the commodification of everything from DJs to their music is expected and supported; and pseudo-individualization is utilized by events and key actors such as DJs in order to "perform authenticity" and distinction.

As a final aside and further clarifying "the money over all else" practices that are often visible in today's dance music culture industry, Martin Garrix, along with Afrojack, David Guetta, Tiësto, Steve Aoki, and, of course,

Peggy Gou all played at the *MDL Beast Festival* in Riyadh, solidifying their collective willingness to ignore ongoing human rights abuses in Saudi Arabia for a large paycheck. Yet, they got away with it by employing a muted form of *authenticity maneuvering*—refusing to address their problematic behavior and, instead, making statements such as "I went there to play music for my fans" or "This is my expression." They also, of course, got away with it because they're simply playing the dance music culture industry game; their business practices are closely aligned with the features listed above and, in the long run, only make them more financially successful as DJs/producers.

Another Way: 59 Rue de Rivoli

As my final research trip came to a close, I spent my last few days with family in Paris and made sure I saw as many last-minute spots as I could before my plane left the following morning. One of those spots was 59 Rivoli (@59rivoli), a "non-profit association that exists with the goal of promoting all forms of artistic and cultural expression" (also, see 59 Rivoli's *Facebook* page).[22] In existence for over 20 years, 59 Rue de Rivoli is unique in so many ways:

> In 1999, a trio of artists managed to break down the doors and began cleaning the place up. *They started exhibiting their works to members of the public. Within weeks, a dozen more artists moved in and began exhibiting their art to the public as well.* 59 Rue de Rivoli had become a movement in itself. . . . In 2000, the French state tried to evict the artists. However, luckily this failed due to the combination of a good lawyer and growing attention from the media. *'Squart'—a mixture of squat and art—was the name given to this unique atelier that was rapidly growing in popularity.* For years, the artists remained in residence; tolerated by the state—*although still officially illegal. Finally, in 2005, the newly elected Mayor of Paris purchased 59 Rue de Rivoli on behalf of Paris so that it would be safe for generations to come. Prior to his election, he had visited the building and fallen in love with it. One of the key points of his campaign was to make the ateliers legal.* He kept true to his word. In 2009, the building was re-opened and can be visited today. (Nadeau 2016, my emphasis).[23]

I fell in love with it, too. It was almost impossible not to as art was everywhere, wrapping up and around the staircases to each floor, in the form of a Grandmother's living room, in process in artists' studios, in every empty corner, often challenging the viewer with cheeky statements such as "choose life, choose a job, choose a career" or in Gaspard Delanoë's *Ne Travaillez Jamais/Never Work* painting, haphazardly on display in the middle of a perfectly cluttered studio space.

I was immediately struck by the possibility of this space, free and open to the public, with multiple artists displaying their art and often working "live" as visitors observed their studios and ongoing process. While artists asked for donations (often with messages on locked boxes), the space was not dictated by capitalism. There was no gift shop, no hierarchical display of art and artists and instead an emphasis on art as process, art as community, as free and open to the public, and as a starting point for resistance and alternative forms of cultural and creative expression.

As I was making my way up to étage/floor 6, I saw the following sign:

There it was, again, so beautiful and true, referenced in @edkarney's description of Trouw (see above), experienced in the time I spent at *Geluk*, and captured during my first rave—that sweet spot that kept me coming back 20 years ago and again over the last 4 years. "This Must Be the Place" is the place that David Byrne sings about: a place, a community, a space that puts "always for love, never for money" at its center, a place that builds this philosophy into its veins, that uses this philosophy to guide its principles, to interact with community, to build community, and to survive. With late capitalism and everything that commercialism has and continues to produce, spaces like this are few and far between. Philosophies like this are increasingly more difficult to practice. Yet, 59 Rivoli was certainly "the place," one that truly lives by a "love over money" philosophy and the beauty that grew out of it was undoubtedly rich and "incredibly interesting" (Nadeau 2016).

Zak "DVS1" Khutoretsky's S.O.S. (Support, Organize, Sustain) captures this ethos, an ethos centered in art rather than commerce. DVS1 was frustrated with how gray everything in dance music had become: "people that

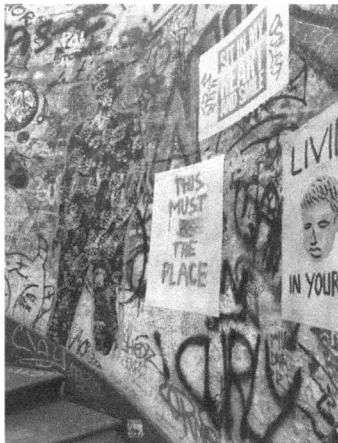

Figure C.5   Picture of "This Must Be The Place" art in 59 Rue de Rivoli.

were asking me to speak at their events were industry, and their topics were completely generic and industry-only focused: social media, marketing, management, and I was unhappy with the topics. And you either sit around complaining, or you do something about it" (Heath 2019).[24] DVS1, like so many of us in dance music today, are deeply aware of today's dance music entertainment machine, "an industry that seemed to have lost sight of its roots" (ibid.). Directly taking on this issue, in October 2019, S.O.S. organized a free-to-attend conference in Amsterdam that covered topics that intersect with my research findings: scene ethics and guidelines, space for marginalized communities, the artistic voice, no-camera/phone policies, and global drug policy, thus "focusing on the *social, artistic, and creative side of techno culture* as opposed to how best to maximize your marketing reach or increase your social media likes" (ibid., my emphasis). While he is under no illusions that we're ever going to be able to go back to the 1990s ("It's a machine. And I get it, there's no going back"), S.O.S. opens up space for "navigating [and directly addressing] that tension between commerce and culture, between money and art," (ibid.) a tension that is undoubtedly here and requires vigilant attention and creative solutions that actually represent a rave ethos.

"We Still Believe" This Must be the Place

Returning to TBM's 2016 DJ of the Year interview with *Mixmag*, she reflects on what she brings to the scene: Then I come in and I'm like, 'Hey, what's up you guys! Love yooooou!' Less heart hands, more hand on heart, Marea is the inverse of emotionless techno guy: excitable, articulate… maternal? 'You know, there's a little mom thing in it too. Totally. Totally!' But if she's dance music's mom, she's a rad, weird and decidedly cool mom" (Brailey 2016).[25]

Since 2016, the scene has certainly changed. While cisgender, white men still largely dominate DJ lineups at major events and there is a huge disconnect between PLUR-related philosophies and how some "top" DJs, promoters, and clubbers are behaving in dance music, gradations of "the underground" will always be present and is experiencing a resurgence (Garber 2014). Matos (2019) makes some predictions:

> *Going big, in fact, is increasingly frowned upon in dance music.* This summer, the dance site Resident Advisor ran a feature about how DJ culture can help combat the climate crisis—a sharp reversal from the doomsday-flouting expenditures of peak EDM. And the blaring fist-pump of EDM-pop that ruled the first half of the 2010s has fluttered out, in favor of Xanaxed-out depressive

pop—perhaps the long hangover after EDM's nonstop serotonin rush. If it's not precisely a backlash, it sounds close enough. (Matos 2019, my emphasis)[26]

Building upon this idea and reflecting what my research shows, Maiolo (2020) makes a similar argument as he reflects on the import of "The Disco Soundsystems That Birthed Modern Dance Music":

I had gone in with the common notion that dance spaces were mostly packed with vain people getting assaulted by over-hyped bass, to understanding the "oneness" aspect of it. François Kevorkian once commented on clubs that don't get this concept when he said, *"They don't understand that it's the crowd that makes the venue, not the furniture."* (Maiolo 2020, my emphasis)[27]

Precisely and those who understand this point are making moves. That is, there are respected, seasoned DJs, producers, promoters, and clubbers who are speaking up, calling out those who position "money over love" and putting their own money where their mouth is.[28] These challenges and pockets of resistance come in many forms: TBM using her fan following to promote and raise money for issues she cares about; Honey Dijon and Kiddy Smile speaking out about the important and often forgotten history of house music; *Geluk* and similar spaces offering models of "love over money" in how they run their club and art space; folks on social media calling Peggy Gou and others out when they agree to perform at festivals like *MDL Beast*; Octo Octa and Eris Drew raising thousands of dollars for the Sylvia Rivera Law Project;[29] and on and on.[30] While dance music "has always been fucked up, and it will always be fucked up," these examples offer some hope that people are making moves that will continue to directly resist the ongoing "money over love" practices that we've seen so clearly over the last 20 or more years.[31]

In reflecting on her collaborations with TBM, Georgia describes her own experience at a TBM show:

I went to see the "We Still Believe" party at the beginning of this year and it honestly changed my whole existence of how music can be performed and how to create a safe space for the audience to feel like they can express themselves and be who they want to be and it doesn't matter what background you're from, what you identify with. When you enter that space you can be whoever you want to be and I think that's the message of Chicago house. People had to be like that because Chicago back in the 80s—it still is a massive segregated community— so people found their communities within House music and I definitely felt like The Bl[essed] Madonna just totally brought that to London and it was such an amazing thing to witness and it really inspired me and I love her dearly.[32]

Although it often functions as a branding strategy, TBM nonetheless constantly reminds us that "love is the message," and, given where dance music is at today, this message must be vigilantly practiced and supported in new, creative and unexpected ways.[33] This means dance music must continuously reflect on its inclusive and fraught history, a history that continues to teach us how to come together and opens up space for tough conversations about what coming together even means. This means cultivating practices that always position "love over money" and combating actions that use this message and PLUR-like philosophies to, in fact, commercialize the message and make more money, with little regard for actual connection, respect, crossing boundaries, inclusion, safety, and love.

This Must Be the Place is not just a set of words. *This Must Be the Place* is an intentional practice, much like what we experienced at *Geluk*. Behind this statement is a physical, emotional, and intellectual place that values our bodies, our connections, and our shared love for the music, scene, each other, dancing, or whatever draws us back to the dance floor. While TBM is a "big act" and certainly no longer "underground," her actions continue to resurrect this idea—retain the magic of "love over all else." A magic that is never simply words but also, importantly, how we treat one another, how we treat ourselves, and how we—vigilantly—support ethical, consensual pleasure in all areas of our lives and especially in our dance music spaces.

NOTES

1. https://www.vice.com/en_us/article/9avw4e/seth-troxler-rallies-against-ketamine-inauthenticity-and-aoki-again

2. https://www.documentjournal.com/2019/10/30-minutes-with-the-black-madonna-a-dj-restoring-dance-musics-holy-spirit/

3. As I continue to show in this chapter, Gou's recent decisions have positioned her as problematic, particularly as someone who calls herself a house music (or, at the very least, non-EDM) DJ; I take up this ongoing conversation and debate below.

4. As their re-posted *Instagram* stories often show, they also engage in branding with the help of their consumers or fans; dance music brand culture entails "a process of transforming and *shifting cultural labor into capitalist business practices* [and t]his channeling of labor into business practices is precisely what mobilizes the building of brand cultures by individual consumers and what distinguishes brand culture in the contemporary moment" (Banet-Weiser 2012, 8, my emphasis). Future research on how dance music cultural labor (particularly the cultural labor of individual consumers) has shifted into capitalist business practices is needed.

5. https://www.stereogum.com/1697589/steve-aoki-defends-throwing-cake-at-his-fans/video/

6. https://www.grammy.com/professional-development/video/steve-aoki-talks -documentary-ill-sleep-when-im-dead

7. https://www.thedailybeast.com/dj-steve-aoki-to-cake-or-not-to-cake

8. The meme included a picture of her smiling (with DJ Solomon) at the DJ booth with the following message: "TFW/[That Feeling When] You Land a Six Figure Gig . . . and a Chance to Chop It Up With the Saudi Royal Family."

9. Improper grammar, spelling, and so on, reflect the actual writing included in this thread and other social media posts in this chapter. Also, *Facebook* references included in data archive.

10. https://www.popdust.com/saudi-arabia-emily-ratajkowski-2641673480.html

11. https://www.arabianbusiness.com/arts/435407-200000-fans-expected-to -attend-mdl-beast-festival-in-saudi-arabia

12. https://i-d.vice.com/en_uk/article/5dmbz3/interview-peggy-gou-korean-dj

13. *Geluk* had a fairly strict "rager-free door policy." I learned this lesson quickly the first time I went to *Geluk*, especially as I watched clubbers in front of me in the line get schooled by the woman working the front desk. She had very little patience for clubbers complaining about the cost of tickets (tickets were as low as 10 euros), not paying cash, and/or talking over her as she processed their entry. In order to get past the first security guard, clubbers also had to know what they were doing by answering a few simple questions such as, "Who are you here to see?" If they failed this question, they had trouble that was often coupled with a number of additional screening questions. During my second visit to *Geluk*, after answering this question quickly and with confidence, the security guard let us pass swiftly, welcoming us in.

14. https://www.instagram.com/p/B66hpcugzk4/

15. Pseudonyms are used for these events.

16. In reference to keeping people out of clubs/events (such as drunk men who harass women and other clubbers), Gilbert and Pearson (1999) pose the following questions: "Even this argument is problematic, however, for how are those men ever going to learn to act differently if they are excluded from your club or party? By only allowing people with the same values to mix with one another, are you not preventing those values from spreading?" (161). *Geluk*'s policies answer these questions; first, (men) clubbers will act differently if they really want to be in the space; and second, PLUR-like values will spread whether or not certain (men) club-bers make it into the club. While club policies have been criticized for being elitist (Thornton 1996), *Geluk* avoids that critique by focusing specifically on how club-bers are expected to behave (not how they're dressed or who they know). Much like the sexuality classes I teach, if a student is not yet ready to have challenging con-versations about sex and sexuality, then they should wait to take the class. Similarly, if a clubber is not yet ready to take responsibility for their own behavior and com-mitted to creating a space that everyone can enjoy, then they should wait to enter that club. *Geluk* lays out their expectations and screens clubbers for their knowledge and commitment to the scene; if a clubber isn't ready to fulfill those expectations or provide *Geluk* with simple answers to questions about what's happening in the club that night, then they should better prepare themselves next time and think deeply about how to contribute to a positive club environment. *Geluk*'s approach flips the

script, requiring clubbers to do the extra, necessary work of creating a positive vibe that everyone—not just themselves and their friends—can enjoy. This set of expectations is absolutely "spreading" PLUR-like values; if a clubber can't get into or gets removed from a club because they don't hold and practice those values, then they learn quickly what values they need to think about and adopt if they want to return.

17. During my visit to *Geluk* over the NYE 2018/2019 season, I did not find this space so it was either not yet built or I simply missed it.

18. This festival was canceled due to the pandemic.

19. As I will show, *Pleasure* and *Massive* were a lot like the EDM events that Conner (2015) studied, large events where people rarely spoke to him and were generally cold.

20. While the burgeoning literature on heteronormativity (see Ward 2020, in particular) might very well consider toxic heteronormativity redundant, I use toxic here to emphasize how thoroughly alienating and uncomfortable these spaces were, especially for clubbers looking for a "positive environment" as defined by *Geluk*.

21. In line with the heteronormative, patriarchal foundation of bro culture, women in this culture have been described as "prostitots" or "girls who dress up like prostitutes, who go to the events in just their bra and underwear" (Matos 2015 in Conner 2015, 148). As per usual, women marked as "prostitots" are typically expected to wear less than men in bro culture and, at the same time, are criticized for dressing "inappropriately" by those outside the culture. Given my research, while patriarchal and whorephobic (Berg 2021) terms such as "prostitot" are extremely problematic and sexist, I was primarily concerned with how bro culture was actually realized, particularly with how gendered harassment and aggressive, hostile behavior often intersected with the presence of bro culture in any one space. Also, while women wore far less clothing than men at some of the events I attended (*Massive* and the Edinburgh club, for example), I did not attend festivals and never saw other bro culture markers such as shirtless men or hot pants and pasties, clothing that Conner (2015) describes in his own research.

22. http://www.59rivoli.org/accueil/

23. https://www.solosophie.com/59-rue-de-rivoli/

24. https://djmag.com/longreads/dvs1-support-organise-sustain

25. https://mixmag.net/feature/the-black-madonna-is-the-dj-of-the-year

26. https://www.npr.org/2019/11/13/778532395/the-mainstreaming-of-edm-and-the-precipitous-drop-that-followed

27. https://reverb.com/news/the-disco-soundsystems-that-birthed-modern-dance-music

28. As we emerge from the pandemic, key actors and stakeholders have been vocal about re-imagining dance music. Whether or not we will see major changes remains to be seen.

29. On April 3, 2020, Octo Octa released "Love Hypnosis," a new mix and limited edition cassette on *Bandcamp* wherein 50 percent of the profits were donated to the @sylviariveralawproject, an organization that "works to guarantee that all people are free to self-determine their gender identity and expression, regardless of income or

race, and without facing harassment, discrimination, or violence" (@octoocta, April 3, 2020). This was one of many donations both Eris Drew and Octo Octa made to the Sylvia Rivera Law Project during my research.

30. Conner and Katz (2020) point to precisely what some participants in dance music are currently engaged in—ongoing discussions and practices that aim to disrupt the current state of dance music: "By way of immanent critique (see Antonio, 1981), resistance may lie in the participants of the EDM subculture pointing out the ironic fate that has befallen the subculture in order to restore it to a more politically dissident subculture" (461). Gadir (2016) also ends her article with some hopeful possibilities, pointing to "an increasing number of DJs of all genders (though largely women) . . . engaging in extensive social media discussions in which practical ideas for change are proposed and debated" (125). The social media data I collected reflects these proliferating discussions that are often coupled with direct digital and physical action.

31. Rietveld (2013) discusses the "heterotopian qualities of DJ culture" that can be found in any dance music space, "as counter-spaces (Foucault 2000), perhaps forged by necessity, rather than by choice . . . [where] the dance event may be understood as a communal celebration of togetherness in the context of social marginalization, away from the perhaps offensive differentiating daylight, a powerful celebration embodied in the shared sensuous force of the bass" (96–97). For many actors in dance music, heterotopian dance spaces like this are the desired goal, one that requires careful, ongoing reflection, discussion, and action.

32. https://www.youtube.com/watch?v=yL6Pd2Lww0w

33. Malbon (1999) reflects on what clubbing offers, arguing that it is "less about rather rigid conceptions of 'resistance' . . . and more about notions of gaining 'strength to go on' through the sharing of a crowd ethos, about fluxing between notions of (egocentric) identities and of (logocentric) identifications, and about finding a space in which—even if just for a fleeting instant—to forget oneself" (182-183).

Bibliography

59 Rivoli. 2020. "59 Rivoli Homepage." Accessed June 11, 2020. http://www
.59rivoli.org/accueil/

Abraham, Amelia. 2019. "Honey Dijon on Whether Dance Music Can Save Us."
Dazed, September 10, 2019. https://www.dazeddigital.com/music/article/45643/1
/honey-dijon-dj-club-culture-comme-des-garcons

Adorno, Theodor W. 1975. "Culture Industry Reconsidered." Translated by Anson G.
Rabinbach. *New German Critique*, no. 6 (Fall): 12–19.

Anderson, Tammy L. 2009a. *Rave Culture: The Alteration and Decline of a
Philadelphia Music Scene*. Philadelphia, PA: Temple University Press.

Anderson, Tammy L. 2009b. "Understanding the Alteration and Decline of a Music
Scene: Observations from Rave Culture." *Sociological Forum* 24, no. 2 (June):
307–336.

Anderson, Tammy L. 2009c. "Better to Complicate, Rather than Homogenize, Urban
Nightlife: A Response to Grazian." *Sociological Forum* 24, no. 4 (December):
918–925.

Aoki, Steve. 2017. "DJ Steve Aoki: To Cake or Not to Cake." *Daily Beast*, July 12,
2017. https://www.thedailybeast.com/dj-steve-aoki-to-cake-or-not-to-cake

Aoki, Steve. 2019. "We may come from different cultures of sound but we all
share the same purpose to make u feel something special and bring happiness to
everyone." Instagram photo, December 2, 2019. https://www.instagram.com/p/
B5l35PCDNvY/

Arditi, David. 2020. *Getting Signed: Record Contracts, Musicians, and Power in
Society*. New York: Palgrave Macmillan.

Arkenbout, Chloë. 2015. "The Black Madonna: 'Clubs Are Dangerous for Women.'"
Vice News, September 2, 2015. https://www.vice.com/en_us/article/pg8g3k/the
-black-madonna-clubs-are-dangerous-for-women

Attias, Bernardo, Anna Gavanas and Hillegonda Rietveld, eds. 2013. *DJ Culture in
the Mix: Power, Technology, and Social Change in Electronic Dance Music*. New
York: Bloomsbury.

Banet-Weiser, Sarah. 2012. *Authentic: The Politics of Ambivalence in a Brand Culture*. New York: New York University Press.

Berg, Heather. 2021. *Porn Work: Sex, Labor, and Late Capitalism*. Chapel Hill, NC: The University of North Carolina Press.

Berg, Maggie and Barbara K. Seeber. 2016. *The Slow Professor: Challenging the Culture of Speed in the Academy*. Toronto: University of Toronto Press.

Berlant, Lauren. 2008. *The Female Complaint: The Unfinished Business of Sentimentality in American Culture*. Durham, NC: Duke University Press.

Bey, Hakim. 1991. *T.A.Z.: The Temporary Autonomous Zone, Ontological Anarchy, Poetic Terrorism*. Brooklyn, NY: Autonomedia.

The Black Madonna. 2016. "Artist of the Year: The Black Madonna on the Beautiful Paradox of Being a Catholic DJ." *Vice News*. December 29, 2016. https://www.vice.com/en/article/kb5pkn/artist-of-the-year-the-black-madonna-catholic-faith-essay

The Blessed Madonna (@blessedmadonnachi). 2017. "Tonight I turn 40 years old." Instagram photo, October 21, 2017. https://www.instagram.com/p/BahXnJmhV85/

The Blessed Madonna (@blessedmadonnachi). 2017. "I am remembering the morning this picture was taken." Instagram photo, August 30, 2017. https://www.instagram.com/p/BYbBT-1h7rI/

The Black Madonna. 2018. "The Black Madonna's Guide to Protecting Your Mental Health When Touring." *Dazed*. May 15, 2018. https://www.dazeddigital.com/music/article/40039/1/the-black-madonna-mental-health-touring

The Blessed Madonna (@blessedmadonnachi). 2018. "They say home is the place where, when you have to go there, they have to take you in." Instagram photo, March 31, 2018. https://www.instagram.com/p/Bg_p10aBGVK/

The Blessed Madonna (@blessedmadonnachi). 2018. "Pro-tip: Don't fucking scam my fans." Instagram photo, October 21, 2018. https://www.instagram.com/p/BpNiG1UgdUB/

The Blessed Madonna. 2019. "I'm beyond excited to announce my Choose Love tour which will cross the globe to raise funds and awareness for Help Refugees and Say It Loud." Instagram photo, September 26, 2019. https://www.instagram.com/p/B230QxjHmDG/

The Blessed Madonna (@blessedmadonnachi). 2020. "I have changed my name to The Blessed Madonna." Instagram photo, July 20, 2020. https://www.instagram.com/p/CC3BKAQnc2S/

Brailey, Louise. 2016. "The Black Madonna is the DJ of the Year." *Mixmag Asia*, December 22, 2016. https://mixmag.asia/feature/the-black-madonna-is-the-dj-of-the-year/12

Bratches, Taylor. 2020. "Dance Floor Epiphanies." Accessed June 4, 2020. https://www.residentadvisor.net/features/3584

Brewster, Bill and Frank Broughton. 1999. *Last Night a DJ Saved My Life: The History of the Disc Jockey*. New York: Grove Press.

Bridge, Sam. 2019. "200,000 Fans Expected to Attend MDL Beast Festival in Saudi Arabia." *Arabian Business*, December 13, 2019. https://www.arabianbusiness.com/arts/435407-200000-fans-expected-to-attend-mdl-beast-festival-in-saudi-arabia

Bromwich, Jonah Engel. 2019. "Peggy Gou Is Kicking Her Electronic Music Career to the Next Level." *New York Times*, July 3, 2019. https://www.nytimes.com/2019/07/03/arts/music/peggy-gou-dj-kicks.html

Brownbill, Colin. 2016. "Mind Dimension: DJs are Finally Opening Up about Mental Health." *Mixmag*, March 4, 2016. https://mixmag.net/feature/mind-dimension-djs-are-finally-opening-up-about-mental-health

Buckland, Fiona. 2002. *Impossible Dance: Club Culture and Queer World-Making*. Middletown, CT: Wesleyan University Press.

Butler, Mark J., ed. 2012. *Electronica, Dance and Club Music*. Burlington: Ashgate.

Campbell, Scott. 2020. "Berghain: How to Get Into Berlin's Most Exclusive Nightclub." *The Telegraph*, May 19, 2020. https://www.telegraph.co.uk/travel/destinations/europe/germany/berlin/articles/Berghain-how-to-get-into-Berlins-most-exclusive-nightclub/

Clark-Flory, Tracy. 2021. *Want Me: A Sex Writer's Journey into the Heart of Desire*. New York: Penguin Books.

Cliff, Aimee. 2019. "Just Gou It: How Peggy Gou Became the World's Hippest DJ." *The Guardian*, August 8, 2019. https://www.theguardian.com/music/2019/aug/08/freedom-fashion-and-being-scouted-on-facebook-how-peggy-gou-became-the-worlds-coolest-dj

Collin, Matthew. 2009. *Altered State: The Story of Ecstasy Culture and Acid House*. London: Serpent's Tail.

Collin, Matthew. 2018. *Rave On: Global Adventures in Electronic Dance Music*. Chicago: The University of Chicago Press.

Conner, Christopher T. 2015. "Electronic Dance Music: From Deviant Subculture to Culture Industry." Ph.D. dissertation, University of Nevada, Las Vegas.

Conner, Christopher T. and Nathan Katz. 2020. "Electronic Dance Music: From Spectacular Subculture to Culture Industry." *YOUNG* 28, no. 5: 445–464.

Couvreur, Eelco. 2015. "The Black Madonna Manifesto." *Djbroadcast*, May 22, 2015. https://www.djbroadcast.net/article/121812/the-black-madonna-manifesto

Csikszentmihalyi, Mihaly. [1975] 2000. *Beyond Boredom and Anxiety: Experiencing Flow in Work and Play*. San Francisco, CA: Jossey-Bass Publishers.

Dijon, Honey. 2020. "Kim Jones and Honey Dijon on the Place Where Fashion and Nightlife Meet." *Interview*, April 8, 2020. https://www.interviewmagazine.com/culture/honey-dijon-and-kim-jones-dior-air-jordan

Dijon, Honey (@honeydijon). 2018. "We need more black female identified and queer people of color DJs on lineups at clubs and festivals." Instagram photo, June 5, 2018. https://www.instagram.com/p/Bjp1qWeBWYU/

Dijon, Honey (@honeydijon). 2018. "Chez Damier @chez.damier asked me once what was my reason for being a dj." Instagram photo, November 9, 2018. https://www.instagram.com/p/Bp9v4mIFf8R/

Dijon, Honey (@honeydijon). 2019. "Because djing is not just choosing a few tunes." Instagram photo, June 2, 2019. https://www.instagram.com/p/ByMyaokCU1E/

Dijon, Honey (@honeydijon). 2019. "Oh you know that time when people used to dance at the club and get so lost in the music that they fell out on the floor cause it was too much!" Instagram photo, April 24, 2019. https://www.instagram.com/p /Bwo2RJOFc2s/

Dijon, Honey (@honeydijon). 2019. "The minute you become more than the music, you're through! – Frankie Knuckles." Facebook, January 29, 2019.

Dijon, Honey (@honeydijon). 2019. "Dreams do come true. Coming soon.….." Instagram photo, August 29, 2019. https://www.instagram.com/p/B1vur-WCQ9F/

Dijon, Honey (@honeydijon). 2019. "Goodmorning." Instagram photo, March 4, 2019. https://www.instagram.com/p/BulRFKuFRap/

Dijon, Honey (@honeydijon). 2019. "Reading the book Keep Going by @austinkleon I was struck by these quotes." Instagram photo, June 4, 2019. https://www.instagram.com/p/BySMUewiiPP/

Dijon, Honey (@honeydijon). 2019. "There is enough for all of us." Instagram photo, April 18, 2019. https://www.instagram.com/p/BwaYp7BF40s/

Dijon, Honey (@honeydijon). 2019. "What if you let go of fear?" Instagram photo, February 23, 2019. https://www.instagram.com/p/BuO8jUKlx65/

Dijon, Honey. 2021. "What I Learned From Honey Dijon About Living a Creative Life." Interview by Georg Stuby, *Portal To Creation Podcast*, May 10, 2021, audio, 50:07. https://open.spotify.com/episode/3ZABhFxhGOk6EQ905KGy33?si =QhLNq3FvROmSWnLnTs2gqA&nd=1

djmagofficial (@djmagofficial). 2019. "Congratulations @honeydijon" Instagram photo, May 29, 2019. https://instagram.com/p/ByDboTnjCXo

Do The Bay. "The Black Madonna at Phoenix Hotel, 9/22/2019." *Do The Bay*, Accessed June 9, 2020. https://dothebay.com/events/2019/9/22/the-black-madonna -tickets

Donovan, Louise. 2019. "Ready, Peggy, Go!" *Elle*, December 3, 2019. https://www .elle.com/uk/life-and-culture/a26793999/peggy-gou-interview/

Dowling, Marcus. 2021. "Baby Weight is the Dolly Parton-Loving DJ Who's Here to Take Tech-House Back from the Big Room Bros." *Mixmag*, May 12, 2021. https:// mixmag.net/feature/impact-baby-weight-dj-mix-feature-interview

DVNFLX, 2018. "I Was There When House Took Over the World." Accessed June 4, 2020. https://www.youtube.com/watch?v=9Rah1F1zq1k

Fabric (@fabriclondonoffficial). 2021. "fabric is London's home for underground music, always aiming to create a feeling of self-expression on the dance-floor." Instagram photo, June 28, 2021. https://www.instagram.com/p/CQq8qaxFRsh/

Farrugia, Rebekah. 2012. *Beyond the Dance Floor: Female DJs, Technology and Electronic Dance Music Culture*. Bristol: Intellect.

Fatsoma. 2020. "Peggy Fucking Gou: How The K-House Was Built." *Ideas for Life*, September 16, 2020.

Ferreira, Pedro Peixoto. 2008. "When Sound Meets Movement: Performance in Electronic Dance Music." *Leonardo Music Journal* 18: 17–20.

Fikentscher, Kai. 2013. "'It's Not the Mix, It's the Selection': Music Programming in Contemporary DJ Culture." In *DJ Culture in the Mix: Power, Technology, and Social Change in Electronic Dance Music*, edited by Bernardo Alexander

Attias, Anna Gavanas, and Hillegonda C. Rietveld, 123–149. New York: Bloomsbury.

Flynn, Paul. 2020. "Honey Dijon on the Sacred Nightclub Experience, Stolen by the Pandemic." *Love Magazine*, May 1, 2020. https://www.thelovemagazine.co.uk/article/honey-dijon-on-the-sacred-nightclub-experience-stolen-by-the-pandemic

Foucault, Michel. 1978. *The History of Sexuality, Volume 1: An Introduction.* Translated by Robert Hurley. New York: Vintage Books.

Friedman, Aron. 2014. "Laidback Luke: 'I Got Sucked into the Mainstream'." *Vice News*, June 16, 2014. https://www.vice.com/en_us/article/mg4zn3/laidback-luke-i-got-sucked-into-the-mainstream

Fritz, Jimi. 1999. *Rave Culture: An Insider's Overview.* Victoria, BC: SmallFry Enterprises.

G., David. 2019. "KFC Bought Colonel Sanders A DJ Slot At Ultra Music Festival In Miami." *One EDM*, March 31, 2019. https://oneedm.com/music-business/kfc-colonel-sanders-ultra-music-festival/

Gadir, Tami. 2016. "Resistance or Reiteration? Rethinking Gender in DJ Cultures." *Contemporary Music Review* 35, no. 1: 115–129.

Garber, David. 2014. "How to DJ with Integrity, According to John Digweed." *Vice News*, March 18, 2014. https://www.vice.com/en_us/article/qkmgy5/how-to-dj-with-integrity-according-to-john-digweed

Garcia, Luis-Manuel. 2013. "Doing Nightlife and EDMC Fieldwork: Guest Editor's Introduction." *Dancecult: Journal of Electronic Dance Music Culture* 5, no. 1: 3–17.

Gavanas, Anna and Rosa Reitsamer. 2013. "DJ Technologies, Social Networks and Gendered Trajectories in European DJ Cultures." In *DJ Culture in the Mix: Power, Technology, and Social Change in Electronic Dance Music*, edited by Bernardo Alexander Attias, Anna Gavanas, and Hillegonda C. Rietveld, 51–77. New York: Bloomsbury.

Georgia. "Georgia: Seeking Thrills." *Apple Music*, Accessed June 10, 2020. https://music.apple.com/us/album/seeking-thrills/1479573983

Giddens, Anthony. 1984. *The Constitution of Society: Outline of the Theory of Structuration.* Berkeley, CA: University of California Press.

Gilbert, Jeremy and Ewan Pearson. 1999. *Discographies: Dance Music, Culture and the Politics of Sound.* London: Routledge.

Glaser, Barney G. and Frances Strauss. 1999. *The Discovery of Grounded Theory: Strategies for Qualitative Research.* London: Routledge.

Goffman, Erving. 1961. *Encounters: Two Studies in the Sociology of Interaction.* Indianapolis, IN: Bobbs-Merrill Co.

Gordon, Eden Arielle. 2019. "The Implications of Visiting Saudi Arabia: Emily Ratajkowski, BTS, Nicki Minaj, and the Politics of Performance." *PopDust*, December 23, 2019. https://www.popdust.com/saudi-arabia-emily-ratajkowski-2641673480.html

Gou, Peggy (@peggygou_). 2019. "I noticed my immune system got low recently from my crazy schedule and it's right time for me to take some holiday." Instagram photo, July 9, 2019. https://www.instagram.com/p/BztAQYmIqlb/

Gou, Peggy (@peggygou_). 2020. "Sick of people who write shit just to get attention." Instagram video, January 6, 2020.

Goulding, Christina and Avi Shankar. 2011. "Club Culture, Neotribalism and Ritualised Behaviour." *Annals of Tourism Research* 38, no. 4: 1435–1453.

Grammy Awards. 2020. "Steve Aoki Talks Documentary 'I'll Sleep When I'm Dad'" *Recording Academy Grammy Awards*, Accessed June 10, 2020. https://www.grammy.com/professional-development/video/steve-aoki-talks-documentary-ill-sleep-when-im-dead

Grazian, David. 2008. *On the Make: The Hustle of Urban Nightlife*. Chicago: The University of Chicago Press.

GQ. 2021. "Peggy Gou Is Reclaiming Her Headspace." *GQ*, September 28, 2021. https://www.gqmiddleeast.com/culture/peggy-gou

Haidari, Niloufar. 2019. "What the Hell Is Business Techno?" *Mixmag*, October 23, 2019. https://mixmag.net/feature/what-the-hell-is-business-techno

Hari, Johann. 2018. *Lost Connections: Uncovering the Real Causes of Depression – and the Unexpected Solutions*. London: Bloomsbury Circus.

he.she.they (@he.she.they). 2021. "At @he.she.they On 11th September when it's our London Pride comeback special." Instagram photo, June 28, 2021. https://www.instagram.com/p/CQsVfaRg9mB/

Heath, Harold. 2019. "DVS1: Support. Organise. Sustain." *DJ Mag*, December 11, 2019. https://djmag.com/longreads/dvs1-support-organise-sustain

Hidalgo, Danielle Antoinette. 2009. "Expressions on a Dance Floor: Embodying Geographies of Genders and Sexualities in Bangkok Nightclubbing." Ph.D. dissertation, University of California at Santa Barbara.

Hidalgo, Danielle Antoinette and Tracy Royce. 2016. " 'Tonight, You Are a Man!': Negotiating Embodied Resistance in Local Thai Nightclubs." In *Cultural Politics of Gender and Sexuality in Contemporary Asia*, edited by Tiantian Zheng, 57–73. Honolulu, HI: University of Hawai'i Press.

Honoré, Carl. 2004. *In Praise of Slowness: How a Worldwide Movement Is Challenging the Cult of Speed*. New York: HarperCollins Publishers, Inc.

Horkheimer, Max and Theodor Adorno. [1944] 1972. *Dialectic of Enlightenment*, Translated by John Cumming. New York: Continuum.

Hutson, Scott R. 1999. "Technoshamanism: Spiritual Healing in the Rave Subculture." *Popular Music and Society* 23, no. 3 (September): 53–77.

Hutson, Scott R. 2000. "The Rave: Spiritual Healing in Modern Western Subcultures." *Anthropological Quarterly* 73, no. 1 (January): 35–49.

Hutton, Fiona. 2006. *Risky Pleasures?: Club Culture and Feminine Identities*. Hampshire: Ashgate.

Jackson, Phil. 2004. *Inside Clubbing: Sensual Experiments in the Art of Being Human*. Oxford: Berg.

Jaguar. 2021. "Welcome to UTOPIA Talks!" *Utopia Talks Podcast*, Accessed August 4, 2021. https://open.spotify.com/episode/1UPq39AIAWhtAj7OnKhnM5?si=-OVWp5Y4TYOAmWNsSwlq-Q&context=spotify%3Ashow%3A3JJDwKDjajLeSE01byNl8O&dl_branch=1&nd=1

Jaimangal-Jones, Dewi. 2018. "Analysing the Media Discourses Surrounding DJs as Authentic Performers and Artists Within Electronic Dance Music Culture Magazines." *Leisure Studies* 37, no. 2: 223–235.

Jaimangal-Jones, Dewi, Annette Pritchard and Nigel Morgan. 2010. "Going the Distance: Locating Journey, Liminality and Rites of Passage in Dance Music Experiences." *Leisure Studies* 29, no. 3: 253–268.

Jayda G (@jaydagmusic). 2021. "@motionbristol / @boilerroomtv !! Thank you!!" Instagram photo, July 24, 2021. https://www.instagram.com/p/CRtyQU8AWfg/

Kale, Sirin. 2018. "Social Media is Dangerously Affecting DJs' Mental Health." *Mixmag*, January 22, 2018. https://mixmag.net/feature/social-media-is-dangerously-affecting-artists-mental-health

Karney, Ed (@edkarney). 2020. "I took these pictures at around 11am on the Sunday morning of the closing of Trouw in Amsterdam exactly five years ago today." Instagram photo, January 4, 2020. https://www.instagram.com/p/B66hpcugzk4/

Kavanaugh, Philip R. 2015. "The Social Organization of Masculine Violence in Nighttime Leisure Scenes." *Criminal Justice Studies* 28, no. 3: 239–256.

Khawaja, Jemayel. 2015. "Seth Troxler Rallies Against Ketamine, Inauthenticity, and Aoki (Again)." *Vice News*, March 23, 2015. https://www.vice.com/en_us/article/9avw4e/seth-troxler-rallies-against-ketamine-inauthenticity-and-aoki-again

Kiddy Smile (@kiddysmile). 2019. "The Way This Woman Got My Back and It's mutual !" Instagram photo, February 28, 2019. https://www.instagram.com/p/BubClNTlqtD/

Kim, Michelle. 2019. "Georgia: 'About Work the Dancefloor.'" *Pitchfork*, March 28, 2019. https://pitchfork.com/reviews/tracks/georgia-about-work-the-dancefloor/

Krook, Justin, dir. 2016. *I'll Sleep When I'm Dead*.

Lawrence, Tim. 2003. *Love Saves the Day: A History of American Dance Music Culture, 1970–1979*. Durham: Duke University Press.

Li, Nicolaus. 2019. "Peggy Gou Discusses Her Career & Inspiration Behind Fashion Line, Kirin." *Hypebeast*, September 25, 2019. https://hypebeast.com/2019/9/peggy-gou-dj-kirin-fashion-launch-interview

Loiseau, Benoit. 2020. "Peggy Gou Discusses Online Criticism and Her Resolutions for 2020." *i-D*, January 8, 2020. https://i-d.vice.com/en_uk/article/5dmbz3/interview-peggy-gou-korean-dj

Lupton, Deborah. 2015. *Digital Sociology*. London: Routledge.

Macias, Ernesto. 2019. "Techno Queen Peggy Gou Shows Us Her Camera Roll." *Interview*, March 26, 2019. https://www.interviewmagazine.com/culture/techno-queen-peggy-gou-shows-us-her-camera-roll

Maiolo, Alex. 2020. "The Disco Soundsystems That Birthed Modern Dance Music." *Reverb*, June 9, 2020. https://reverb.com/news/the-disco-soundsystems-that-birthed-modern-dance-music

Malbon, Ben. 1999. *Clubbing: Dancing, Ecstasy and Vitality*. London: Routledge.

Maloney, Liam. 2018. "…And House Music Was Born: Constructing a Secular Christianity of Otherness." *Popular Music and Society* 41, no. 3: 231–249.

Marcus, Bert and Cyrus Saidi, dir. 2017. *What We Started*.

Marcuse, Herbert. 1964. *One-Dimensional Man: Studies in the Ideology of Advanced Industrial Society*. Boston, MA: Beacon Press.

Matos, Michaelangelo. 2015. *The Underground is Massive: How Electronic Dance Music Conquered America*. New York: HarperCollins Publishers.

Matos, Michaelangelo. 2019."The Mainstreaming of EDM And The Precipitous Drop That Followed." *NPR Music*, November 13, 2019. https://www.npr.org/2019/11/13/778532395/the-mainstreaming-of-edm-and-the-precipitous-drop-that-followed

McIver, Joel. 2018. "Avicii obituary." *The Guardian*, April 22, 2018. https://www.theguardian.com/music/2018/apr/22/avicii-obituary

McLeod, Kembrew. 2001. "Genres, Subgenres, Sub-Subgenres and More: Musical and Social Differentiation Within Electronic/Dance Music Communities." *Journal of Popular Music Studies* 13, no. 1: 59–75.

McRobbie, Angela. 1993. "Shut Up and Dance: Youth Culture and Changing Modes of Femininity." *Cultural Studies* 7, issue 3: 406–426.

Mitchell, Aurora. 2018. "Peggy Gou: Welcome to the Age of Gou-Mania" *Mixmag*, February 22, 2018. https://mixmag.net/feature/peggy-gou-welcome-to-the-age-of-gou-mania

Montano, Ed. 2013. "DJ Culture and the Commercial Club Scene in Sydney." In *DJ Culture in the Mix: Power, Technology, and Social Change in Electronic Dance Music*, edited by Bernardo Alexander Attias, Anna Gavanas, and Hillegonda C. Rietveld, 173–194. New York: Bloomsbury.

Moore, Ralph. 2021. "From Leftfield House to the Grammys: Jayda G is Taking Her Sound to Another Level." *Mixmag*, May 4, 2021. https://mixmag.net/feature/jayda-g-cover-interview-grammy-dj-kicks

MTV ASIA. 2019. "Introducing Georgia (MTV Push Exclusive Interview)." *MTV Push*, Accessed December 5, 2021. Video, 4:07. https://www.youtube.com/watch?v=yL6Pd2Lww0w

Murphy, Sam. 2020. "Georgia Wants You to Feel It All on the Dancefloor." *The Interns*, January 7, 2020. https://theinterns.net/2020/01/07/georgia-wants-feel-dancefloor/

Musgrave, George. 2020. "Avicii: True Stories." *Dancecult: Journal of Electronic Dance Music Culture* 12, no. 1: 94–97.

Nadeau, Sophie. 2016. "59 Rue de Rivoli: An Artist's Atelier in the Heart of Paris." *SoloSophie*, Accessed December 5, 2021. https://www.solosophie.com/59-rue-de-rivoli/

Nicolov, Alice. 2016. "Thirty Years Later and Rave Still Hasn't Left the Dancefloor." *Dazed*, February 23, 2016. https://www.dazeddigital.com/music/article/29976/1/thirty-years-later-and-rave-still-hasn-t-left-the-dancefloor

Octo Octa (@octo_octa). 2020. "House music doesn't get enough credit for being a genre that has so much weird and experimental elements to it." Twitter, May 27, 2020. https://twitter.com/octo_octa/status/1265693958254059527

Olaveson, Tim. 2004. "'Non-Stop Ecstatic Dancing': An Ethnographic Study of *Connectedness* and the Rave Experience in Central Canada." Ph.D. dissertation, University of Ottawa.

Olufemi, Tope. 2021. "'Never Constrained by Anything': TAAHLIAH's Fearless Creativity Fuses Emotion, Pop and Experimental Electronics." *Mixmag*, May 27, 2021. https://mixmag.net/feature/taahliah-impact-mix-interview

Ongley, Hannah. 2019. "30 Minutes With The Black Madonna, a DJ Restoring Dance Music's Holy Spirit," *Document Journal*, October 16, 2019. https://www .documentjournal.com/2019/10/30-minutes-with-the-black-madonna-a-dj-restoring-dance-musics-holy-spirit/

Oxford Union. 2020. "Peggy Gou: Full Q&A at The Oxford Union." Accessed June 9, 2020. https://www.youtube.com/watch?v=gESqFUcia6o

Palamar, Joseph J. and Marybec Griffin. 2020. "Non-Consensual Sexual Contact at Electronic Dance Music Parties." *Archives of Sexual Behavior* 49: 909–917.

Pini, Maria. 2001. *Club Cultures and Female Subjectivity: The Move from Home to House*. New York: Palgrave Macmillan.

Pink, Sarah. 2009. *Doing Sensory Ethnography*. Thousand Oaks, CA: SAGE Publications.

Ravens, Chal. 2019. "Bitch, She's The Black Madonna: Meet the Coolest Woman in Music." *TimeOut*, June 5, 2019. https://www.timeout.com/london/music/bitch -shes-the-black-madonna-meet-the-coolest-woman-in-music

Redfield, Audrey and Marie I. Thouin-Savard. 2017. "Electronic Dance Music Events as Modern-Day Ritual." *International Journal of Transpersonal Studies* 36, no. 1: 52–66.

Redford, Patrick. 2016. "The White Sox's Disco Demolition Riot Was Even More Insane Than You Thought." *Deadspin*, July 5, 2016. https://deadspin.com/the -white-soxs-disco-demolition-riot-was-even-more-insa-1783162273

Resident Advisor. 2016. "Between the Beats: The Black Madonna." Published August 11, 2016 at *Resident Advisor*. https://www.residentadvisor.net/features/2793

Resident Advisor. 2018. "How Punk Shaped Electronic Music." Published March 27, 2018 at *Resident Advisor*. https://www.residentadvisor.net/features/3192

Rettig, James. 2014. "Steve Aoki Defends Throwing Cake at His Fans." *Stereogum*, August 10, 2014. https://www.stereogum.com/1697589/steve-aoki-defends-throwing-cake-at-his-fans/video/

Reynolds, Simon. [1998] 2012. *Energy Flash: A Journey through Rave Music and Dance Culture*. Berkeley, CA: Soft Skull Press.

Rietveld, Hillegonda C. [1998] 2018. *This is Our House: House Music, Cultural Spaces and Technologies*. London: Routledge.

Rietveld, Hillegonda C. 2013. "Introduction." In *DJ Culture in the Mix: Power, Technology, and Social Change in Electronic Dance Music*, edited by Bernardo Alexander Attias, Anna Gavanas, and Hillegonda C. Rietveld, 1–14. New York: Bloomsbury.

Rill, Bryan. 2006. "Rave, Communitas, and Embodied Idealism." *Music Therapy Today* VII, no. 3: 648–661.

Rill, Bryan. 2010. "Identity Discourses on the Dancefloor." *Anthropology of Consciousness* 21, issue 2: 139–162.

Ritzer, George. 2019. *The McDonaldization of Society: Into the Digital Age*. Thousand Oaks, CA: SAGE Publications.

Ross, Annabel. 2020. "Women Provide Accounts of Sexual Harassment and Assault by Derrick May." *Resident Advisor*, November 13, 2020. https://ra.co/features/3780

SceneNoise Team. 2018. "Noise 101: Peggy Gou." *SceneNoise*, September 19, 2018. https://scenenoise.com/Interviews/noise-101-peggy-gou

Schaap, Julian and Pauwke Berkers. 2020. "'You're Not Supposed to Be into Rock Music': Authenticity Maneuvering in a White Configuration." *Sociology of Race and Ethnicity* 6, no. 3: 416–430.

Scott, Clara. 2020. "Peggy Gou, the Universal DJ." *Michigan Daily*, January 12, 2020. https://www.michigandaily.com/section/music/peggy-gou-universal-dj

Shukur, Natalie. 2021. "Honey Dijon and Kim Jones on What Happened to Nightlife." *CR FASHION BOOK*, March 9, 2021. https://www.crfashionbook.com/culture/a35509582/honey-dijon-kim-jones-cr18/

Siokou, Christine. 2002. "The Melbourne Rave Scene." *Youth Studies Australia* 21, no. 1: 11–18.

Snickars, Pelle and Patrick Vonderau, eds. 2012. *Moving Data: The iPhone and the Future of Media*. New York: Columbia University Press.

St John, Graham, ed. 2001. *FreeNRG: Notes from the Edge of the Dance Floor*. Melbourne: Common Ground Publishing.

St John, Graham. 2006. "Electronic Dance Music Culture and Religion: An Overview." *Culture and Religion* 7, no. 1: 1–25.

St John, Graham. 2012. *Global Tribe: Technology, Spirituality and Psytrance*. Sheffield: Equinox.

Stoller, Paul. 1997. *Sensuous Scholarship*. Philadelphia, PA: University of Pennsylvania Press.

Sylvan, Robin. 2005. *Trance Formation: The Spiritual and Religious Dimensions of Global Rave Culture*. New York: Routledge.

Takahashi, Melanie and Tim Olaveson. 2003. "Music, Dance and Raving Bodies: Raving as Spirituality in the Central Canadian Rave Scene." *Journal of Ritual Studies* 17, no. 2: 72–96.

Terry, Josh. 2019. " 'Disco Demolition Night' Was a Disgrace, and Celebrating it Is Worse." *Vice News*, June 12, 2019. https://www.vice.com/en_us/article/8xzke5/disco-demolition-night-was-a-disgrace-and-celebrating-it-is-worse

Thebault, Reis and Katie Mettler. 2019. "Instagram Influencers Partied at a Saudi Music Festival—But No One Mentioned Human Rights." *The Washington Post*, December 24, 2019. https://www.washingtonpost.com/technology/2019/12/23/instagram-influencers-partied-saudi-arabian-music-festival-no-one-mentioned-human-rights/

Thornton, Sarah. 1996. *Club Cultures: Music, Media and Subcultural Capital*. Middletown, CT: Wesleyan University Press.

Trax Magazine. 2016. "The Black Madonna: 'I Discovered Underground Resistance with the First Guy Who Hit Me.'" *Trax Magazine*, May 24, 2016. https://www.traxmag.com/the-black-madonna-jai-decouvert-underground-resistance-avec-le-premier-mec-qui-ma-frappee/

Troxler, Seth. 2014. "Seth Troxler: 'Dance Festivals Are the Best and Worst Places in the World.'" *Vice News*, May 20, 2014. https://www.vice.com/en_uk/article

/bmb953/seth-troxlers-guide-to-dance-music-festivals-clubbing-and-not-being-a
-terrible-human

Tsikurishvili, Levan, dir. 2017. *Avicii: True Stories.*

Turkle, Sherry. 2011. *Alone Together: Why We Expect More from Technology and Less from Each Other.* New York: Basic Books.

Turner, Victor. 1967. *The Forest of Symbols: Aspects of Ndembu Ritual.* Ithaca: Cornell University Press.

Turner, Victor. [1969] 2017. *The Ritual Process: Structure and Anti-Structure.* New York: Routledge.

Vandenberg, Femke, Michaël Berghman and Julian Schaap. 2021. "The 'lonely raver': Music Livestreams During COVID-19 as a Hotline to Collective Consciousness?" *European Societies* 23, no. S1: S141–S152.

Vincentelli, Elisabeth. 2017. "The Black Madonna, an Activist D.J., Wants to Turn Dance Music Upside Down." *New York Times*, November 30, 2017. https://www.nytimes.com/2017/11/30/arts/music/the-black-madonna-dj.html

Wade, Lisa. 2017. *American Hookup: The New Culture of Sex on Campus.* New York: W. W. Norton & Company.

Waisbord, Silvio, ed. 2014. *Media Sociology: A Reappraisal.* Cambridge: Polity Press.

Ward, Jane. 2020. *The Tragedy of Heterosexuality.* New York: New York University Press.

Warren Carol A. B. and Tracy X. Karner. 2005. *Discovering Qualitative Methods: Field Research, Interviews, and Analysis.* Los Angeles, CA: Roxbury Publishing Company.

Weber, Max. [1925] 1978. *Economy and Society*, 2 vols. Translated and edited by Guenther Roth and Claus Wittich. Berkeley, CA: University of California Press.

Whitmer, Jennifer M. 2019. "You Are Your Brand: Self-Branding and the Marketization of Self." *Sociology Compass* 13, no. 3: 1–10.

Wilson, Brian. 2006. *Fight, Flight, or Chill: Subcultures, Youth, and Rave into the Twenty-First Century.* Montreal: McGill-Queen's University Press.

Wray, Adam. 2020. "Meet, Mate, and Create: The Life of Honey Dijon." *SSense*, n.d. https://www.ssense.com/en-gb/editorial/music/meet-mate-and-create-the-life-of-honey-dijon

Index

Page references for figures are italicized.

Abloh, Virgil, 107
"About Work the Dancefloor–The Blessed Madonna Remix", 74–75
Adorno, Theodor, 6, 16n44, 131
Afrojack, 135, 153
alcohol consumption, and harassment, 86–87, 99nn20–22
Alejandro (friend of author), 31, 39n26
Alone Together (Turkle), 55
Anderson, Tammy L., 6, 7, 10n4, 12n12, 13n25, 16n43, 17n46, 21, 37n8, 50, 69, 71, 72, 74, 79, 86, 88, 98n9, 99n18, 100n29, 124n4
Aoki, Steve, 64n15, 129–35, 138, 151–53
Arabian Business/Lifestyle (magazine), 135
Attiah, Karen, 136
authenticity: as a brand, 11n10, 106; branding as, 3, 12nn13–14, 62–63; of dance music, 37n5, 106, 125n18; in dance music spaces, 2–3, 71–72, 96–97, 105–6, 150–51; defined, 11n6; discursive, 110; of DJs, 37–38n8, 123–24; as a social construct, 11n11. *See also* authenticity maneuvering
authenticity imperative, 110, 119

authenticity maneuvering: Aoki's failure at, 131, 133–34; and the authenticity imperative, 110, 119; as a branding practice, 124–25nn5–6; by clubbers and fans, 125n19; defined, 9–10, 106, 109–10, 125n16; by Dijon, 10, 62–63, 64n7, 110–13, 116–19, 123–24, 130, 135; and discursive authenticity, 110; by DJs, 109–11, 118–19, 126n29, 134–35, 138–39, 154; examples of, 110; "giving back" theme, 126n29; by Gou, 10, 62–63, 110–12, 119–20, 123; Schaap and Berkers's use of term, 110; by TBM, 10, 62–63, 64n7, 109–10, 113–16, 123–24
autoethnography, 5–6, 14n29, 15n35, 15n40
Avicii, 32–33, 35, 40nn28–29, 120, 122

Banet-Weiser, Sarah, 3, 11n8, 11n10, 12n13, 62, 124n5
Becky (club-goer), 87
Bentley, Jason, 131
Berg, Heather, 118
Berg, Maggie, 24
Berkers, Pauwke, 110

Redfield, Audrey, 65n20
Reitsamer, Rosa, 12n14, 126n25
Resident Advisor (online publication), 34
Reynolds, Simon, 39n18; *Energy Flash*, 15n36
Rietveld, Hillegonda C., 161n31
Rill, Bryan, 14n32, 37n4
Ritzer, George, *The McDonaldization of Society*, 108
Ross, Annabel, 38n10

Sasha (DJ), 53
scene insiders, 110, 124nn3–4, 125n17
SceneNoise, 119, 138
Schaap, Julian, 110
Seeber, Barbara K., 24
Sensuous Scholarship (Stoller), 10n3
sexual harassment, 25, 83–87, 97, 99nn18–23, 144, *144*, 147–48, *147*, 160n21
Shankar, Avi, 38n13, 56
"Shut Up and Dance" (McRobbie), 37n3, 82
Siokou, Christine, 31
slow practices, 24
smartphones, in dance music spaces, 29, 53–55, 64n13, 75–76, 90–95, 97, 101n30
Smile, Kiddy, 52, 57–58, 157
social differences, in dance music spaces, 29–31, 39n25
social media, 6, 8, 93, 101n32, 106–9, 118–19, 122. *See also* branding; technology; *specific platforms*
"Social Media is Dangerously Affecting DJs' Mental Health", 122
spatiotemporal embodied relations, 5–6, 15n36
spirituality, of dance music spaces, 77–78
stakeholders, 124n4

Stamper, Marea, 13n23. *See also* The Blessed Madonna (TBM)
"Stanley's Get Down (No Parking on the DF)" remix, 54, 75
"stay in the moment" policies, 93
St John, Graham, 14n33, 38n13
Stoller, Paul, *Sensuous Scholarship*, 10n3
Support, Organize, Sustain (S.O.S.), 156
Sylvia Rivera Law Project, 157, 161n29

Takahashi, Melanie, 11n9, 14nn32–34, 53
taste discourses, 109, 119–20, 123, 125n15, 129, 134, 151–52
TBM. *See* The Blessed Madonna
technology: pandemic livestreams, 55; smartphones, in dance music spaces, 29, 53–55, 64n13, 75–76, 90–95, 97, 101n30. *See also* social media
Terry, Josh, "'Disco Demolition Night' Was a Disgrace and Celebrating it Is Worse", 49
"This must be the place", as a practice, 156, 158
Thornton, Sarah, 2, 11n9, 125nn16–17
Thouin-Savard, Marie I., 65n20
Tiësto, 153
timelessness, 23–26, 38nn13–14, 38n16, 74–75, 88–90, 92, 98n6, 98n11, 100n25, 124n2
Tong, Pete, 131
transcendence, 23–24, 38n12, 77–79, 98n11
Traxman (DJ), 27
Trouw (club), 139–40, 156
Troxler, Seth, 20–21, 28, 56, 103, 110, 129, 153
Turkle, Sherry, *Alone Together*, 55
Turner, Victor, 14n32
Ultra Music Festival, 153